THE METAMORPHIC TRADITION
IN MODERN POETRY

THE

METAMORPHIC TRADITION

IN MODERN POETRY

Essays on the work of

EZRA POUND · WALLACE STEVENS

WILLIAM CARLOS WILLIAMS · T. S. ELIOT

HART CRANE · RANDALL JARRELL

and

WILLIAM BUTLER YEATS

By

Sister M. Bernetta Quinn

NEW YORK
GORDIAN PRESS, INC.
1966

Originally Published 1955
Reprinted 1966

Copyright 1966
Published by Gordian Press, Inc., by
Arrangement with the Trustees of Rutgers College in New Jersey
Library of Congress Catalog Card No. 66-19365

Designed by Andor Braun

Printed in U.S.A. by
EDWARDS BROTHERS, INC.
Ann Arbor, Michigan

To Our Lady of Peace

ACKNOWLEDGMENT

I AM deeply grateful for the kind interest of Ezra Pound, Wallace Stevens, William Carlos Williams, and Randall Jarrell, whose suggestions through correspondence have been of inestimable help in the preparation of *The Metamorphic Tradition in Modern Poetry*. Appreciation is also due Allen Tate for reading the sections on Williams, Pound, and Jarrell; to Ray B. West, Jr., for his advice on the Stevens and Pound chapters; and to Ruth Wallerstein for generously reading and commenting upon the pages dealing with Pound. To the Sisters of my congregation, The Sisters of Saint Francis, Rochester, Minnesota, and to my colleagues at the College of Saint Teresa, Winona, Minnesota, I owe my sincere gratitude for their prayerful and enheartening interest in the progress of this book. I wish also to thank the University of Wisconsin library staff, for services graciously proffered. Chiefly, however, I am indebted to Frederick J. Hoffman of the University of Wisconsin, under whose patient and stimulating direction most of these ideas on metamorphosis in modern poetry were formulated.

CONTENTS

THE METAMORPHIC TRADITION
IN MODERN POETRY

INTRODUCTION

THE principal aim of *The Metamorphic Tradition in Modern Poetry* is to give a sense of direction in the exploration of what to many readers is a New World, the world of contemporary verse. Like Wallace Fowlie's *The Clown's Grail,* which traces love in its literary expression, it seeks to isolate one aspect of art, not only in order to illuminate the meanings of that aspect itself but also to draw attention to and facilitate the understanding of the work of those who have made the present century distinctive in poetry. Any one of a number of themes might have served with equal effectiveness as a focal point in such an examination, directed at bringing to bear on poetry the concentration necessary for sympathetic reception. Metamorphosis, however, summarizing as it does man's desire and need to transcend the psychologically repressive conditions of his mechanized *milieu,* is fitted to serve as the subject for a study that is intended to do more than supply an Ariadne's thread as guide for the willing reader. Metamorphosis begins and ends the history of man, from baptism to resurrection, affecting the world within him and the world without.

Much of the apathy, even antagonism, felt for long poems such as *The Cantos, The Bridge, The Waste Land,* and *Paterson* is that these are considered only in their parts, not as wholes. Just as any lifetime—and surely the first and last of these works represent the lifetimes of their authors—cannot be evaluated until viewed as a unit, so must an extensive poem be regarded as what it is, a tissue of relationships. Any criticism, then, which does not take into account reflexive reference is a partial criticism and leads to an unfair appraisal of the modern poet. Too many of the exegetical essays on *The Waste Land*, for instance, concentrate on minutiae of erudition; too many studies of *The Bridge* are focused on ambiguity in lyrical passages removed from context, rather than on Crane's attempts, at times brilliantly successful, to secure thematic continuity.

Often the intellect, recoiling in dismay from a major poem, frightened at its scope, may even take its revenge in blaming the parts rather than trying to comprehend the whole. It is true that when there were only thirty Cantos the problem of seeing the work in its entirety was a much simpler one than it is today; even though sound critics from the first realized that judgment must be deferred, it was easier to discuss *Paterson* I or II or III than it is to write of the complete poem. Yet this difficulty is no excuse but rather a challenge. One of the chief services which criticism can render — a service of more value than awarding praise or condemning — is to construct with humility and a perseverance brightened with sympathy some map drawn from a position in the upper air of objectivity and designed to reduce the effort required for appreciation — a short cut, if you will, to the reader's rightful joy in the full aesthetic realization of the poem.

By pursuing the metamorphic principle as it informs the larger poetic experiments of the twentieth century, as well as briefer ones, this book tries to reveal the unifying forces at work within each, forces not obvious and without patience and charity likely to remain undiscovered. Not only does such an approach lend itself to exposing the ways in which a long poem is integrated; it also furnishes insights into and at last familiarity with the mind of the artist himself. An ever-deepening acquaintance with someone, growing into friendship as time moves on, provides us with knowledge that reinterprets all he says and does in the light of what he is. Thus a long-range view of how Ezra Pound explains *rerum naturae;* of how Wallace Stevens sees imagination, reality, and their interdependence; of what Randall Jarrell believes about the human condition, with its marginal regions of the supra- and sub-rational, ought to make every poem by Pound or Stevens or Jarrell more meaningful for the reader who possesses such an understanding of their premises.

The seven poets examined at length—Ezra Pound, Wallace Stevens, William Carlos Williams, T. S. Eliot, Hart Crane, Randall Jarrell, and William Butler Yeats—have been chosen not because of their stature in contemporary letters (although six of them are major poets and it is the author's belief that the seventh will become so); rather, they were selected because of the predominance of metamorphic themes and effects in their work and also because each illustrates divergent facets of the metamorphic principle. Metamorphosis will be understood in the widest possible sense. At the core of the treatment will be the general meaning given in dictionaries, expressed thus by *The New "Standard" Dictionary of the English Language:* "A passing from one form or shape into another; transformation with or without change of matter: especially applied to change by means of witchcraft, sorcery, etc." But beyond this, the chapters will involve most of the subsidiary meanings—for instance, the significance which the term *metamorphosis* has in biology, chemistry, music, zoology, geology. All of these senses, however, can perhaps be grouped under Webster's definition in the *New International:* "a striking alteration in appearance, character, or circumstances."

It may be helpful to indicate here, in an elliptical manner, the variations of the metamorphic theme in this century which the chapters themselves expand. Metamorphosis will be shown to be one resolution of the question of transience, since in the cyclic character of the universe, "All things doo chaunge. But nothing sure dooth perish." (Golding's Ovid.)

Ezra Pound, particularly, has stressed this apparent immortality which the absolute confers upon beauty, drawn
forth time and time again in fresh media. Such a thesis is
perhaps as close as writers like Pound come to the supernatural, this insistence upon perfection waiting and longing
to break through the façade of the quotidian. Immersed in
materialism, then, the poet yet serves the ideal.

In the plane of action, every abstraction must be transformed to the concrete if it is to have any practical significance; thus justice is inoperative until a just act is per-
formed. Likewise, in art, as long as ideas and emotions remain universal, they do not really exist except in the logical
order. Metamorphosis is a way of giving them bodies, from
which gift springs their power to appeal to men in human
terms. When time or its conclusion, death, is turned to the
flesh and blood of Medusa, the grisly terror strikes deep in
our hearts. Every metamorphosis in Ovid dramatizes the
cold, bare statement at its center; every new version of his
or other ancient metamorphoses fulfills an identical function.

In a period marked by disguise of the subjective rather
than by an emphasis upon autobiography in poetry, it is
not strange that poets should turn, as in Augustan England,
to the mythic allegories of Greece and Rome as a means of
incarnating ideas; indeed, such a rebirth of neo-classicism is
especially likely in view of the fact that most of the leading
poets have had university training. Though Narcissus,
Daphne, and the other *personae* of transformation histories
no longer stand for what they did to the ancients, the Renaissance, or the Age of Enlightenment, they retain an im-
personality behind which a writer may hide and by means of
which he may establish communication with others who remain part of an intellectual tradition long after they have
broken with all spiritual ones. These symbolic persons have
acquired more complicated significations through their em-
ployment in psychoanalysis, among other sources of new

connotations; yet in tragic or comic masks they play a stylized version of contemporary *ennui,* passion, aspiration, and despair, speaking the lines of each unique script in the accents of the ages.

One such abstract idea, the search for an absolute—a topic suggestive of a philosophical treatise rather than a lyric—is invested with living beauty when such a poet as Yeats seizes upon a story that reaches back to the childhood of his race to supply an artistic realization of this theme. In the legends of Aengus the longing for perfect beauty that burns in a Celtic heart can be dramatized. The danger as well as the difficulty of attaining an ideal vivifies under mythic treatment just as did Galatea under Pygmalion's chisel. Daphne in her arboreal disguise, renewed in loveliness each blossomtide, or Persephone and Vertumnus as in the *Cantos,* bring to all of the senses the truth, among other truths, that what perishes will reappear according to a primordial plan. The eighteenth century could write without apology and directly upon such abstractions as melancholy, the vanity of human wishes, imagination; the twentieth requires that these be translated into the concrete, and the personages of myth and folklore stand ready in the poet's mind to accomplish the translation.

A second reason for the selection of ancient metamorphoses by today's writers is that they can serve so well as verbal equations for contemporary emotional situations. On the level of the individual, Medusa has in turn symbolized unrequited love, hate, fear; on a larger scale, the emotional situation of a whole society may be concretized by the same mythical character. Unlike the arbitrary items of the list in Lewis Carroll's "The Mad Gardener's Song" (in which an Elephant turns into a letter from the speaker's wife, a Buffalo into his Sister's Husband's Niece, a Rattlesnake into the Middle of Next Week, etc.), each change in the best lyrics is deliberately selected in order to bring out a facet of man's psychic involvement with his fellow man or

with the material universe around him. Two advantages ac-
crue from treating emotional relationships in these terms:
the subjective element is given universal appeal, and the
isolated instances are dignified by being caught up in a
stream of legend flowing out of a heroic past where life itself was dignified, unlike the fragmentary, raucous *milieu*
in which many of today's children are forced to suffer out
their days. By integrating *la condition moderne* with the
splendor of its cultural sources, whatever influences have
interposed to dull that splendor, the poet hopes to achieve
an expression worthier of his vision than if he confined himself to his own age.

One of Randall Jarrell's lyrics is entitled, "Falling in
Love Is Never As Simple As That." This might be paraphrased to express a conviction that has been gathering
force in man ever since Descartes: "Knowing the World Is
Never As Simple As That." Common sense no longer appears a sufficiently fine instrument to guarantee that what
man sees and feels and hears is really there, and corresponds
to his perceptions. Wallace Stevens among American poets
is pre-eminently fascinated with this problem, choosing
metamorphosis as the best explanation. Not only do the
senses transform reality; language too changes it. Everything, in fact, is in delicate relationship to everything else.

In Stevens, agent or environment or words exert a power
mysterious as invisibility and irresistible except to those objects the properties of which are too positive to undergo
mutation by these three forces. Such a philosophy of becoming is not without misgivings, regrets that Stevens voices
in "This Solitude of Cataracts":

> *He wanted the river to go on flowing the same way,*
> *To keep on flowing. He wanted to walk beside it,*
>
> *Under the buttonwoods, beneath a moon nailed fast.*
> *He wanted his heart to stop beating and his mind to rest*
>
> *In a permanent realization, without any wild ducks*

Or mountains that were not mountains, just to know how it
*   would be,*
Just to know how it would feel, released from destruction,
To be bronze man breathing under archaic lapis,
Without the oscillations of planetary pass-pass,
Breathing his bronzen breath at the azury center of time. *

But this is an exceptional mood; usually, together with
Pound and Jarrell, he is willing, even eager, to accept
change as the basis of life.

And since poetry and reality for Stevens are built upon
the same structural plan, since they continue to function on
identical principles, a metamorphic aesthetic is fully as essential as a metamorphic epistemology. The resemblances
which link together the parts of nature connect the elements
of lyrics, but with the added advantage that poetry can
not only order but improve upon actuality through "the
shaping spirit," imagination.

Writers of far less importance than Wallace Stevens or the
other poets considered in this study have used "the difference we make in what we see" as a subject for poetry. Richard Wilbur's "The Beautiful Changes" phrases it better than
most of these, in a perhaps too easy yet colorful sequence
of images:

> *One wading a Fall meadow finds on all sides*
> *The Queen Anne's lace lying like lilies*
> *On water; it glides*
> *So from the walker, it turns*
> *Dry grass to a lake, as the slightest shade of you*
> *Valleys my mind in fabulous blue Lucernes.*
>
> *The beautiful changes as a forest is changed*
> *By a chameleon's tuning his skin to it;*
> *As a mantis, arranged*
> *On a green leaf, grows*

* From *The Collected Poems of Wallace Stevens,* copyright
1923, 1931, 1935, 1936, 1937, 1942, 1943, 1944, 1945, 1946,
1947, 1948, 1949, 1950, 1951, 1952, 1954 by Wallace Stevens.
By permission of Alfred A. Knopf, Inc.

Into it, makes the leaf leafier, and proves
Any greenness is deeper than anyone knows.

Your hands hold roses always in a way that says
They are not only yours; the beautiful changes
In such kind ways,
Wishing ever to sunder
Things and things' selves for a second finding, to lose
For a moment all that it touches back to wonder. *

Here the metamorphosis is a matter of appearances rather than of reality, an approach, however, which focuses attention on the difficulty for many minds of separating appearances from reality.

Besides treating metamorphosis as descriptive of the natural world and the way in which that world is known, poets have seized upon it as a means of unifying their longer works, even to the extent of creating, as William Carlos Williams does, new myths in which a super-human character adopts identity after identity while yet retaining a recognizable self. Such a character is Paterson, a modern god of place, whose drama refreshes for us the ancient realization that the where and when of each life become a part of its what. As Susanne K. Langer says, "The 'making' of mythology by creative bards is only a metamorphosis of world-old and universal ideas." (*Philosophy in a New Key*, 161.)

Other poets—for example, Eliot and Crane—do not rest content with one setting as Williams does, but accompany their mutations of character with those of place. Thus *The Waste Land* expresses a common theme by means of interchangeable characters, using parallel myths in a metaphorical sense, all rooted somehow in the Fisher King legend and unified by coming to us through the sensibility, a dual one, of Tiresias. Crane carries this technique even further in *The Bridge*, as he meticulously and subtly converts one

* From *The Beautiful Changes and other Poems*, copyright, 1947, by Richard Wilbur. Reprinted by permission of Harcourt, Brace and Company, Inc.

image into another, the poem itself becoming its subject: a bridge from one insight to another until the reader reaches the bank of final illumination, opposite the bank of uncertainty on which is built the terrestrial hell of Manhattan.

These chapters will endeavor to show that to write a poem is in itself to effect a metamorphosis, and that the process has been so treated by modern theorists whose practice is herein discussed. One need not stop with the special group of artists known as the Symbolists in applying the following statement by Elizabeth Drew: "The Symbolists held as the central doctrine of their poetic creed that poetry must transmute life into a new incarnation of image and rhythm." (*T. S. Eliot: The Design of His Poetry,* 22.) Such an aesthetic has been advanced by Eliot in particular, through his analogy of the catalytic agent, and by Pound through his prose comments on the way in which poetry (as well as its translation), sculpture, painting, music, give new life to original vision, which in turn depends upon an absolute beauty. In his theory of resemblance and his criticism based on the eternity of forms, Wallace Stevens, too, has affirmed that the poetic act utilizes metamorphosis—indeed, consists of it.

Freud, Jung, and the other twentieth-century writers on psychology have realized how traditional metamorphoses embody the conflicting urges at war within the soul, employing them in accounts of the various complexes deforming personality. After an examination of psychoanalysis in the service of metamorphic myth and vice versa, the reader feels more at home in the *Märchen*-filled, dreamy, mythic regions of Randall Jarrell's poetry. Because human nature remains always the same, the impulses which led primitive peoples to devise their tales of transformation, to view the objects in their surroundings as animated by strange intelligences, are not without relevance even today:

> To a large proportion of human beings at the present day
> beasts and birds, trees and plants, the sea, the mountains,

the wind, the sun, the moon, the clouds and the stars, day
and night, the heaven and the earth, are alive and possessed of the passions and the cunning and the will they
feel within themselves. The only difference is that these
things are vastly cleverer and more powerful than man.
(Edwin Sidney Hartland, *The Science of Fairy Tales: An
Inquiry into Fairy Mythology*, 25.) *

Such people, if they were to read modern poetry, would take
the poet's figures literally, like the child who expects to see
real animals when his elders tell him it is raining cats and
dogs. On a more sophisticated level, pathetic fallacies are
but another evidence of this tendency to humanize Nature.
Men, and most of all poets, are not satisfied to leave their
non-human settings untouched by the imagination; thus in
speculation John Nerber changes the wood of a house back
to its pristine boughs inhabited by nightingale and swallow:

> *How would this house react, were leaves*
> *To come again upon its common wood—*
> *The wood bird nesting where its rafters*
> *Stood in the grey gloomed dusk, where now*
> *We stand like children staring*
> *At its nest upon the topmost bough.*
>
> *When to the sessions of its change*
> *The mind romantic to extremity*
> *Converts at will the dead or dying wood*
> *Back to a life, green-boughed, of sensitivity,*
> *And myth returns the wood bird to its range*
> *In the warm glooms, by a new destiny pursued—* †
>
>   ("Romance" in *The Spectre Image*)

The world itself is separated into time and eternity, the
human and the divine, the sentient and the inanimate. Beings who share the properties of both worlds or who progress from one to another (Zeus, Tiresias, the Sidhe) stand
for far more than the simple or involved narrations of which

* Reprinted by permission of Charles Scribner's Sons.
† From *The Spectre Image* by John Nerber. Simon and Schuster.

they are the heroes or heroines. Because man is no longer at home in any world, he seeks these links between stages of existence which will somehow bridge the terrifying isolation in which he finds himself.

Each of the proper names belonging to the hero or heroine of an age-old metamorphic story really functions in modern poetry as a concentrated metaphor, a single word in the vocabulary of the imagination, radiating all the accretions of meaning which century upon century have given it. Philomel remains for us, as for Ovid, beauty and those who love beauty suffering amidst evil and ugliness, even though, as John Crowe Ransom points out, our ironic times can no longer romanticize the nightingale:

> *Procne, Philomela, and Itylus,*
> *Your names are liquid, your improbable tale*
> *Is recited in the classic numbers of the nightingale.*
> *Ah, but our numbers are not felicitous.*
> *It goes not liquidly for us . . .*
>
> *Philomela, Philomela, lover of song,*
> *I am in despair if we may make us worthy,*
> *A bantering breed sophistical and swarthy;*
> *Unto more beautiful, persistently more young*
> *The fabulous provinces belong.**

The poets of today go on alchemizing the old names and legends, Grecian or Teutonic or Celtic. In the lexicon of a contemporary writer like Pound, Circe is not merely a lovely wizard; she is also a synonym of usury. Leda for Yeats crystallizes the fascinating problem of whether man can ever participate in the omniscience of deity. Just as the Renaissance emblems operated as hieroglyphics, pictorial units often complex in design, so their verbal counterparts, built into the ever-changing mosaics of poems, carry a catholic significance which permits the transmission of emotion and

* From *Selected Poems* by John Crowe Ransom, copyright 1924, 1945 by Alfred A. Knopf, Inc. Reprinted by permission of the publisher.

idea from the poet to his reader. Even on the walls of the dark cave of positivism these metamorphic figures blazon a chronicle of soul, both individual and collective.

Finally, these chapters treat metamorphosis in its highest finite forms: baptism and its culmination, the resurrection of the body to glory. The primitive concept of survival, just as does the modern religious concept, stressed the persistence of life even after destruction of its material dwelling-place:

> The belief in metamorphosis involves opinions on the subject of death which are worth a moment's pause. Death is a problem to all men, to the savage as to the most civilized. Least of any can the savage look upon it as extinction. He emphatically believes that he has something within him that survives the dissolution of his outward frame. This is his spirit, the seat of his consciousness, his real self. (Hartland, *The Science of Fairy Tales: An Inquiry into Fairy Mythology*, 27.)

The end of life and its beginning are questions of such tremendous interest to men that they could hardly escape being reflected in the poetry of this or any age.

The Waste Land abounds in baptismal references, and even Paterson, at the end of Williams's poem, emerges renewed from the sea. The idea of resurrection is implicit in the *Quartets*. John Nerber's "Romance" represents in a slighter key the longing to see the dead vivified, even in the non-human realm. This divinely implanted desire of man to achieve a more perfect existence than this life affords is one reason why the modern poet has been preoccupied with mythic figures who have attained such tangible immortality, as for example Heracles, in Yvor Winters' poem by that name:

> *Grown Absolute, I slew my flesh and bone;*
> *Timeless, I knew the Zodiac my span . . .*
> *Transmuted slowly in a fiery blast,*

Perfect, and moving perfectly, I raid
*Eternal silence to eternal ends.**

The poet will not submit, then, to that chrysalis which rationalists keep telling him is his true domain. Consciously and subconsciously, he wants to transcend the limits of his senses, the boundaries of matter. As a consequence, he struggles; and his struggle, with its outcome, is recorded in that current which is metamorphosis in modern poetry.

* Reprinted from *Collected Poems* by Yvor Winters, by permission of the publisher, Alan Swallow. Copyright 1952 by Yvor Winters.

CHAPTER ONE

✪

EZRA POUND

and the Metamorphic Tradition

AMONG the many approaches to Pound's Cantos which illuminate their design, not the least fruitful is the pursuit of the metamorphic theme. It is indeed surprising that so little critical attention has been given to this aspect of the poem, since Pound has clearly stated on several occasions that metamorphosis is one of the two major themes used to effect continuity in the long work. The best-known expression of his intentions is that confided to William Butler Yeats, who, although he misunderstood what Pound meant by fugal structure, has left us in "A Packet for Ezra Pound" an excellent account of how the metamorphic principle was to be applied. Yeats writes:

> There will be no plot, no chronicle of events, no logic of discourse, but two themes, the descent into Hades from Homer, a Metamorphosis from Ovid, and mixed with these medieval or modern historical characters.*

Pound, eager as always to drive home his meaning, then scribbled on the back of an envelope a diagram based upon a photograph hanging on the wall; it was of a Cosimo Tura decoration in three compartments, the upper representing the Triumph of Love and the Triumph of Chastity; the middle, the Zodiac; and the lower, certain events in the time of Tura himself. Referring to this design, he explained

* *A Vision* by W. B. Yeats. Copyright 1938 by The Macmillan Co. Reprinted by permission of The Macmillan Co.

his plan of using as one theme (ABCD) the descent to Hell, as a second (JKLM) metamorphosis; repeating these; then reversing the first (DCBA) to fit changing circumstances; introducing archetypal persons (XYZ) and a fifth structural unit, symbolized by any letters that never recur, to stand for contemporary events; finally setting all sorts of combinations of ABCD, JKLM, XYZ, DCBA whirling together. Yeats then shows how this algebraic analysis relates to the Cosimo photograph:

> The descent and the metamorphosis—ABCD and JKLM
> —his fixed elements, took the place of the Zodiac, the
> archetypal persons—XYZ—that of the Triumphs, and cer-
> tain modern events—his letters that do not recur—that of
> those events in Cosimo Tura's day.*

That this design is not a discarded hope but one realized in practice can be verified by a careful examination of the Cantos published thus far as a whole, though the evidence is not convincing if one looks only at a single block of the verse. Further proof that Pound did not change his mind about the basic components of his poem is contained in a 1927 letter which he wrote from Rapallo to his father:

> One major theme is: live man goes down to world of
> Dead. Another: the repeat in history. A third: the 'magic
> moment' or moment of metamorphosis, bust thru from
> quotidien into 'divine or permanent world.' Gods, etc.

Five years after that, he says in a letter to John Drummond that the three planes in the Cantos are "the permanent, the recurrent, the casual." In 1937 he writes to John Lackay Brown: "There *is* at start, descent to the shades, metamorphoses, parallel (Vidal-Actaeon)." One can hardly imagine a meticulous craftsman like Pound setting forth certain elements out of which he intends to construct his masterpiece and then abandoning them for the bulk of the poem; the

* *A Vision.*

appearance of the Pisan section with its frequent echoes of the ABCD and JKLM themes indicates that the original scheme is still being followed, and subsequent Cantos will undoubtedly make the pattern unmistakable.

Significantly, Pound's enthusiasm for the master of meta-morphic tale-telling, Ovid, particularly as that poet has been translated by the Elizabethan Arthur Golding, is un-equaled among his fiery espousals of ancient or contempo-rary authors. His letters and criticism are filled with injunc-tions to his fellow-artists to go out and read the *Metamor-phoses,* exalted by him as by the Middle Ages (though for different reasons) to a rank analogous to that of the Scrip-tures. He places it among the five literary works requisite for culture, in such high company as the Confucian Odes, Ho-mer, the Divine Comedy, and the Plays (*Culture,* 236). More than once, he calls Golding's version the most beauti-ful book in the English language (*The A B C of Reading,* 44 and 115), and considers editor W. H. D. Rouse as the person who has given him more pleasure than any man liv-ing, because he is "the man who made Golding's *Ovid* avail-able." (*Polite Essays,* 125.)

Pound's interest in the *Metamorphoses* is twofold: artistic and philosophical. Repeatedly he emphasizes the fact that Golding created a new Ovid and that a knowledge of how he did so is indispensable to an understanding of English (or any other division of) literature. After quoting at length in *The A B C of Reading* from the episode of Cadmus, Pound continues:

> I apologize for the cuts in the story, but I cannot give a whole book of the Metamorphoses here, and I do not honestly think that anyone can know anything about the art of lucid narrative in English, or let us say about the history of the development of English narrative writing (verse or prose) without seeing the whole of the volume ("The xv Bookes of P. Ouidius Naso, entytuled Meta-morphosis, translated oute of Latin into English meeter, by Arthur Golding Gentlemen"). (114–115)

Any English department, he writes to Sarah Perkins Cope
in 1934, "is a farce without it." Like Chapman, the translator Golding, whose version had reached seven editions by
1597, was an authentic poet in his own right and contrib-
uted many beautiful effects not in Ovid, just as Ovid added
things not in Greek literature.

But besides its beauty, the *Metamorphoses* is a great
treasury of wisdom, a depository of truth which could be
registered in this form and in no other. While foreign editor
for *Poetry,* Pound instructed Harriet Monroe, whom he apparently enjoyed shocking, that she should inform the
American public as follows concerning his beliefs: "Say
that I consider the writings of Confucius, and Ovid's *Metamorphoses* the only safe guides in religion." Ovid presents
a world of permanent values, of absolutes, one in which
Pound also is at home and into which he introduces us
whenever he makes allusion in the Cantos to gods and goddesses of classical cultures.

Pound has taken as a subject for criticism another book
of metamorphoses, widely popular but far inferior to Ovid
—the *Golden Ass* of Lucius Apuleius, a second-century
lecturer and author. *The Spirit of Romance* contrasts
Apuleius with Ovid, much to the disadvantage of the
former:

> To find out how these metamorphoses of Apuleius dif-
> fer from preceding Latin, we may compare them with the
> metamorphoses of Ovid. Both men write of wonders, and
> transformations, and of things supernatural.
>
> Ovid, urbane, sceptical, a Roman of the city, writes,
> not in a florid prose, but in a polished verse, with the
> clarity of French scientific prose. . . . His mind, trained
> to the system of empire, demands the definite. The scepti-
> cal age hungers after the definite, after something it can
> pretend to believe. The marvellous thing is made plausi-
> ble, the gods are humanized, their annals are written as
> if copied from a parish register; the heroes might have
> been acquaintances of the author's father. (6–7)

Then Pound goes on to describe admiringly the Ovidian
treatment of Daedalus and Icarus, stressing its verisimili-
tude, and setting it against the extravagance and once-upon-
a-time quality of Apuleius, whose floridity preceded Gon-
gorism and the prolixity of medieval romance. The chief
reason Pound is drawn to the Augustan poet rather than to
the author of the Cupid-Psyche story is given in one sentence, which serves also to illuminate the use of Ovidian
techniques in the Cantos: "Ovid, before Browning, raises
the dead and dissects their mental processes; he walks with
the people of myth; Apuleius, in real life, is confused with
his fictitious hero." However, despite this expression of dis-
approval of Apuleius, at least one critic, Allen Tate, has
seen resemblances between Pound's poetry and the *Golden
Ass:* "The Cantos are a sort of *Golden Ass.* There is a likeness, but there is no parallel beyond the mere historical one:
both books are the product of worlds without convictions
and given over to hard pragmatism." (*Reactionary Essays
on Poetry and Ideas,* 50.)

To understand what role transformation plays in the
Cantos, one might consider the doctrine of changes as it
affects things, then ideas, and finally the creative act itself,
since this is the order in which these three occur in relation
to the artifact. First, metamorphosis of things. Of this,
Pound in "Affirmations" says, "The undeniable tradition of
metamorphosis teaches us that things do not remain the
same. They become other things by swift and unanalysable
process." That he means this statement quite literally is apparent from his interpretation of evolution as this scientific
theory is discussed in the postscript which he wrote for his
translation of Remy de Gourmont's *The Natural Philosophy
of Love:*

> I believe, and on no better ground than that of a sudden
> emotion, that the change of species is not a slow matter,
> managed by cross-breeding, of nature's leporides and
> mules, I believe that the species changes as suddenly as
> a man makes a song or a poem, or as suddenly as he

starts making them, more suddenly than he can cut a
statue in stone, at most as slowly as a locust or long-tailed
Sirmione false mosquito emerges from its out-grown skin.
(174)

The suddenness with which May breaks upon a country-
side, the rapid quenching of day's-end gold and cerise, are
among the natural phenomena involved in Pound's "swift
and unanalysable process." This going-forward of the universe has not escaped comment by his favorite Oriental
sages; it is part of the process meant by Confucius in
Book VII of the Analects: "He said: keep your mind (will,
directio voluntatis) on the process (the way things function)." One of Pound's irritable spots is impatience with
those who regard the tenets of Mencius and Confucius as
static, refusing to pay attention to their frequent use of verbs
indicating change and renewal; he says so vehemently in
a *Criterion* essay, "Mang Tsze," wherein he includes the
ideogram for metamorphosis, used again in Canto LVII:

Among Western thinkers Heraclitus put the same concept
into the two words, "All flows," which appear repeatedly
in the Cantos, besides being paraphrased in "Hugh Selwyn
Mauberley."

Pomona, wooed in Canto LXXIX by Vertumnus, the deity
of the seasons whose very name means "he who changes,"
is used by Pound to represent the cycle of the year; Nature's
recovery from apparent death in the triumph of spring and
its annual surrender to winter is concretized further in the
Cantos by three classical myths. The first, employed merely
as an incidental figure, is that of Atthis: "And many things
are set abroad and brought to mind / Of thee, Atthis, un-
fruitful." (Canto V) Atthis, the Phrygian shepherd beloved
of Cybele who emasculated himself under a fir tree, his
spirit at death passing into the tree and (as in the Hyacin-

thus, Adonis, and Narcissus legends) flowers springing from his blood, stands in Pound's mind for a negative attitude towards the sex instinct. He opposes the Atthis-Adonis mentality to a Mediterranean one in *Make It New,* dividing culture upon that basis:

> By 1934 Frazer is sufficiently digested for us to know that opposing systems of European morality go back to the opposed temperaments of those who thought copulation was good for the crops, and the opposed faction who thought it was bad for the crops (the scarcity economists of pre-history). That ought to simplify a good deal of argument. The Christian in being Christian might at least decide whether he is for Adonis or Atys, or whether he is Mediterranean. (17)

In the following year, he comments in a letter to Henry Swabey on the Atthis element in all Anglo-education.

The second myth relates the history of Adonis, introduced in Canto XXIII with a reference to his having died virgin; Canto XLVII devotes more space to him, using the refrain Καὶ Μοῖραι' 'Άδονιν six times. The anemones Venus caused to rise from his blood are Pound's "flower from the swift seed." An analogue to the Greek narration—the legend of the Babylonian god Tammuz, whose blood was said to stain the waters of a certain river in spring flood times—is incorporated into this Canto, which combines the myths thus: "The sea is streaked red with Adonis." The last of these fertility types is Proserpina, spoken of in the first Canto, hinted at in XXI, and mentioned several times in the Pisan section, especially in connection with the pomegranate. In the seventy-fourth Canto her name is linked with the Sirens, her attendants who were metamorphosed after her abduction by Pluto.

Other kinds of metamorphoses observable in the world about us are the formation of rocks and the much faster decomposition of the human body. Pound has given explicit treatment to the latter, so frequently a subject of poetry, in

Cantos XXVII, XXXVII, and LXXX. The first of these begins: "Formando di disio nuova persona / One man is dead, and another has rotted his end off"; the second refers to such decay as the descent to plant life; the last dramatizes disintegration in this quatrain with its overtones of Victorian verse:

> *Nor seeks the carmine petal to infer;*
> *Nor is the white bud Time's inquisitor*
> *Probing to know if its new-gnarled root*
> *Twists from York's head or belly of Lancaster* *

The Ash Wednesday liturgy of the Catholic Church, which gives tangible form to the belief that man has originated from the dust and must return to it (*Memento, homo quia pulvis es, et in pulverem reverteris*) is reflected in the three Cantos dealing with the Cadmus story, first alluded to in XXVII: "Me Cadmus sowed in the earth / And with the thirtieth autumn / I return to the earth that made me." The myth is picked up again in XXXIII ("whether serpents' teeth sprang up men . . .") and is concluded in LXXVII ("men rose out of Χθόνος" and again, "the forms of men rose out of γεά"). The twenty-eighth Canto begins with a similar picture, except that God the Father has taken the place of the pagan deities:

> *And God the Father Eternal (Boja d'un Dio!)*
> *Having made all things he cd.*
> *think of, felt yet*
> *That something was lacking, and thought*
> *Still more, and reflected that*
> *The Romagnolo was lacking, and*
> *Stamped with his foot in the mud and*
> *Up comes the Romagnolo:*

Eventually these men out of earth return to their mother, Gea, by the nature of the process, and are gathered together in Orcus, the shadowy land of the dead.

---

* Quotations from Ezra Pound's poetry reprinted by permission of New Directions.

A related subject is metempsychosis, mentioned by Pound in Canto LIX as well as in the first of the Pisan Cantos, and expounded much earlier in his lyric "Histrion":

> *No man hath dared to write this thing as yet,*
> *And yet I know, how that the souls of all men great*
> *At times pass through us,*
> *And we are melted into them, and are not*
> *Save reflexions of their souls.*
> *Thus am I Dante for a space and am*
> *One François Villon, ballad-lord and thief*
> *Or am such holy ones I may not write*
> *Lest blasphemy be writ against my name;*
> *This for an instant and the flame is gone.*

The personae device leaps to one's mind at the reading of this poem, Pound's series of forms which project themselves into the translucent golden sphere of the ego—Odysseus, Sordello, the Cid, Actaeon, Vidal, Sigismundo, and the rest. Ovid's Renaissance translator, Arthur Golding, has anticipated "Histrion" in: "For soules are free from death. Howbeet, they leaving ever-more / Theyr former dwellings, are receyved and live ageine in new." Certainly no reader of the Roman poet could escape this extension of the metamorphic theme, as Herman Fränkel points out in *Ovid: A Poet between Two Worlds:* "Furthermore the theme gave ample scope for displaying the phenomena of insecure and fleeting indentity, of a self divided in itself or spilling over into another self." (99) One's entire life is, in a sense, a struggle for complete self-realization. The artist, with his highly receptive sensibility, is more intensely aware of this search, which Pound describes in "Vorticism," a 1914 contribution to the *Fortnightly Review,* wherein he speaks ruefully of how, as soon as one is able to say "I am this," he ceases to be so—a fact making it necessary to go on looking for one's true self though all the masks afforded by the workings of the imagination. (463) Eliot, four years later, described Pound's method as just such a throwing-aside of mask after mask ("The Method of Mr. Pound," *Athenaeum,* October 24, 1919, 1065).

The relation between the terms *personae* and *personality* is an interesting one: Pound's practice has been to use the first for exploration and definition of the second:

> I began this search for the real in a book called *Personae,* casting off, as it were, complete masks of the self in each poem. I continued in a long series of translations, which were but more elaborate masks. ("Vorticism")

The essay from which this passage is taken appeared in 1914, near the beginning of his career—he has since created many fascinating *personae* to express, among other things, the mystery of self. The process is well illustrated by the Cosimo Tura diagram, referred to above, which Pound drew up for Yeats, in relation to which these masks are to be considered as the xyz theme. It is as if a soul (X or Y or Z) went from body to body, throughout the ages, retaining in each transmigration its original character. X, Y, and Z, however, are not the souls of ordinary human beings, but composites, archetypes: X_1 becomes X_2, who changes to X_3 in an inspired metempsychosis which lends unity to the entire poem. As D. S. Carne-Ross points out: "It is a basic principle of *The Cantos* that all related characters can merge, or meet, into one another." (*An Examination of Ezra Pound,* 159.)

The archetypes fall into three major classes: heroes, heroines, and enemies of either sex of the life of value. Among the heroes are found both good rulers of their people and artists of integrity: Odysseus; Kung; Hanno; Roland; the Cid; Provençal troubadours like Vidal, Sordello, William of Poitiers, Piere de Maensac, Savairic Mauleon, Arnaut Daniel; Cavalcanti; Sigismundo Malatesta and Borso D'Este; Pisanello, Titian, Carpathio; American leaders such as John Adams, Jefferson, Van Buren; Pietro Leopoldo; Henry James; Mussolini. In these men, however, the good is not unmixed with evil. Pound's heroines include

Helen of Troy, Eleanore of Aquitaine, Ignez de Castro, Lady Soresmunda, Isotta degli Atti, the Marchesa Parisina d'Este, Cunizza—all of them women whose flesh enshrined a gleam of the eternal beauty. Among the villains are Chi Hoang Ti; Ou-heou; Franz Joseph; Hamilton and Marshall; Churchill; Krupp, Metevsky, and others who reap the evil gains of usury. The gods and goddesses, too, and mythological figures of lower rank (Circe, Terreus, Lycabs) blend one into another, so that the sun god may be called Mithras, Phoebus, Apollo, or Helios; the moon goddess Diana, Artemis, or Titania.

Pound introduced the idea of metempsychosis into his attitudes toward actual as well as fictive characters; always impatient of confinement to the present, he rejoiced in the impression of reincarnation which his young sculptor-friend, Gaudier-Brzeska, awakened in him, an impression of being with someone out of Castiglione, or with the subject of a Renaissance painting. (*Gaudier-Brzeska,* 50.)

Another indication of his interest in metempsychosis is his loving study of the Rimini bas-reliefs, those magnificent carvings in which Agostino di Duccio and other Quattrocento artists united their genius to perpetuate the passionate devotion of Sigismundo, Lord of Rimini, for his third wife, Isotta. An extreme of metempsychosis is reached in one of the Temple chapels, where a figure of Saint Michael the Archangel has the face of Isotta. Pound has also called attention in his criticism to the metempsychosis which informs the long eulogy, *Isottaeus,* written by the court-poet Basinio in honor of his patron's wife. (*Criterion,* XIII, 496.)

Not only does this transformation operate from soul to soul, but also in empathetic fashion between man and nature. Relationships, truths otherwise unsuspected, are revealed through entrance into the life of one's environment. In his brief poem, "The Tree," Pound brings up to date the several Ovidian tales of persons turning into trees (Daphne, the Heliades, Baucis and Philemon, Dryope, Cyparisse,

Myrrha, the Thracian women, the shepherd of Appulia);
the central thought is expressed in these lines:

> I stood still and was a tree amid the wood,
> Knowing the truth of things unseen before;
> Of Daphne and the laurel bow
> And that god-feasting couple old
> That grew elm-oak amid the wold.

Just the reverse of this transformation is presented in the
popular anthology lyric, "A Girl," wherein a tree becomes a
girl, the tree, however, being employed metaphorically to
symbolize her lover:

> The tree has entered my hands,
> The sap has ascended my arms,
> The tree has grown in my breast—
> Downward,
> The branches grow out of me, like arms.

Shortly after quoting from Pound's "The Tree" in his
book *Trends in Literature*, Joseph T. Shipley has this to
say about an important movement in modern aesthetics:

> This inevitable identity of the individual with his sur-
> roundings is made the basis of one of the time's most
> credited theories of beauty. Anything is beautiful, ac-
> cording to the doctrine of Einfuhling, or empathy, that
> draws us into its being. Thus Socerian says "We have
> only one way of imagining things from the inside, and
> that is putting ourselves inside them." Bergson declares
> that the spectator must become actor. Lotze asserts that
> we accomplish the feat: 'We project ourselves into the
> forms of a tree, identifying our life with that of the
> slender shoots that swell and stretch forth, feeling in our
> souls the delight of the branches that drop and poise
> delicately in mid-air.' (271–272) *

All this, as well as Pound's lyric, might be described as the
imagination exercised to the height of its capacity, or even,
for some readers, just a bit beyond.

* *Trends in Literature*. Reprinted by permission of Philosophical
Library.

The underlying use which Pound makes of the metamorphoses of things might best be classified as an epistemological one. Only by accommodating apperception to the nature of things—a nature described by Golding in "In all the world there is not that that standeth at a stay. Things eb and flow, and every shape is made too passe away"—can we attain truth. We must be willing to admit that our version of reality needs constant revision if it is to remain valid. Moreover, the subject as well as the object is continually changing; what served yesterday as an equation for one's personality, or any fragment of it, is no longer satisfactory today. Only the man who keeps voluntary pace with his metamorphoses will succeed as a human being.

Besides using metamorphoses as a way of knowing reality, Pound has taken over the principle as a satisfactory means of uniting the parts of a poem already over six hundred pages long. In a review of Ford Madox Ford's novel, *Parade's End* (a review given over chiefly to a discussion of Pound's innovations in structure), Ambrose Gordon explains this technique as follows:

> For it seems likely that there actually is something inherent in local clarity itself—in the very sharply defined image or, for that matter, idea—which sets it off from all that is exterior to it, which prevents a 'flow.' Thus to mediate between individual brilliant moments,—in a poem or a novel—something rather like a movie 'fade in' or, more accurately, a montage is what is required—if you will, a metamorphosis. (*Furioso*, VI, 85.)

Canto I, for example, contains only one such metamorphosis, since the bulk of it is straight translation from the eleventh book of the Odyssey, via Andreas Divus; that change occurs at the very end, where Ulysses, having consulted Tiresias in the underworld, sails off to the shores of Circe. Suddenly we find ourselves with Aphrodite, still in the Homeric world (the concluding lines refer to the Second Hymn) but in a new sequence of timeless moments, equally luminous. Similarly, in Canto XVI the hideousness of the usurers' hell gives way to the bright serenity of Pound's purgatory only to relapse again into the inferno of war. This is not just progress by association of feeling or ideas; the precision, the knife-edged clarity for which Pound has ever striven wars against the vagueness of the reverie method.

The way in which metamorphosis effects transitions between juxtaposed "brilliant moments" stands out more distinctly in those Cantos containing several classical mutations; an excellent example is Canto II. After an introduction including three waterscapes—Oriental waters churned by So-Shu (King of Soku), a northern sea where seals frolic along with the transformed daughter of the Irish King Lir, and the harbor where the old Greeks admire and condemn Helen at once—this second Canto moves from the story of Tyro taken in love by Poseidon in the form of her river-god husband Enipeus into the story of Bacchus and the Tyrrhenian pirates; so smoothly is this done that one does not even realize the sea touching Scios has replaced the waters where Tyro was seduced. After a lengthy paraphrase of Golding's Bacchus-Acoetes episode, the sea changes to that wherein Ileuthyeria, metamorphosed to coral, gleams in ivory stillness. Pound follows this image with another glimpse of So-Shu and then turns the scene once more into the Tyro-Poseidon setting.

Gordon puts his finger on the success of such a method when he goes on to say:

> It is ultimately a metaphorical device, an affair of identity; for it may quite plausibly be argued that the present local object or situation—in a poem, in drama—always by parody or analogy tends to suggest another object or situation which is not present; e.g. when one is with Claudius one is also with Hamlet senior and vice versa.

Thus Itys and Cabestan (Canto IV) stand in a metaphorical relationship, as do Actaeon and Vidal in the same Canto;

De Tierci and Menelaus (Canto v); both of these rejected husbands with Richard Saint Boniface in the next Canto; Eleanore and Helen (Canto VII). Even the perversions of the positive characters are bound into the whole by their distortions of the pattern; Kung, maker of order, immediately precedes the causers of disorder punished within the filth of Canto XIV.

In addition to treating the metamorphoses of things Pound takes up those of ideas, the effectiveness of which depends upon their renewal, as is epitomized in the title of his 1934 collection of essays, *Make It New*, a direction quoted twice in Canto LII, which also contains the corresponding ideogram. Emperor Tching Tang of the Chang dynasty had this motto painted on his bath tub—the emperor who in Pound's translation of the *Ta Hio* is described as having "kept his gaze fixed ceaselessly upon this bright gift of intelligence which we receive from the sky." (11.) In the ideogram the signs for *new* and *sun* are combined so as to give what might literally be translated as "New, day by day new." Rejuvenation is achieved by clothing the basic thought in fresh particulars, the vitality of which has not been worn down by familiarity.

In *Culture*, Pound labels the *forma*, the concept immortal. (152.) This *concetto*, separable from its materialization only logically, travels through time, seizing upon successive embodiments, each of which shows it in its power, an idea in action. "Nothing is new and all good is renewal," Pound declares in a *Criterion* essay. The jungle, to which Richard Eberhart has compared the Cantos (*Quarterly Review of Literature*, v, 180) is the best example of such re-forming; as Canto XX puts it,

> *Glaze green and red feathers, jungle,*
> *Basis of renewal, renewals;*
> *Rising over the soul, green virid, of the jungle,*
> *Lozenge of the pavement, clear shapes,*
> *Broken, disrupted, body eternal,*

Wilderness of renewals, confusion
Basis of renewals, subsistence;
Glazed green of the jungle

This order out of confusion, incidentally, parallels the cosmos out of chaos with which Ovid begins his *Metamorphoses*. The twenty-fifth Canto, after speaking of the meadows of Phlegethon, phrases the theory thus: "And thought then, the deathless, / Form, forms and renewal, gods held in the air." Just as metempsychosis presupposes a fixed number of souls, so this view of thought binds one to an absolutist position, a World of Ideas, as it were, which changes only in its phenomenal aspects. This is a rigid commitment, but one from which Pound does not shrink:

> I mean or imply that certain truth exists. Certain colours exist in nature though great painters have striven vainly, and though the colour film is not yet perfected. Truth is not un-true'd by reason of our failing to fix it on paper. Certain objects are communicable to a man or woman only 'with proper lighting,' they are perceptible in our own minds only with proper 'lighting,' fitfully and by instants. (*Culture*, 295.)

To make the truth of these ideas perceptible, then, is Pound's aim in following the precept of the Chinese emperor.

One such idea requiring to be made new—an idea which appears in various guises throughout the centuries—is that it is vicious to twist the will, to defraud one's fellow man, as in usury. To get this pivotal truth across, Pound uses two major stories of transformation, as well as a few minor ones. The first to occur is that of Circe; Hugh Kenner calls her the most clearly defined character in the first half of the poem. Allen Tate goes even further:

> Mr. Pound's world is the scene of a great Odyssey, and everywhere he lands it is the shore of Circe, where men 'lose all companions' and are turned into swine. . . . And ironically, being modern and a hater of modernity,

he sees all history as deformed by the trim-coifed goddess. (*Reactionary Essays on Poetry and Ideas,* 48.)

Tate's comment, however, is hardly valid as a description
of Pound's Cantos; while it is true that the world they present is the scene of an Odyssey, not all the points of landing
are comparable to the shores of Circe—certainly not the
ardent re-creations of Chinese, Renaissance, or early American civilization. Moreover, to call Pound a hater of moder-
nity—Pound, who has championed so many artists ahead of
their age—would require a very special definition of that
term.

The initial Canto, which Pound himself describes in
Make It New (137–143) as a close translation from the
Odyssey, says nothing of Circe's sorcery, though it mentions
the trim-coifed goddess five times. Canto xxxii hints at the
mutations she effected: "and thus are become as mere animals / . . . whether in a stye, a stable or in a stateroom."
Canto xxxix is largely devoted to her; it speaks of "Lions
loggy with Circe's tisane"; it gives her parentage (Helios
and Perseis) as well as the name of her sister (Pasiphae);
it also provides an account of the magic diet she prepared
for the victims of her craft:

> First honey and cheese
>> honey at first and then acorns
> Honey at the start and then acorns
> honey and wine and then acorns

In the seventy-fourth Canto, Pound goes back to this central myth, clearly connecting it with usury, that lust for
earthly goods which turns men into swine:

> every bank of discount is downright iniquity
>> robbing the public for private individual's gain
>> nec benecomata Kirkê, mah! κακὰ φαργακ' ἔδωκευ
> neither with lions nor leopards attended
>> but poison, veleno
> in all the veins of the commonweal

Fragments of the story occur in Greek, Latin, English; the last Canto to be published thus far includes a few lines of the Circe myth in Italian, as if the poet wished to emphasize in as many ways as possible the wretched evil of money-lending. In "e poi io dissi alla sorella / della pastorella dei suini" (Canto LXXXIV), he echoes the "and at sunset la pastorella dei suini / driving the pigs home, benecomata dea" of Canto LXXVI. Greed is one of the dangers of modern life, just as it was one of the obstacles facing Ulysses and his men on the way home to Penelope.

By translating this keystone truth into a vivid fiction, Pound hopes to reinstate it in the minds of his contemporaries; besides the Homeric-Ovidian method of doing so, he utilizes the medieval craze to discover an elixir which would change base metal into gold, that dream which brought ruin to so many scientists. Marco Polo is quoted in Canto XVIII as reporting of Kublai's empire: "I have told you of that emperor's city in detail / And will tell you of the coining in Cambaluc / that hyght the secret of alchemy." By spelling the Chinese emperor's name Kahn instead of Khan, Pound telescopes time—not, after all, a factor of great importance in his realm of values; the medieval Khan's scheme for issuing paper money on pearls and other valuables and the modern Kahn's profits from usury, a way of creating money out of nothing, are thus contrasted. Another Chinese ruler, Hien of Tang, Pound informs us in Canto LVII, died seeking the fatal elixir, "seeking the transmutation of metals / seeking a word to make change." This line is immediately followed by the ideogram for metamorphosis.

This ideogram is an interesting one. It consists of a radical meaning *the spoken word,* in center position, bordered on either side by one signifying *silk as a raw material,* and all three are placed over a fourth sign meaning *a literary thing, form, the finished product, anything with art in it;* the latter originally consisted of a meeting of two lines, a cross effected by design—of a very simple type, of course, but still art. Thus the concept is rooted in a concrete analogy, based upon one of the best-known forms of metamorphosis: caterpillar–chrysalis–butterfly. The complete ideogram is defined in the *Concise Dictionary of Spoken Chinese* as meaning *to change*.

The other important development of the usury theme is the Bacchus-Acoetes myth, adapted from the poem of Ovid, via Golding. The differences between Canto II and the two older accounts are chiefly those of condensation and idiom, besides the devices of anaphora and repetition of entire lines as these occur in the latest version. As always in his translations, Pound wishes to preserve the spirit rather than to attain literal accuracy. Colloquial terms such as *loggy, cum' along lad, aye, racket,* make the incident come alive, while the interruptions of direct address create an eyewitness effect. The rhythms of conversation are managed with a sureness of poetic line to make this passage one of the finest in the Cantos. The "god-sleight" (wonderful compound!) is given much more space in Pound than in the two sources, indicating that his absorption in the moment of rapid mutation is perhaps even greater than Ovid's, about whom he says: "No Greek was so interested in the magical instant as was Ovid." (*Criterion*, 1, 155.)

Wherever Pound thinks he can make the transformation more real to the sentient man, he does not hesitate to add ideas not present in the sources; for instance, out of "stetit aequore puppis / haud aliter, quam si siccum navale teneret," which Golding translates as "The ship stoode still amid the Sea as in a dustie docke," he derives "Ship stock fast in sea-swirl," retaining in five simple words the motion of the water around the "frozen" ship. One of his best contributions is "grapes with no seed but seafoam," a reference to their divine origin which has no equivalent in Ovid and Golding. The picture of jungle cats materializing out of the void is accomplished by appeals to all five senses, with each variant expression of the metamorphosis adding to the cumulative effect. The order of sense-impressions is handled with amazing rightness: first, just hot breath on the ankles of Acoetes as if from invisible nostrils, then "Beasts like shadows in glass," at two removes from reality. The immaterial character of these Dionysiac symbols is a high achievement, for which almost none of the credit is due to Pound's models.

Acoetes represents the man of a straight will, of integrity: the merchant seaman who will not betray his god. Contrasted with him are the sailors of perverted wills, whose hunger for worldly riches causes them to break all laws of truth or justice in order to obtain gold. About this, Golding moralizes: "so sore mennes eyes were blinded / Where covetousenesse of filthie gaine is more than reason minded." Their sins are such as are symbolized by the monster Geryon, emblem of Fraud, who figures in Cantos XLIX and LI, as well as in the Divine Comedy. Bacchus does well to punish by reduction to the bestial level human beings as depraved as those are who try to live by bread alone.

In addition to these expanded transformations, Pound employs as a criticism of usury that of Midas (XXI, LXXVII, LXXVIII), whose avarice was so dreadfully rewarded. He also uses the shield of Athena (Justice) in order to win an exit for his dramatic character from the usurers' hell described in Canto XV:

> Prayed we to the Medusa,
>   petrifying the soil by the shield
> Holding it downward
>   he hardened the track
> Inch before us, by inch,
>   the matter resisting,
> The heads rose from the shield,
>   hissing, held downwards.

Departing from the realm of antique transformations but keeping to a similar condemnation, Pound in Canto LXXIV tells about an experience in Tangier, when he saw a snake long as a man's arm bite the tongue of a fakir; from the blood thus drawn, dirty straw stuffed into the fakir's mouth was ignited; this "something" from no adequate cause corresponds to the poet's view of usury, called in the same Canto "lending / that which is made out of nothing," a definition Pound has elaborated earlier in Canto XLVI.

A second crucial idea, given many guises in the poem, is the fact that beauty is hard to possess, as Danäe, Actaeon, Salmacis, the historical Piere Vidal (among others) found out to their sorrow. Danäe's love for Jupiter had been merely a gasp between the clichés of daily life; Pound speaks of her in Cantos IV and V as the bride awaiting the god's touch, awaiting the golden rain. The myth of Actaeon is told at greater length, in the fourth Canto. Pound weaves into his tragedy the lycanthropy of the troubadour Vidal, who dressed in wolf-skins for the love of Lady Loba de Peugnautier (whose name means wolf), even allowing himself to be hunted by dogs and beaten by shepherds. In both these accounts the hunter, paradoxically, becomes the victim, the second being a grim parody of the first, in that Vidal is a self-appointed victim. In *Exultations* (16–19) Pound had published a Browningesque monologue, "Piere Vidal Old," wherein the troubadour, driven through the mountains of Cabaret by hunters with hounds, tells his own story. The last line of this lyric ("Ha! this scent is hot!") shows how completely Vidal had been conquered by his wolf-delusion.

In two lines, Canto IV brings together three famous pools in a way that transcends space and time: Vidal is shown reciting Ovid as he stumbles through the Provençal forest: " 'Pergusa . . . pool . . . pool . . . Gargaphia, / Pool . . . pool of Salmacis.' " Pergusa was the pool near which Proserpina had been playing just before her rape; Gargaphia, that wherein Diana was bathing when seen by Actaeon; Salmacis, that named after the water-nymph enamoured of the beautiful but cold Hermaphroditus and fused with him

into a double-sexed being. Just as the water-bodies of
Canto I are one, so are these. Immediately after the two
lines quoted, Pound summarizes the transformation of
Cygnus into a swan, as Ovid relates it in Book XII; "The
empty armour shakes as the cygnet moves"; thus he depreciates further the significance of chronology. Economy
and rhythmic invention are characteristic of Pound's version, drawn out of Ovid's "arma relicta videt; corpus deus
aequoris albam / contulit in volucrem, cuius modo nomen
habebat." Golding's version is "But nought he in his armor
found. For *Neptune* had as tho / Transformed him too the
fowle whose name he bare but late ago."

A third idea which turns from one mythical context into
another is that love must be free. If, as Hugh Kenner thinks,
Circe dominates the first half of the Cantos, the figure
emerging as primary from the entire work is Venus, the
goddess of love, presented under several other titles: Aphrodite, Cythera, Hathor, Primavera. How necessary Pound
considers this virtue may be seen in the letterhead he has
used for some of his correspondence: *"J'ayme donc je
suis."* No external forces can control this value, not even
the hardships of the Pisan D.T.C. In the last accounting,
nothing truly good comes from violence, whether in public
or private relationships. The myth most powerfully exempli-
fying this axiom is that of Procne and her sister Philomela.
The fourth Canto blends this story with the equally horrible
one from the Provençal *vidas,* in which a banquet of her
lover Cabestan's heart is served to Lady Soremonda by her
husband, Sir Raymond of Castle Rossillon, an atrocity
which causes the young wife to commit suicide. Pound's
delicate combinations of these analogues is worthy of quotation:

> *Ityn!*
> *Et ter flebiliter, Ityn, Ityn!*
> *And she went toward the window and cast her down,*
> *"All the while, the while, swallows crying:*

Ityn!
>   *"It is Cabestan's heart in the dish."*
>   *"It is Cabestan's heart in the dish?*
>   *"No other taste shall change this."*
And she went toward the window,
>   *the slim white stone bar*
Making a double arch;
Firm even fingers held to the firm pale stone;
Swung for a moment,
>   *and the wind out of Rhodez*
Caught in the full of her sleeve.
>   *. . . the swallows crying:*
'Tis. 'Tis. Ytis!

The union of the legends is accomplished, among other ways, by gradually altering the name of the innocent child-victim in the Greek tale: the Latin accusative Ityn (also a union of Itys and Cabestan) > It is > 'Tis > Ytis. Another phase of Pound's skill in blending is the resemblance of these sounds to swallow song. An echo from Horace makes the allusion even richer—*Ityn flebiliter gemens* in Carm. IV, xii, 5. One is surprised that the name of the castle, Rossillon (which suggests nightingale), finds no place in the poem. Toward the close of the Canto the joined ideas occur again: "Cabestan, Terreus, / It is Cabestan's heart in the dish." Echoes also appear later, in Cantos LXXVII and LXXXII. Lust, then, a perversion of the will just as avarice is, and cruel jealousy lead only to suffering.

Daphne, like Philomela, is a woman whose lover seeks to compel, not entreat, affection. Her mutation, which Ovid tells with the liveliest of details, has long fascinated Pound. In "Hugh Selwyn Mauberley" he writes: "Daphne with her thighs in bark / Stretches toward me her leafy hands"; ten years earlier the speaker in "La Fraisne" changes the traditional laurel to dogwood: "By the still pool of Mar-nan-oltra / Have I found me a bride / That was a dogwood some syne." "The Girl," alluded to above, is based on this myth. In the Cantos it is treated only obliquely; the second describes an analogue, which reads like a popular belief concerning the origin of coral:

> And of a later year,
>   pale in the wine-red algae,
> If you will lean over the rock,
>   the coral face under the wave-tinge,
> Rose-paleness under water-shift,
>   Ileuthyeria, fair Dafne of sea-bords,
> The swimmer's arms turned to branches,
> Who will say in what year,
>   fleeing what band of tritons,
> The smooth brows, seen, and half seen,
>   now ivory stillness.

The incident is picked up again in Canto xxix: "(fleeing what band of Tritons)." Ileuthyeria is a personification of freedom, the meaning of the Greek word. At the conclusion of Canto ii, the fauns (symbol of masculine fertility) chide Proteus (the ever-changing one) for being on the side of this composite woman; in triumph the frogs (symbolic of metamorphosis) sing against the fauns.

More subtle compulsion of love is given triple presentation in the wooing of Tyro, Alcmene, and Thetis; in each of these courtships, "god-sleight," craft, replaces force. Neither of the first two women seems to have relished the substitution of a god for her husband—the stratagem of disguise employed by the deities—to judge from Pound's Canto LXXIV:

> between NEKUIA where are Alcmene and Tyro . . .
> femina, femina, that wd / not be dragged into paradise
>   by the hair

For sheer loveliness of imagery, nothing in the Cantos surpasses the description of Tyro's possession by Neptune, which juxtaposes the color-words *blue-gray glass, glare azure, sun-tawny, sun-film, black azure, hyaline, bright welter, buff sands, glass-glint, grey, salmon-pink* in such a way as to create an unforgettable amalgam of shade and radiance.

That the third, Thetis, did not want to be dragged *out* of paradise by her hair, the Roman poet implies in these lines: "tum demum *ingemuit,* 'neque' ait "sine numine vincis' / exhibita estque Thetis" [italics mine]. According to Ovid, Peleus beheld the sea-nymph Thetis as she slumbered in her Thessalian cave and determined to have her for his bride; she, being equally resolved that he should not, transformed herself from bird to tree to tigress; Peleus, however, prayed to the deities of the sea, in response to which petition Chiron, the Centaur, advised him to hold the maiden fast, no matter what form she might assume. The Peleus-Thetis story is not developed in Pound; he merely glances at it in Cantos XXXVI and LXXVI, as a way of reinforcing his treatment of modes of love and violence. Canto LXXIV alludes to another mortal unwilling to love a deity: Tithonus, whom Aurora changed to a grasshopper when she saw the sad consequences of Jove's gift to him of eternal life without eternal youth.

A somewhat similar courtship, that of Venus and Anchises, forms the bulk of the Second Homeric Hymn to Aphrodite, quoted from in Canto I; it is unlike the Tyro-Alcmene situation in that Anchises recognized the divinity of his visitor, even though she tells him that she is the daughter of Otreus, King of Phrygia; he most willingly agrees to the union, which bears fruit in the hero Aeneas. Aphrodite announces herself in her assumed identity at the close of Canto XXIII; two Cantos later she repeats, "King Otreus, my father"; a shadowy allusion to the story occurs in the first of the Pisan group ("as by Terracina rose from the sea Zephyr behind her / and from her manner of walk-

ing / as had Anchises"); finally a striking particular is given
in Canto LXXVI:

> or Anchises that laid hold of her flanks of air
> drawing her to him
>   Cythera potens, Κύθηρα δεινά
> no cloud, but the crystal body
>   the tangent formed in the hand's cup
>   as live wind in the beech grove
>   as strong air amid cypress.

Since this plan was devised by Love herself, the outcome
was free of reluctance.

Each metamorphosis of an idea, then, presents a change
within a change. First of all, Pound uses the various transformations (Circe, Actaeon, etc.) as exempla—ways of setting ideas in action. Like any great teacher, he realizes that
concepts of goodness are effective only in so far as they are
in operation; like any great artist he knows that only what
has been actuated (i.e., changed from potency to act) can
be an object for contemplation.

The last type of metamorphosis to be considered is that
which Pound equates with the artistic process. Nowhere has
he better explained what he means by this identification
than in this passage from a 1915 *New Age* essay, "Affirmations":

The first myth arose when a man walked sheer into "nonsense," that is to say, when some very vivid and undeniable adventure befell him, and he told someone else who
called him a liar. Thereupon, after bitter experiences,
when he said that he "turned into a deer," he made a
myth—a work of art that is—*an impersonal or objective
story woven out of his emotions,* as the nearest equation
that he was capable of putting into words. That story,
perhaps, then gave rise to a weakened copy of his emotions in others, until there arose a cult, a company of
people who could understand each other's nonsense
about the gods. [italics mine] (246)

After this definition, he expostulates about using myths for purposes other than this type of communication–for political or ethical good, allegorically or as a fable. One speculates as to what he might say about the moralized Ovids so common in the late Middle Ages and early Renaissance.

This aesthetic theory suggests scholastic definitions of form, substance, and accident. The artist has the form in his mind before he begins work: "as the sculptor sees the form in the air / before he sets hand to mallet." (Canto XXV) This is not, however, the Platonic notion of forms as types but a unique concept. Pound reverses one aspect of scholastic philosophy by transforming the accidents while retaining the substance. Thus, for example, Dante's epic and the Analects may be substantially the same though their verbal manifestations (the accidents) may vary. In *Make It New* Pound significantly remarks that Guido Cavalcanti used the whole poem to define an accident. (360)

Not only in literature does this principle of metamorphosis operate but also in sculpture. One of Pound's favorite periods in sculpture is the fifteenth century, an era in which artists regarded sculpture as a fight through to the surface of the life of the stone itself. Pound expresses the same idea in Canto LXXIV when he writes: "stone knowing the form which the carver imparts it / the stone knows the form." He treats this aspect of sculpture at greater length in *Make It New:*

> We might say: The best Egyptian sculpture is magnificently plastic; but its force comes from a non-plastic, i.e. the god is inside the statue . . . The god is inside the stone, *vacuos exercet aera morsus.* The force is arrested, but there is never any question about its latency, about the force being the essential, and the rest 'accidental' in the philosophic technical sense. The shape occurs. (349)

This Latin quotation (from Ovid's seventh book of the *Metamorphoses*) was also used by Pound in 1920 as pro-

logue for the second part of "Hugh Selwyn Mauberley," the
fourteenth section of which concludes:

> *Mouths biting empty air,*
> *The still stone dogs,*
> *Caught in metamorphosis, were*
> *Left him as epilogues.*

Again, Pound puts this idea in the mouth of Count William
of Poitiers, troubadour, in Canto VI: "The stone is alive in
my hand."

Adrian Stokes devotes much space in his book *Stones of
Rimini* to the distinction between carving and modeling—
between letting a form imprisoned in stone emerge and im-
posing a form from without—relating his critical pronounce-
ments to the exquisite bas-reliefs of Agostino di Duccio
which ornament the Tempio Malatesta. The several Cantos
dealing with the Tempio, as well as scattered references, are
evidences of Pound's passionate interest in this Quattrocento
wonder of sculpture. Stokes identifies the "goddess" in
whose honor the Tempio was built (Isotta) with Diana herself (252), one of the dominant figures in the Cantos, appearing also under her Greek title of Artemis—the feminine
principle (moon) as opposed to the masculine principle
(sun); the rose, Isotta's emblem, to the elephant, Sigismundo's emblem; Yang to Yin, as the Chinese express the
opposition. A most striking representation of Diana's power
is the Duccio relief, "Influxion of the Moon," wherein waves
achieve the stasis of mountains, and trees are rooted in the
swirling deep as moonlight softens, even obliterates, the
differences between the elements.

Stokes also has a fascinating book on another Italian city,
Venice, which might indeed be called the city of metamorphosis and which forms the heart of one of the most beautiful descriptions in the Cantos (XVII). Though Venice is not
mentioned by name, the details given, plus the line "Thither
Borso, when they shot the barbed arrow at him" (a misfor-

tune which Canto x tells us happened to Borso D'Este in Venice), warrant considering the scene as Venetian:

> *A boat came,*
> *One man holding her sail,*
> *Guiding her with oar caught over gunwale, saying:*
> "   *There, in the forest of marble,*
> "   *the stone trees—out of water—*
> "   *the arbours of stone—*
> "   *marble leaf, over leaf,*
> "   *silver, steel over steel,*
> "   *silver beaks rising and crossing,*
> "   *prow set against prow,*
> "   *stone, ply over ply,*
> "   *the gilt beams flare of an evening"*
> *Borse, Carmagnola, the men of craft, i vitrei,*
> *Thither, at one time, time, after time,*
> *And the waters richer than glass,*
> *Bronze gold, the blaze over the silver,*
> *Dye-pots in the torch-light,*
> *The flash of wave under prows,*
> *Stone trees, white and rose-white in the darkness,*
> *Cypress there by the towers,*
> *Drift under hulls in the night.*

The twenty-fifth Canto adds further details to the picture of this city, the Renaissance *Regina del Mare*.

In *Venice: An Aspect of Art* Stokes lets his imagination dissolve the barriers between the limestone carvings of Venice and the life these resemble, likening the balustrade-supports of the old prison's windows to penguins, referring to sea-birds as stones released from the buildings which they once ornamented, calling the food given to the pigeons of Saint Mark's an offering to the stones themselves. (6) In his earlier volume on Rimini he had already pointed out the metamorphic nature of Venice: "In Venice the world is stone. . . . There, the lives of generations have made exteriors, acceptable between sky and water, marbles in-

habited by emotion, feelings turned to marble." (16–17)
Over ten years later, he re-defines this sense of transformation which is peculiarly Venetian:

> We have seen a principle of interchange inspiring Quattro Cento architecture; we have seen that Venice herself inspires a lively sense of poetry, of metamorphosis, of interchange, of inner in terms of outer. (*Venice: An Aspect of Art,* 55.)

This concept, which the rather florid style of Stokes takes pages to establish, is crystallized by Pound in a few lines, near the end of the Canto last quoted from:

> *And shipped thence*
> *to the stone place*
> *Pale white, over water,*
> *known water,*
> *And the white forest of marble,*
> *bent bough over bough,*
> *The pleached arbour of stone . . .*

In painting, too, the metamorphic principle applies; e.g., the drawing forth of forms from the air of the poet's imagination, so wonderfully expressed by Sandro Botticelli (whose Dafne is mentioned in Canto LXXVI) in his "Venus Rising from the Sea," by its background starred with aerial flowers of miraculous origin. Pound might almost be describing this picture in Canto XXVII: "But in sleep, in the waking dream, / Petal'd the air," and again, " 'The air burst into leaf.' / 'Hung there flowered acanthus.' " The eightieth Canto credits Sandro Botticelli with knowing secrets of his art never suspected by Velasquez, who was "lost in the brown meat of Rembrandt / and the raw meat of Rubens and Jordaens."

In music, also, metamorphosis functions. The entire seventy-fifth Canto, except for a few lines of introduction, consists of the transcription for violin by Gerhart Münch (*per metamorfosi,* as the Ms. says) of Clement Janequin's bird-song chorale. (The special meaning of *metamorphosis* in music is the repetition of a musical figure or idea with modifications giving it a new character.) Pound's comments in his criticism and letters on this "Canzone degli Uccelli" invariably present this work as a unit of eternal beauty which has traveled down through the ages, seizing upon various media to manifest itself. Through Pound's influence, after correspondence with the Princess Edmond de Polignac to obtain the score, the canzone was presented at Rapallo on October 10, 1933. The following passage from *Culture* points out its metamorphic nature:

> Janequin's concept takes a third life in our time, for catgut or patent silver, its first was choral, its second on the wires of Francesco Milano's lute. And its ancestry I think goes back to Arnaut Daniel and to god knows what 'hidden antiquity.' (152)

Later in the same book, while again tracing the life of Janequin's birds back to Francesco da Milano and to Arnaut, Pound says: "One of the rights of masterwork is the right of rebirth and recurrence." (251) The inclusion of the Janequin score in the midst of the Cantos is no irrelevance, as those who adhere to the "rag-bag" school of Poundian criticism declare; rather it strengthens the several allusions to actual birds forming ever-new ideograms on the electrically charged wires of the Pisan D.T.C. (James Blish, *Sewanee Review,* 58, 219.) Canto LXXV hints to us that the birds in LXXVII and LXXXII are writing on their wire staff a musical score, truly a *Canzone degli Uccelli.*

Furthermore, though this is not evident at present, Canto LXXV has been prepared for in one of the Cantos omitted from the New Directions edition (those between LXXI and LXXIV); in a section from these which Pound sent to his Japanese friend, Katue Kitasano, this line occurs: "We have heard the birds praising Janequin." It should be remembered, too, that Pound naturally desires the reader to play, or have someone else play, the Canto, so that the ear may reinforce that sense of permanent loveliness which the poem as a whole repeatedly opposes to corrupted values. This is a type of positive metamorphosis which is set against the degradation of the Circean kind.

Allied to the art of original creation is that of translation. Pound's versions of Latin, Tuscan, Provençal and Chinese literature prove him a translator worthy to be ranked among the finest, despite the outcries of purists. The root meaning of *translate,* to change from one condition to another, sets Pound's translations securely within the metamorphic tradition. All men when they exercise the act of cognition are imitators, reproducing in the intellect the material object. The real translator is not, of course, a copyist, but rather an imitator. (As Pound puts it in *Culture:* "Golding made a new Ovid.") The translator's work consists in causing a thing to recur in matter different from the original. The excellence of the result depends upon the exactness with which he works out the ratio of A : B : : C : D (original vision : poem : : his own vision : translation). If the sides balance, the metamorphosis is acceptable as art.

Pound's most extensive Canto experiment in this type of metamorphosis is Canto XXXVI, the first eighty-four lines a very close rendering of Guido Cavalcanti's canzone, *Donna mi priegha,* an alternate translation of which is included in *Make It New.* (353–356) Pound's choice of Cavalcanti is not due entirely to his strong conviction that the Italian poet has much to teach artists of the twentieth century, nor to his intense pleasure in Cavalcanti's songs. The reason why so much space is given to this lyric is this:

> In Guido the 'figure,' the strong metamorphic or 'picturesque' expression is there with purpose to convey or to interpret a definite meaning. In Petrarch it is ornament, the prettiest ornament he could find, but not an irreplaceable ornament, or one that he couldn't have used just about as well somewhere else. (*Make It New,* 351.)

What does Pound mean by "the strong metamorphic or 'picturesque' expression"? Like Guido, and unlike Petrarch, he uses his words in an exact sense, and here to refer to a truth so important that when he told it to T. E. Hulme, the latter exclaimed, after reflection, that he had never read in any book or heard any man say a more interesting thing. (*Make It New,* 361.) He means that Guido, preoccupied with sophisticated points of analyses as to what goes on inside a lover, devised imagery which would take the abstract definition of an emotional situation out of the realm of logical discourse and into the world of breathing, rejoicing, suffering men and women; which would turn the science of psychology (long before it was so called) into the art of poetry. Just as one idea is utterly discrete from all others (the selection of the connotatively right words safeguarding this), so only one rhythm will suffice to render the unique emotion which matches the idea. In the introduction to his Cavalcanti translations, Pound states in a most explicit and uncompromising way the requisites of ideal translation:

> As for the verse itself: I believe in an ultimate and absolute rhythm as I believe in an absolute symbol or metaphor. The perception of the intellect is given in the word, that of the emotions in the cadence. It is only, then, in perfect rhythm joined to the perfect word that the twofold vision can be recorded. I would liken Guido's cadence to nothing less powerful than line in Blake's drawing. (xxi)

The problem in translating Cavalcanti, then, is to retain the substance while replacing one set of accidents with another. This is not the problem in translating such a poet as Baudelaire, where (for ugly rather than as in Petrarch for pretty effect) many figures may be substituted for the original one. (*Imaginary Letters,* 49.)

Ideograms, the units of Chinese literature, are constantly being "made over" in the later Cantos. Hugh Kenner in the study mentioned above compares Pound's translations from the Chinese to "Mr. Eliot's metamorphic processing of St. John of the Cross, the Ferrar community, the Gouvernour, his childhood memories, Dante and a rose-garden." (122) Although it is harder for the average reader to judge this side of Pound than it is to evaluate Eliot's mutations, an unbiased study of the Chinese characters as these appear in the Cantos reveals that they add richness, visual interest, and scope to the work, not obscurity, since they are nearly always accompanied by English equivalents.

A branch of Poundian translation most pertinent to this chapter is the work he has done on the Noh plays, based upon Ernest Fenollosa's studies in Japanese drama. As early as 1917 Pound had published, working on Fenollosa's unfinished drafts, 'Noh' or Accomplishment: A Study of the Classical Stage of Japan. The plot of one of the plays in this collection ("Awoi No Uye") is completely metamorphic. The lovely Awoi, married to Genji Yugawo, is so jealous that her own passion appears to her, first in the form of the Princess Rakujo (her rival), then in the guise of a demon or "hannya." Pound explains these two transformations as follows:

> The passion makes her [Awoi] subject to the demon-possession. The demon first comes in a disguised and beautiful form. The prayer of the exorcist forces him first to appear in his true shape, and then to retreat.
>
> But the 'disguised and beautiful form' is not a mere abstract sheet of matter. It is a sort of personal or living mask, having a ghost life of its own; it is at once a shell of the princess, and a form, which is strengthened or made more palpable by the passion of Awoi. (196–197)

Just before this analysis Pound has said: "Western students of ghostly folk-lore would tell you that the world of spirits is fluid and drifts about seeking shape." Such a view is particularly intriguing when considered in relation to his personae technique.

Ezra Pound writes of the metamorphoses of things, making the changes real, available to the sentient man. He gives us the metamorphoses of ideas—e.g., the evil of usury, the difficulty of beauty, the unwisdom of violence—by embodying them in the shifting histories of Circe, the seamen who tried to deceive Bacchus, and other figures from classical poetry. He describes the metamorphosis of the creative act, showing how it operates in sculpture, painting, music, literature. If he is able to complete his poetic restatement of the metamorphic theme as it informs the Cantos, he will have as valid a right as had Ovid to predict:

> *And tyme without all end*
> (*If Poets as by prophesie about the truth may ame*)
> *My lyfe shall everlastingly bee lengthened still by fame.*

☆

CHAPTER TWO

WALLACE STEVENS:

His "Fluent Mundo"

> The romance of the precise is
> not the elision
> Of the tired romance of impreci-
> sion.
> It is the ever-never-changing
> same,
> An appearance of Again, the
> diva-dame.*

WHAT is constant in Wallace Stevens's poetry, as well as in his theory of poetry, is emphasis on change, or, as he expresses the principle with greater nicety in the first of "Three Academic Pieces," on metamorphosis. He concerns himself first of all with the structure of reality; secondly, with the way in which man knows his world; and finally, with the transfigurations of that world as imagination acts upon it. Each succeeding year of his critical prose and his verse further defines metamorphosis as it functions in the areas of metaphysics, epistemology, and aesthetics, the latter term including life itself considered as the highest of the arts. For idealists, being and knowing cannot be separated, as indicated in that familiar crystallization of one idealist position, *esse est percipe;* thus metaphysics and epistemology, for practical purposes, become one. And since Stevens belongs to the idealist tradition, any discussion of his excursions into the first branch of philosophy will be interwoven with his poetical and critical treatment of the second.

* From *The Collected Poems of Wallace Stevens,* copyright 1923, 1931, 1935, 1936, 1937, 1942, 1943, 1944, 1945, 1946, 1947, 1948, 1949, 1950, 1951, 1952, 1954 by Wallace Stevens. All quotations from the poetry of Wallace Stevens reprinted by permission of Alfred A. Knopf, Inc.

A primary aspect of metamorphosis in Stevens is the effect of the senses on extra-mental reality. No one sees quite the same rose as anyone else does; there is, in fact, a semantics of perception, wherein sense "is like a flow of meanings with no speech / And of as many meanings as of men." ("Bouquet of Roses in Sunlight.") What connotation is to a word, the action of the senses is to a physical object. In "Sombre Figuration" Stevens remarks that reality is that which impresses us: "As a church is a bell and people are an eye, / A cry, the pallor of a dress, a touch"; such a point of view relates him to impressionistic painting, a kinship made doubly clear by his habit of giving lyrics titles which might equally well apply to pictures ("Study of Two Pears," "Girl in a Nightgown," "Landscape with Boat," "Woman Looking at a Vase of Flowers," "Man Carrying Thing," "Large Red Man Reading," to mention only a few). This variety of synecdoche is a consequence of the selection made by the senses from the ineffably multiple phenomena comprising the flux which overwhelms human consciousness from instant to instant.

In "Bouquet of Roses in Sunlight," Stevens phrases the metamorphosis of perception thus:

> *Our sense of these things changes and they change,*
> *Not as in metaphor, but in our sense*
> *Of them. So sense exceeds all metaphor.*
> *It exceeds the heavy changes of the light.*

The "difference that we make in what we see" is more transforming than any rhetoric, so that as one of the three theories propounded in "Metaphors of a Magnifico" suggests, there are as many realities as observers. In this poem Stevens records the speculations of a magnifico—the term a good example of his ironic diction—who is watching men cross over a bridge into a village; there are, the speaker reflects, three possibilities: (a) twenty men crossing twenty bridges into twenty villages (b) one man crossing one bridge into one village (c) twenty men crossing a bridge into a village. The vivid particulars of the village itself, its first white wall and fruit-trees, drive out the intricacies of epistemology from the magnifico's mind, like the words of an old song one cannot quite remember: "This is old song / That will not declare itself. . . ."

The choice which is here put first—that there is a different bridge for each man who crosses and a different village for him to enter—is the metaphor Stevens usually prefers. As early as 1916 he was employing it; in his prize-winning poetic drama, "Three Travelers Watch a Sunrise," one of the three Chinese who serve as main characters philoso-phizes thus beside the body of a suicide, as dawn brightens the sky:

> *"Sunrise is multiplied,*
> *Like the earth on which it shines,*
> *By the eyes that open on it,*
> *Even dead eyes,*
> *As red is multiplied by the leaves of trees."*
> (*Poetry,* VIII, 178.)

The second choice, however, finds articulation in "Thinking of a Relation between the Images of Metaphors," in which the problem of perception is again presented in metaphori-cal terms: "In the one ear of the fisherman, who is all / One ear, the wood-doves are singing a single song." The third choice is obviously too naive a solution, convincing only to those who have not posed the problem of perception to themselves or had it posed.

The word Stevens uses for the difference made by the subject in the object is description, which is "a little different from reality"; it is neither what is described nor an imitation of it, but rather something artificial that exists no place, only in the spirit's universe, that intangible "locale" of all seem-ing. This somewhat elusive view of appearance is elaborated upon in the fifth section of "Description without Place":

about the restricted meaning he gives to *description,* Stevens
here says:

> *It is an expectation, a desire,*
> *A palm that rises up beyond the sea,*
>
> *A little different from reality:*
> *The difference that we make in what we see*
>
> *And our memorials of that difference,*
> *Sprinklings of bright particulars from the sky.*

The term Stevens makes synonymous with such description
is *revelation,* the Biblical connotations of which he underlines in the sixth part of the poem; there he speaks of description as the double, though not too closely the double,
of our lives—artificial, visible, intense; then he defines it as

> *A text we should be born that we might read,*
> *More explicit than the experience of sun*
>
> *And moon, the book of reconciliation,*
> *Book of a concept only possible*
>
> *In description, canon central in itself,*
> *The thesis of the plentifullest John.*

The fullest illustration of the "difference that we make in
what we see" is the early and widely anthologized lyric, "Sea
Surface Full of Clouds," the five sections of which ring a
single setting through five changes. The setting in question
is a November seascape near Tehuantepec, at daybreak. Ar-
ranged in six tercets, each part of the poem delineates a view
of the ocean that reflects the highly colored Mexican sky:
Stevens worked out his five-paneled picture with exquisite
balancing of syntax, delicately adjusted shadings of diction,
using for every twelfth line an explanatory sentence in
French to indicate how the shifting selves of the observer
remodel this "fluent mundo" of sea and cloudy heavens, how
in turn they evolve protean cloud-blossoms in marine gardens. The poem has been intelligently explicated in detail

by John Pauker in *Furioso;* Pauker concludes his essay thus:

> "The sea / And heaven rolled as one" and they presumably proceed to present an infinity of new combinations to the observer, "fresh transfigurings of freshest blue," subject to his understanding and his will. We have the assurrance, however, that these metamorphoses can no more be problematical or ominous. (v, 46.)

This is the victory of the imagination over brute facts of sensory stimuli, a conquest to be treated at greater length later in this chapter.

One of the poet's finest accounts of the process of perception is in "Woman Looking at a Vase of Flowers":

> *It was as if thunder took form upon*
> *The piano, that time: the time when the crude*
> *And jealous grandeurs of sun and sky*
> *Scattered themselves in the garden, like*
> *The wind dissolving into birds,*
> *The clouds becoming braided girls, . . .*
>
> *Hoot, little owl within her, how*
> *High blue became particular*
> *In the leaf and bud and how the red,*
> *Flicked into pieces, points of air,*
> *Became — how the central, essential red*
> *Escaped its large abstraction, became,*
> *First, summer, then a lesser time,*
> *Then the sides of peaches, of dusky pears.*
>
> *. . . The crude and jealous formlessness*
> *Became the form and the fragrance of things*
> *Without clairvoyance, close to her.*

To the subject of the lyric, the bouquet becomes thunder, summer, the sides of peaches and pears; the abstract red and blue turn into particulars. Colors and shapes powerfully stir the woman; she is conscious of related impressions, which have a metamorphic nature: "The wind dissolving into birds, / The clouds becoming braided girls, . . ." These comparisons point out that the mind as well as the eye has its metamorphoses.

The spectator walking about New Haven on an ordinary evening regards certain chapels and schools as transformed men, openly displaying in their new identities the secrets they hid while human:

> *It is as if*
> *Men turning into things, as comedy,*
> *Stood, dressed in antic symbols, to display*
>
> *The truth about themselves, having lost, as things,*
> *That power to conceal they had as men. . . .*
>   ("An Ordinary Evening in New Haven")

In Ovid trees frequently are not really trees but victims of love; stones, rivers, stars, not actually inanimate settings of man's life but men and women removed to lower realms of existence. Stevens adapts the principle of mutation to accord with the exigencies of his twentieth-century world by making the buildings of a Connecticut city exteriorizations of its inhabitants, at least in the mind of one beholder.

A universally valid example of how the minds transfigures sensory detail is the way in which, to one indulging in summer reverie, clouds turn into one thing and then another as they form and re-form in endless progress across the sky. Besides braided girls (a specialized image not apt to occur to anyone but Stevens), clouds become fortresses, sheep, groves of blossoming trees, ships, and thousands of other objects preserved in the cliches of minor poetry. "Sunday Morning," first published in 1915, had called the earth an island afloat in space; twenty-five years later "An Ordinary Evening in New Haven" depreciates our planet still further by reducing it to a cloud. In the sixth section of "The Auroras of Autumn," Stevens experiments with this idea:

It is a theatre floating through the clouds,
Itself a cloud, although of misted rock
And mountains running like water, wave on wave,

Through waves of light. It is of cloud transformed
To cloud transformed again, idly, the way
A season changes color to no end,

Except the lavishing of itself in change,
As light changes yellow into gold and gold
To its opal elements and fire's delight,

Splashed wide-wise because it likes magnificence
And the solemn pleasures of magnificent space.
The cloud drifts idly through half-thought-of forms.

The conversion of earth to cloud and mountain to water,
with the implied change of ocean to light (air) to fire, is
only an apparent one; yet it belongs to that extensive literature dealing with transmutation of the four elements, of
which Plato, Lucretius, and Ovid among the ancients and
John Donne in such poems as the Anniversary elegies furnish only a few examples. Mountains are not really converted to water here; they appear like water ("running like
water"). The poem celebrates chiefly a "trick of the light":
the earth is a cloud because light transforms it as light transforms the clouds through "half-thought-of forms." Solidity
has nothing to do with the change; light as seen transforms
rock and vapor alike.

Besides the transformations effected by perception, things
are changed by the words used to refer to them; nomencla-
ture adds to the image on the retina, the vibrations on the
eardrum. In "Certain Phenomena of Sound" Sister Eulalia
is created of her name, just as is the dark-syllabled Semiramide:

You were created of your name, the word
Is that of which you were the personage.
There is no life except in the word of it.
I write Semiramide and in the script
I am and have a being and play a part.
You are that white Eulalia of the name.

Earlier in this poem the Roamer, telling to the background
of music what things he has seen as he wanders through the
redwoods, constructs what he speaks of: "A sound producing the things that are spoken." The same process, creation
through music, occurs in "The Auroras of Autumn":

> *As if the innocent mother sang in the dark*
> *Of the room and on an accordion, half-heard,*
> *Created the time and place in which we breathed.* . . .

The subjunctive mode in this poem, and the use of the verb
seem in "Certain Phenomena of Sound," prevent one from
ascribing to Stevens such a thorough-going idealism as
might otherwise be warranted by these passages. "A Post-
card from the Volcano" declares that what is said about
a mansion becomes a part of it. Stevens affirms the same
belief in "An Ordinary Evening in New Haven": "The poem
is the cry of its occasion, / Part of the res itself and not
about it." These are, perhaps, extreme instances of reifica-
tion, but they serve to show his conviction that the perceiving agent greatly alters reality.

Some objects, on the other hand, resist the catalysts of
language and sense; among these are

> *The weight of primary noon,*
> *The A B C of being,*
>
> *The ruddy temper, the hammer*
> *Of red and blue, the hard sound—*
> *Steel against intimation—the sharp flash,*
> *The vital, arrogant, fatal, dominant X.*

From the testimony of this poem ("The Motive for Metaphor") Stevens apparently considers summer as a fullness
of expression too much itself to need or sustain metaphor,
unlike the half-seasons of autumn and spring, which some
persons prefer to a complete reality. Certain roses in sunlight are

> *Too much as they are to be changed by metaphor,*
> *Too actual, things that in being real*
> *Make any imaginings of them lesser things.*

Although ordinarily man can, at least in theory, make things over, some objects like the two pears in a lyric from *Parts of a World* impose their own qualities so violently that they "Are not seen / As the observer wills," but as they are. Other examples wherein two forces pull in opposite directions, victory going to the real over the fictive, are the rising sun, calm sea, and moon hanging in the sky of "Notes toward a Supreme Fiction," which Stevens declares "are not things transformed. / Yet we are shaken by them as if they were."

The perceiving agent is symbolized often by the wind, called Jumbo in the poem of that name, a "companion in nothingness" who although a transformer is himself transformed. Although the sounds of the sea are meaningless, the sounds of the wind are speech, as in the quatrain, "To the Roaring Wind," the last poem in *Harmonium*, wherein the wind, credited with consciousness, searches for a word; or in "Page from a Tale," where unlike the water, which utters no accurate syllable, the wind cries *so blau, so lind, so lau.* Human speech imitates the wind rather than the other way around:

> Let this be clear that we are men of sun
> And men of day and never of pointed night,
> Men that repeat antiquest sounds of air
> In an accord of repetitions. Yet,
> If we repeat, it is because the wind
> Encircling us, speaks always with our speech.
> ("Evening without Angels")

The superiority of the wind's voice over man's is summarized in "The Auroras of Autumn" thus: "What company, / In masks, can choir it with the naked wind?"

In the poem significantly called "Metamorphosis" the wind plays around with the names of the months, which are as vitally connected with their referents as are the names of characters in a Jonsonian comedy:

> *Yillow, yillow, yillow,*
> *Old worm, my pretty quirk,*
> *How the wind spells out*
> *Sep—tem—ber. . . .*
>
> *Summer is in bones.*
> *Cock-robin's at Caracas.*
> *Make o, make o, make o,*
> *Otu—otu—bre.*
>
> *And the rude leaves fall.*
> *The rain falls. The sky*
> *Falls and lies with the worms.*
> *The street lamps*
>
> *Are those that have been hanged,*
> *Dangling in an illogical*
> *To and to and fro*
> *Fro Niz—nil—imbo.*

From the very start the wind is shown taking liberties with its autumn world, altering *yellow* to *yillow* as illustration of how September leaves lose their clear yellow to the brown stains of decay. Of summer, only the skeleton is left; the robin, symbol of summer, has migrated to Venezuela. At the end of stanza two, the sound of September has been distorted by the wind to *Oto—otu—bre;* after evidences of seasonal change the word finally becomes *Niz—nil—imbo,* a blending of *frozen, nil,* and *limbo,* with of course a suggestion also of *November.* It is no shock to hear that leaves and rain fall, since this is their natural behavior, though the adjective *rude* as a modifier for leaves causes some surprise. But when the sky falls, to lie with the worms, one realizes that a meaningful universe where things happen according to expected patterns has been replaced by a surrealistic one, void of reason, as different as possible from things of August, a world where street lamps are crazily pushed to and fro by the wind, as if they were Villon's hanged men.

Older than Narcissus, the wind stands for a self which

creates in the best idealistic fashion its rocks and stones.
Jumbo is

> *Ancestor of Narcissus, prince*
> *Of secondary men. There are no rocks*
> *And stones, only this imager*

Nature, as in the Narcissus myth, is a mirror of the psyche,
but of a constantly changing psyche:

> *If, while he lives, he hears himself*
> *Sounded in music, if the sun,*
> *Stormer, is the color of a self*
> *As certainly as night is the color*
> *Of a self, if, without sentiment,*
> *He is what he hears and sees and if,*
> *Without pathos, he feels what he hears*
> *And sees, being nothing otherwise,*
> *Having nothing otherwise, he has not*
> *To go to the Louvre to behold himself.*
>   ("Prelude to Objects")

The young men walking in the woods in "The Pediment of
Appearance" cry: "The world is myself, life is myself, /
Breathing as if they breathed themselves." "Theory" affirms:
"I am what is around me"; if man influences what he sees
or names, the non-ego in turn has power over him, giving
him a character, says the poet in this proposition, which by
an exchange of the subject and predicate nominative would
be merely a restatement of the young men's proclamation.

This theory that the perceiving agent causes his world to
exist as a projection of himself, present in several others of
Stevens's poems, is forcefully stated in the essay which forms
the first of "Three Academic Pieces." Narcissus has traditionally been regarded as the supreme egoist, his infatuation
with the reflection of himself given back by external reality
as a great folly. This is a mistaken attitude toward the myth,
according to Wallace Stevens, since after all Narcissus was
only acting in harmony with the principles of his nature and
ours:

Yet Narcissus did not expect, when he looked in the stream, to find in his hair a serpent coiled to strike, nor, when he looked in his own eyes there to be met by a look of hate, nor, in general, to discover himself at the center of an inexplicable ugliness from which he would be bound to avert himself. On the contrary, he sought out his image everywhere because it was the principle of his nature to do so and, to go a step beyond that, because it was the principle of his nature, as it is of ours, to expect to find pleasure in what he found. Narcissism, then, involves something beyond the prime sense of the word. It involves, also, this principle, that as we seek out our own resemblances we expect to find pleasure in doing so, that is to say, in what we find. So strong is that expectation that we find nothing else.*

It is only natural, then, that we should rejoice in the resemblance of ourselves which we find in the world outside us, a resemblance conferred by our longing to discover it there.

The relation of subject to object is a metaphysical problem Stevens likes to meditate upon, as shown by "An Ordinary Evening in New Haven," a poem which constitutes over sixty pages of *The Auroras of Autumn.* In the second section, he supposes that "these houses are composed of ourselves," with the result that New Haven becomes "an impalpable town," its bells, "transparencies of sound"; if this be true, then it follows that New Haven is "So much ourselves, we cannot tell apart / The idea and the bearer-being of the idea." Further on he advises us to consider "Reality as a thing seen by the mind, / Not that which is but that which is apprehended." If these suppositions are valid, man might be regarded as a magician who makes phenomena real. The flowering Judas, dark-spiced branches of trees, cat-bird's gobble are "real only if I make them so."

A final step in this tracing of the metamorphoses undergone by the objective world is the way in which a whole age takes character from one powerful figure. The term *Eliza-*

* *The Necessary Angel* by Wallace Stevens. Copyright 1942, 1944, 1947, 1948, 1949, 1951 by Wallace Stevens. By permission of Alfred A. Knopf, Inc.

bethan as applicable to the golden period of the sixteenth
century is too dulled by use for flaming details of its origin
to leap in the minds of average men, but Stevens, with incredible alertness, looks afresh at the hackneyed phrase
Elizabethan age and sees Elizabeth as a green queen in a
summer of sun, the greenness and sunlight created by her
own splendor:

> *Her green mind made the world around her green*
> *The queen is an example. . .. . This green queen*
>
> *In the seeming of the summer of her sun*
> *By her own seeming made the summer change.*
> ("Description without Place")

There are various kinds of queens—red, blue, green, argent
—each of whom bestows an identity upon her *milieu*. John
Malcolm Brinnin, in the Wallace Stevens number of *Voices*
(Spring, 1945), emphasizes the importance for this poet
of the human agent acting upon externality:

> For Stevens, as for Plato, there is 'no single truth' in the
> world about us, neither is there real change. There are,
> rather, endless interpretations and rearrangements of
> sense data, and infinite refinements of the perceiving sen-
> sibility itself. (31)

Those individuals most capable of swaying popular imagination, then, determine what forms the metamorphoses of
sense data will take.

Just as metamorphosis links the objective and the subjective worlds, so it connects the realm of reality with the realm
of the imagination. In fact these are not two realms at all,
but one—the realm of resemblance. And since the structure
underlying them is the same, a complex and ever-flowing
system of resemblances, it follows that one theory will explain them both. All referents for poetry are found in reality,
though not all of them are material.

Everything in our environment is, in certain respects, like

everything else, bound together in an inescapable relationship which is the basis of appearance. In "Three Academic
Pieces" Stevens shows how this truth operates by analyzing
the colors of a seascape:

> Take for example, a beach extending as far as the eye can
> reach, bordered, on the one hand, by trees and, on the
> other, by the sea. The sky is cloudless and the sun is red.
> In what sense do the objects in this scene resemble each
> other? There is enough green in the sea to relate it to the
> palms. There is enough of the sky reflected in the water
> to create a resemblance, in some sense, between them.
> The sand is yellow between the green and the blue. In
> short, the light alone creates a unity not only in the reced-
> ings of distance, where differences become invisible, but
> also in the contacts of closer sight. So, too, sufficiently
> generalized, each man resembles all other men, each
> woman resembles all other women, this year resembles
> last year. The beginning of time will, no doubt, resemble
> the end of time. One world is said to resemble another.*

It is easy to see how like things resemble each other (man
and man, woman and woman, year and year); it is not so
easy to apply this principle to dissimilar objects, such as
sand and water, palm tree and sky. But Stevens's ingenuity
in using color as a bond is persuasive enough to let the illustration stand as a foundation for his aesthetic theory.

Resemblance is omnipresent in Nature; poetry, however,
must supply resemblances to its fictions if these are to be
truly supreme. Fortunately, it has two ways of doing so
denied to Nature:

> In metaphor (and this word is used as a symbol for the
> single aspect of poetry with which we are now concerned
> —that is to say, the creation of resemblance by the imagi-
> nation, even though metamorphosis might be a better
> word) —in metaphor, the resemblance may be, first, be-
> tween two or more parts of reality; second, between

* *Ibid.,* pp. 71–72.

> something real and something imagined . . . and, third,
> between two imagined things. . . .*

For the second way, Stevens gives as an example music and that which music evokes in us; for the last he has in mind two abstractions.

The importance of equations in the critical prose of Wallace Stevens can hardly be over-stated, a sign of intellectual exactitude found also in the criticism of Ezra Pound; indeed, Pound's Imagist tenets are the equivalent of Stevens's passion for finding metaphors that come ever closer and closer to the ideal resemblance. The essay which is the first of the "Three Academic Pieces" is rich in equations: accuracy of literature is equated with accuracy of the structure of reality; reality, with the central reference for poetry; the desire for resemblance, with the desire to enjoy reality; and both these with the desire for elegance; false exaggeration, with the disturbance of balance between imagination and reality; life in metaphor, with the imagination. Stevens here discusses six topics: (a) poetry (b) metaphor (c) metamorphosis (d) resemblance (e) partial similarity between two dissimilar things (f) activity of the imagination. If these are considered anonymously, as letters, an analysis of the essay reveals that $a = b = c = d = e = f$. He clarifies his terms carefully, excluding identity and imitation from the meaning of resemblance, and hence from the meaning of the six topics synonymous with it, for instance, from metamorphosis.

This is not the only instance in his criticism where Stevens uses metamorphosis and poetry interchangeably. In "Effects of Analogy," delivered at Yale as a Bergen lecture in 1948, he says:

> Poetry is almost incredibly one of the effects of analogy.
> This statement involves much more than the analogy of
> figures of speech since otherwise poetry would be little
> more than a trick. But it is almost incredibly the outcome

* *Ibid.*

of figures of speech or, what is the same thing, the outcome of the operation of one imagination on another,
through the instrumentality of the figures. To identify
poetry and metaphor or metamorphosis is merely to ab-
breviate the last remark.*

The same article elucidates an equation even more stimulating than those in "The Realm of Resemblance": the poet's
sense of the world = the poet's world = the poet's subject = reality plus imagination. Such meditations in philosophy, carried on with an extraordinary seriousness, make
the term hedonist, accorded to Stevens by more than one
critic, hardly an appropriate one; they invalidate likewise
the view that he is merely a strummer of nuances on a guitar.
an exponent of preciosity, a dandy.

Four years before the Bergen lecture on analogy, another
Stevens essay, "The Figure of the Youth as Virile Poet," laid
the critical foundations for a metamorphic concept of poetry. After reviewing the difficulties of defining poetry,
Stevens here remarks that at times we feel confident of
reaching a center around which variations of the definition
may cluster: "We say that poetry is metamorphosis and we
come to see in a few lines descriptive of an eye, a hand, a
stick, the essence of the matter." (45) The "matter" which
Stevens is referring to here is the *vis* or *noeud vital* which
might constitute the center of poetry, discovery of which is
a prerequisite for any valid definition. The philosopher, rely-
ing only upon reason, can never come to such a definition.
Can the poet? Enigmatically, Stevens puts his answer to this
question in a suppositional manner, confusing us by his
introduction of the indicative form *was* into the conditional
clause:

> Suppose the poet discovered and had the power there-
> after at will and by intelligence to reconstruct us by his
> transformations. He would also have the power to de-
> stroy us. If there was, or if we believed there was, a
> centre, it would be absurd to fear or to avoid its discovery.

* *Ibid.,* pp. 117–118.

This dangerous nature of poetry finds further articulation in "Poetry Is a Destructive Force." Stevens reveals one source of the idea central to this poem when he writes: "Does not the saying of Picasso that a picture is a horde of destructions, also say that a poem is a horde of destructions?" ("The Relations between Poetry and Painting," *The Necessary Angel*, 161.) One might imagine these lines as describing one of Ovid's transformations, since in these, when human beings were made beasts, reason was always transferred into the body of the irrational creature:

> *That's what misery is,*
> *Nothing to have at heart.*
> *It is to have or nothing.*
>
> *It is a thing to have,*
> *A lion, an ox in his breast,*
> *To feel it breathing there.*
>
> *Corazon, stout dog,*
> *Young ox, bow-legged bear,*
> *He tastes its blood, not spit.*
>
> *He is like a man*
> *In the body of a violent beast.*
> *Its muscles are his own. . . .*
>
> *The lion sleeps in the sun.*
> *Its nose is on its paws.*
> *It can kill a man.*

The last six lines might almost apply to Hippomenes in Book Ten of the *Metamorphoses*, when after his successful wooing of Atalanta he meets doom at the hands of Venus, whose temple he has defiled; he is turned into a lion, together with his bride, and condemned to roam the Caledonian forest. Stevens is not content to state that poetry is metamorphosis; he must also write a poem wherein it shows itself to be so.

There are different degrees of excellence in poetry considered as metamorphosis, depending upon the things compared. To return to "The Realm of Resemblance," if these are two unlike things of adequate dignity, the resemblance transfigures, sublimates them. The common property is made brilliant. When the human mind moves from some exquisite earthly scene, such as a moonlit evening on a Caribbean island, to the thought of Paradise, both ideas gain in glory. In such a manner poetry transfigures, though not always so ambitiously. About this, Stevens says:

> However, not all poetry attempts such grandiose transfiguration. Evereyone can call to mind a variety of figures and see clearly how these resemblances please and why; how inevitably they heighten our sense of reality. The images in Ecclesiastes:
>
> > *Or ever*
> > *the silver cord be loosed, or the golden bowl be*
> > *broken, or the pitcher be broken at the fountain,*
> > *or the wheel broken at the cistern—*
>
> these images are not the language of reality, they are the symbolic language of metamorphosis, or resemblance, of poetry, but they relate to reality and they intensify our sense of it and they give us the pleasure of "lentor and solemnity" in respect to the most commonplace objects.*

The silver cord, golden bowl, pitcher, and wheel are parts of the tangible world though used in this passage as symbols to effect metamorphosis or resemblance or poetry—here Stevens makes no attempt to differentiate among the three. The destruction of the body, which these represent figuratively, borrows an imaginative radiance from then, just as they, inanimate creatures, acquire a new lustre from their association with human death. Poetry satisfies our desire for resemblance but more than that, by the activity of the imagination in discovering likeness, it intensifies reality, enhances it, heightens it.

* *Ibid.*, p. 78.

A knowledge of this theory of resemblance helps greatly in understanding Stevens's work. The originality for which he has frequently been praised and which has caused his reading public to grow but gradually (since people are frightened of the unfamiliar) is accounted for by the uniqueness of resemblance, first in nature and then, as a consequence, in art. The chief symbol for the anti-mechanical changes in the physical world is the sea. "Sea Surface Full of Clouds" comes to the mind at once; there are many less obvious examples of this "sea-change."

No two waves, leaves, hands, sunsets, men are like. Believing this, the poet cannot write in conventional tropes; what the neo-classical age considered part of the resources open to an artist, Stevens repudiates as static, lifeless, and hence fatal to poetry. Such a credo has given rise to the amazing and exact verbal equations characteristic of him, for instance the twelve metaphors for a pineapple in the second of "Three Academic Pieces":

1. *The hut stands by itself beneath the palms.*
2. *Out of their bottle the green genii come.*
3. *A vine has climbed the other side of the wall.*

4. *The sea is sprouting upward out of rocks.*
5. *Symbol of feasts and of oblivion . . .*
6. *White sky, pink sun, trees on a distant peak.*

7. *These lozenges are nailed-up lattices.*
8. *The owl sits humped. It has a hundred eyes.*
9. *The coconut and cockerel in one.*

10. *This is how yesterday's volcano looks.*
11. *There is an island Palahude by name—*
12. *An uncivil shape like a gigantic haw.*

One more point, in a discussion of how poetry is metamorphosis in the writing of Wallace Stevens, is that art, by erasing the defects of its original, results in the ideal, in the universal unlimited by the particular, though drawn from it. In his most complete poetic statement on aesthetics, "Notes toward a Supreme Fiction," which concludes *Transport to Summer,* Stevens presents the poem as transmuting life to Eden-like perfection: "The poem refreshes life so that we share, / For a moment, the first idea. . . ." Later in the same work he rephrases the proposition thus: "The freshness of transformation is / The freshness of a world." Stevens works in the opposite direction from the Platonic theory. For Plato a poetic figure about a plum (A) was a copy of a real plum (B) which might perhaps have a bad spot on its underside and which itself was copied from the perfect plum (C) existing in the world of ideas. For Stevens, C drops out and A is superior to B. He is, indeed, closer to Aristotelian imitation, in spite of his repugnance for the term *imitation* as expressed in "The Realm of Resemblance." To Aristotle mimesis was not a mere copying of the object as it existed in nature; it was a resemblance worked out into perfection in so far as the maker was able to do so. All aspects of the object extraneous to its perfection were eliminated. The supreme fiction must give pleasure, it must change, but it must also be abstract—the Stevensian word for ideal.

The ideal, moreover, is the absolute. One can think of ideas as going an endless journey through matter, realizing here more and there less of their original perfection as they progress toward their end which is their beginning. A similar concept, as applied to art, underlies Henri Focillon's *The Life of Forms in Art,* which Stevens has called one of the really remarkable books of the day, drawing upon it twice in the course of his essay, "The Figure of the Youth as Virile Poet." Focillon, interestingly enough, bases his aesthetic upon metamorphoses. He believes that plastic forms constitute an order of existence, alive and in motion, and that they are continually renewed by metamorphosis:

Plastic forms are subjected to the principle of metamorphoses, by which they are perpetually renewed, as well
as to the principle of styles, by which their relationship
is, although by no means with any regularity of recurrence, first tested then made fast, and finally disrupted.
(6)

The work of art may seem to be fixed, but in reality it
is born of change and moves on to other changes, a truth
shown by an examination of preliminary sketches by Rembrandt or any other artist. One might imagine that designs
so apparently static as the arabesque of Moslem ornament,
the product of geometry rather than emotion, would be ex-
ceptions to this ever-varying life of forms. Quite the contrary; about such patterns, Focillon says:

But deep within them, a sort of fever seems to goad on
and to multiply the shapes; some mysterious genius of
complication interlocks, enfolds, disorganizes, and reor-
ganizes the entire labyrinth. Their very immobility spar-
kles with metamorphoses.

Romanesque sculpture is analogous to this, with chimerical
creatures ceaselessly reborn in a mocking flight from fixa-
tion:

Form becomes a *rinceau,* a double-headed eagle, a mermaid, a duel of warriors. It duplicates, coils back upon,
and devours its own shape. Without once trespassing its
limits or falsifying its principles, this protean monster
rouses up, and unrolls its demented existence—an existence that is merely the turmoil and the undulation of a
single, simple form.

Even the human body, declares Focillon, controlled as
its depiction is by the fact that the artist takes it from Nature and not from his imagination, is capable of inexhausti-
ble variety; a metamorphosis as astonishing as Daphne's
and far more subtle has occurred between Raphael's Or-
leans Madonna and the Madonna of the Chair.

Form may, however, become formula, canon—and it is this descent to the stereotyped for which Stevens feels an intense repugnance. Certain landscapes, in or out of art, distress us because of this hardening process:

> *It means the distaste we feel for this withered scene*
>
> *Is that it has not changed enough. It remains,*
> *It is a repetition.*
>
> ("Notes toward a Supreme Fiction")

But primarily form is life, moving ahead restlessly toward the absolute through the medium of the artist who incarnates it:

> Even as the artist fulfills his function of geometrician and mechanic, of physicist and chemist, of psychologist and historian, so does form, guided by the play and interplay of metamorphoses, go forever forward, by its own necessity, toward its own liberty. (Focillon, 76.)

Just as in "The Realm of Resemblance" Stevens identifies the activity of the imagination in poetry with metamorphosis, so M. Focillon heads one of the sections of his book: "Technique as the instrumentation of metamorphosis and as epistemological mode." (42) In the passage following this title he declares that he regards technique not as automatism or as a system of rules but as a poetry of action and "as the means for the achievement of metamorphoses." Analysis of preliminary forms of any masterpiece—the stages by which an artifact climbs to its perfection—will, he feels, show how valid this view is. While the emphasis in *The Life of Forms in Art* is not primarily a literary one, the book is illuminating in a study of Stevens because of the close similarity between its tenets and those of his own critical prose. Both Focillon and Stevens have a passion for nicety of distinctions and a Platonic attraction for the immaterial as opposed to a positivistic interpretation of reality.

One more phase of Focillon's thesis which resembles the

practice and theory of Wallace Stevens is the French critic's affirmation that substances (by which he means media) are interchangeable; forms undergo a metamorphosis as they pass from one to another, the initial, simple idea remaining incorrupt, so that an engraving made from a painting is only a transposition. Flaubert's reference to the Parthenon's being black as ebony is explained thus by Focillon:

> He wished, perhaps, to indicate an absolute quality—the absolute of a measure that dominates matter and even metamorphoses it, or to put it more simply, the stern authority of a single, indestructible thought.

One manifestation of such an interest in Stevens is the way in which he has always been drawn by the problem of interrelationships among the arts. His imagery taken from music, sculpture, architecture, painting, helps him to present in different realms whatever single, pure form his genius has invented or discovered, to exhibit it in several ways, attempting to come ever closer to its ideal existence in the world of eternal forms. His constant devotion to nuances, to variations on a theme, is another mark of belief in an immortal root-concept.

The lecture which Stevens gave at the Museum of Modern Art in New York on January 15, 1951, is impregnated with the notion of a Platonic ideal world. As is usual with him, however, the diction is so cautious that one is never absolutely sure of his beliefs. What he states categorically he quickly qualifies:

> There is a universal poetry that is reflected in everything. This remark approaches the idea of Baudelaire that there exists an unascertained and fundamental aesthetic, or order, of which poetry and painting are manifestations, but of which, for that matter, sculpture or music or any other aesthetic realization would equally be a manifestation.*

* *Ibid.,* p. 160.

Thus there may be many poetries—of mankind, of children, in words, in paint—though in a larger sense all poetry is one; in some types of art it is as if poetry and life itself were the same thing.

"Effects of Analogy," "The Realm of Resemblance," and "The Figure of the Youth as Virile Poet" are insistent that a theory of poetry is also a theory of reality. Tennyson felt that if he could understand a fragment of reality (the flower in the crannied wall) he could understand the whole; Stevens feels that if he can understand poetry he can understand the entire structure of things. If one is able to write poetry deserving the title of supreme fiction, or if he can read it as it should be read—also a creative activity—he has learned a secret which is as radical to life as it is to letters. Perhaps by way of vindicating himself from the libel of hedonism, Stevens returns again and again to this coming-together of what have been traditionally regarded as two spheres:

> We have been trying to get at a truth about poetry, to get at one of the principles that compose the theory of poetry. It comes to this, that poetry is a part of the structure of reality. If this has been demonstrated, it pretty much amounts to saying that the structure of poetry and the structure of reality are one or, in effect, that poetry and reality are one, or should be.*

"Effects of Analogy" presents poetry as an analogue of the world. The thirty-odd years of Stevens's career as a poet have been dedicated to an anatomy of the world, which has proved to be at the same time an anatomy of poetry.

The world is a changing world. One aspect of this principle of change is that it results from a union of opposites, each depending upon the other: man on woman, day on night, the imagined on the real, winter on spring, music on silence, morning on afternoon, North on South, sun on rain.

* *Ibid.,* pp. 80–81.

("Notes toward a Supreme Fiction") From this metaphysical law pleasure arises:

> —*a law of inherent opposites,*
> *Of essential unity, is as pleasant as port,*
> *As pleasant as the brush-strokes of a bough,*
> *An upper, particular bough in, say, Marchand.*
> ("Connoisseur of Chaos")

The ordinary man may not be able to put the matter into precise syllogisms, but he suffers from this primitive need of his nature to achieve integrity through the reconciliation of opposites—a paradox which is at the core of the Christian dispensation. About such plain men Stevens says:

> *They only know a savage assuagement cries*
> *With a savage voice; and in that cry they hear*
> *Themselves transposed, muted and comforted*
>
> *In a savage and subtle and simple harmony,*
> *A matching and mating of surprised accords,*
> *A responding to a diviner opposite.*
>
> *So lewd spring comes from winter's chastity.*
> ("An Ordinary Evening in New Haven")

As "Study of Images II" puts it, the imagination mimics this fusion of unlike things found in nature, relating opposites, even marrying them; it conceives moons composed of shade, women with other lives (perhaps snakes) in their hair, mermaids: "As if, as if, as if the disparate halves / Of things were waiting in a betrothal known / To none. . . ." By means of opposites ("by aid of land and sea, / Night and day, wind and quiet") the cloudy world produces other nights, days, clouds, worlds. ("Variations on a Summer Day") Not only the arsis but also the thesis is an essential unit for absolute music. The very title of Stevens's first book, *Harmonium* (1923), epitomizes his desire to reconcile. Whatever the word owes to Baudelaire's "Harmonie du

Soir," it points toward "the whole, / The complicate, the
amassing harmony" by combining the reference of a small
reed organ with that of a just adaptation of parts one to
another. *Ideas of Order,* published in 1936, continues this
assemblage of pieces, this time of a mental reality. *Parts of
a World* (1942) sums up the process in "Parochial Theme,"
which begins the collection: "Piece the world together, boys,
but not with your hands." Having put his world together,
Stevens in *Transport to Summer* (1947) invites man to
enter it.

What are these parts to be harmonized by the individual?
They resolve themselves into a formidable display of opposites. All the imaged world consists of antitheses, which
must undergo a change more powerful than vehicles in
metaphors exert on their tenors before man can be content

In a world that shrinks to an immediate whole,

That we do not need to understand, complete
Without secret arrangements of it in the mind.
                    ("Description without Place")

Yet actually this transformation should not be difficult, because each of the terms in a pair depends by nature upon
the other and this very contingency is the origin of change;
the singulars unite easily into a Heracleitan "plural" which
is really another singular: "And sun and rain a plural, like
two lovers / That walk away as one in the greenest body."
("Notes toward a Supreme Fiction")

In *Transport to Summer* Stevens begs men to resist the
pressure of reality, which he considers the deciding artistic
factor in any age, to abandon action for contemplation long
enough to think of how spring and autumn, art and reality,
life and death, form a whole. Approach to such an ordering
of experience is to be made through poetry, which succeeds
in achieving harmony on the level of the fictive since it can
rearrange the real, on which it depends, through imagination—according to Stevensian criteria, the will of things.

Certain pairs of opposites, however, can never be recon-
ciled: the poor and the rich, for instance. This denial of the
possibility of economic leveling indicates the anti-Marxist
attitude of the poet.

Another characteristic of the world of Wallace Stevens
is the fluidity of essence. Besides this union of opposites in
Nature, there is also a mysterious transference of essences.
Now that the concept of essence is no longer taken for
granted—at least in several schools of modern philosophy
—this interference with quiddity requires less suspension of
disbelief than it would have in earlier periods. One instance
of such mutations occurs in the middle section of "Notes
toward a Supreme Fiction": the water of the lake, says the
poet, was "Like a momentary color, in which swans / Were
seraphs, were saints, were changing essences." In "Variations on a Summer Day," the rocks of the cliffs are heads
of dogs that turn into fishes and plunge into the sea; this,
of course, occurs only in the imagination, though the de-
sideratum is "To change nature, not merely to change
ideas."

"The Apostrophe to Vincentine" begins with the poet's
imagining Vincentine as a small, nude, nameless creature
between single-colored earth and dark blue sky; then he
actually sees her, and she changes to a warm, clean girl in
a whited green dress (green standing as it usually does in
Stevens for reality); when she approaches, talking, he adds
her emotions to his conception of her, since what others feel
makes a difference in what we see:

> *And what I knew you felt*
> *Monotonous earth I saw become*
> *Came then.*
> *Illimitable spheres of you,*
> *And that white animal, so lean,*
> *Turned Vincentine,*
> *Turned heavenly Vincentine,*
> *And that white animal, so lean,*
> *Turned heavenly, heavenly Vincentine.*

The monotonous earth metamorphoses into illimitable spheres of Vincentine, and she herself has turned from the lean white animal with which the poem started to just the opposite of animality—to *heavenly* Vincentine, the adjective here heightened by repetition and by the ambiguity of its first use. Stevens has meticulously chosen his heroine's name, for reasons of sense as well as of sound, since Vincentine means *conquering;* the word not only serves as a rhyme for *between, lean, clean,* and *green,* but signifies the victory of consciousness over inanimate being.

Still one more illustration of the fluidity of essence is the poem "The House Was Quiet and the World Was Calm," in which "The reader became the book; and summer night / Was like the conscious being of the book," a progression which identifies the reader with the summer night. Again Stevens surprises by using the indicative where accepted grammar would demand the subjunctive, as if to obliterate the distinction between wish and fulfillment; the scholar hears the words of the book spoken "as if there was no book." The poet goes on to say that truth itself is summer, the night, the reader—a blending of essences reminiscent of Eliot's "music heard so deeply that you are the music" in the *Quartets.* The entire lyric is but another phrasing of the exchanges between man and his environment, a topic which Stevens has been experimenting with since the 1917 publication in *Poetry* of his play, "Carlos Among the Candles." This brief drama opens with the entrance of Carlos, carrying a lighted taper. His first speech includes in embryo all that Stevens has later enunciated on the instability of essence:

> How the solitude of this candle penetrates me! I light a candle in the darkness. It fills the darkness with solitude, which becomes my own. I become a part of the solitude of the candle . . . of the darkness flowing over the house and into it . . . Just to go through a door, and the change . . . the becoming a part, instantly, of that profounder room . . . and equally to feel it communi-

cating, with the same persistency its own mood, its own
influence . . . and there, too, to feel the lesser influences of the shapes of things, of exhalations, sounds.
. . . (116)

Whatever the shortcomings of this piece as theater, its
epistemological foreshadowings are noteworthy.

In "Anecdote of Men by the Thousand" a necessary relationship is set up between an environment and its inhabitants, wherein the men of the East are the East, the men of
a province equal that province, the men of a valley and the
valley itself are the same thing; even mandolins and dresses
are the places they are found in, Aristotle's laws of contra-
diction and identity notwithstanding. According to such
reasoning, man is natureless; his essence depends upon his
whereabouts: "The soul, she said, is composed / Of the external world." The guest at the Palaz of Hoon announces: "I
was the world in which I walked, and what I saw / Or
heard or felt came not but from myself." As Crispin's education proceeds in "The Comedian as the Letter C" he
rearranges the proposition, "Man is the intelligence of his
soil," to "his soil is man's intelligence." "The statue is the
sculptor, not the stone," in "A Duck for Dinner." Not only
essences but accidents are interchanged; witness the
myriad *correspondances* in Stevens: the voices of the
wind in "Parochial Theme," which "Are sounds blown by a
blower into shapes," Liadoff's "epi-tones, the colors of the
ear."

To disbelieve in the separateness of things, to believe that
man may participate in the existence of species further down
the ladder of creation, is to court pantheism. Wordsworth,
to whom Stevens has been compared, is popularly (whether
justifiably so or not) associated with this type of thinking.
John Malcolm Brinnin's essay cited above has called attention to Stevens's propensity to equate man with lower forms
of being:

"Poetry is the supreme fiction," and the will is harnessed
to its creation. In this sense, will becomes imagination.

> Its function is to unite itself with unthinking things—a
> stone, a snow man, a blackbird—and thereby to realize
> some taste of primal beingness or, in modest realization
> of its creative powers, to become part of an elaborate
> commentary upon a static thing. (32)

Amidst the irritations, tedium, and discouragement of life,
the desire to become some unsusceptible object is not an
uncommon one—the desire to be, for example, a sun-
drenched rock on a sweep of Hawaiian beach, a thinking
stone soothed by sea-wind and palm-shadows, detached
from all burdens of humanity. Such tales as Niobe's are
perhaps due to the longing to escape from grief; escapism,
incidentally, is a term to which Stevens has never objected.
No one can better suggest this imaginary metempsychosis.
After commenting on how closely Stevens approaches romantic pantheism, Brinnin goes on to say: "If it is possible
to understand how it feels to be a pear, a green light on the
sea, a bowl of flowers, Stevens manages, with necromantic
conviction, to say that he does."

Pantheism is, of course, one variety of monism. Ordinarily we are aware, often unpleasantly so, of the peculiarity
of things rather than of their oneness. Perhaps the leading
reason why we are at present "unhappy people in a happy
world" is this lack of rapport between parts of the universe;
in contradistinction to the general Christian tradition, Stevens feels that man ought to be at home in this world, one
with it, and not just a pilgrim en route to eternity. Sometimes, in moments of great emotion, peculiarity disappears
and we are overwhelmed with the oneness of all experience.
"World without Peculiarity" presents a young man enduring
intense suffering: his father "lies now / In the poverty of
dirt"; "what his mother was returns and cries on his
breast"; "she that he loved turns cold at his light touch."
What he needs to learn is that the earth itself is humanity,
his mother, the day, the moon. When he discovers that all
is one,

. . . *difference disappears*

> *And the poverty of dirt, the thing upon his breast,*
> *The hating woman, the meaningless place,*
> *Becomes a single being, sure and true.*

The dirt, his mother, and the woman he loved fuse with the night into a consoler, one upon whom he can finally depend.

After seeing how, in Stevens, the theories that govern the structure of poetry and the structure of reality are identical, one can proceed to apply the principle of metamorphosis, at the heart of every poem, to life itself. Once man understands the nature of his world and of poetry he will, particularly if he is an artist, re-fashion reality in such a way as to achieve happiness in what will then become a terrestrial paradise. Adam was capable of something close to this:

> *His mind made morning,*
> *As he slept. He woke in a metaphor: this was*
> *A metamorphosis of paradise,*
>
> *Malformed, the world was paradise malformed.*
> ("The Pure Good of Theory")

According to this view, imaginative activity is a way of rendering man divine, in the sense that he shares God's creative power; the "Pastoral Nun" in the last year of her age feels she has discovered this to be true and that if she lives in harmony with her faith in the oneness of poetry and apotheosis:

> *Everything becomes morning, summer, the hero,*
> *The enraptured woman, the sequestered night,*
> *The man that suffered, lying there at ease,*
> *Without his envious pain in body, in mind,*
> *The favorable transformations of the wind*
> *As of a general being or human universe.*

The nun, Stevens's ironic version of the pastoral character, corresponds to the man with the blue guitar, who was "a shearsman of sorts."

In the critical essay, "The Figure of the Youth as Virile Poet," Stevens also makes poetry synonymous with apotheosis. He characterizes the creative process thus:

> The way a poet feels when he is writing, or after he has written a poem that completely accomplishes his purpose is evidence of the personal nature of his activity. To describe it by exaggerating it, he shares the transformation, not to say, apotheosis, accomplished by the poem.*

The relevance of this to the Stevensian doctrine of resemblance, or metamorphosis, is obvious. In "A Pastoral Nun" Stevens underlines the connection of poetry, apotheosis, and resemblance by pointing out that the first two resemble each other in that "Each matters only in that which it conceives," a comment close in meaning to the scriptural "By their fruits you shall know them."

Re-molding reality is not confined to men; even a rabbit can create through imagination a more satisfactory world than that of actuality, or so Stevens would convince us in one of his empathetic excursions into other than human consciousness, "A Rabbit as King of the Ghosts." Here the rabbit reduces the cat from a monument to a bug in the grass, little and green, whereas he himself grows to a self that fills the four corners of night." Everything in his environment now exists only for him—the trees, the vastness of night; he becomes more and more important in the cosmos until his head rises beyond the atmosphere of earth into space itself. The poem as a whole is a satiric expression of anthropomorphism.

This creative power, this sorcerer's gift capable of producing a terrestrial paradise, does not function automatically; it is an act of will, since imagination is the will of things. Nowhere is the conscious striving to effect a mutation of *milieu* more concretely brought out than in "Human Arrangement": on a rainy evening the speaker projects an imagined wooden chair into the sky, so that it becomes

* *Ibid.,* p. 49.

> . . . *the clear point of an edifice,*
>
> *Forced up from nothing, evening's chair,*
> *Blue-strutted curule, true—unreal,*
>
> *The center of transformations that*
> *Transform for transformation's self,*
>
> *In a glitter that is a life, a gold*
> *That is a being, a will, a fate.*

This imaginary chair in the real rainy sky reminds one of Marianne Moore's imaginary gardens with real toads in them and serves much the same purpose in emphasizing the interpenetration of the actual and the fictive in any true work of art.

At the present time, realization of the resources of the imagination is intermittent, confined to "moments of awakening, / Extreme, fortuitous, personal," which correspond to Eliot's intuitional flashes in the *Quartets*. But the day will come when earth will constitute all the heaven that a savage race hungers for, a primal paradise regained through courage. It does not seem to bother Mr. Stevens that he probably will not be around to enjoy it; for him, there is always the solace of the blue guitar. Yet he is not entirely without misgivings in thus fashioning his *Weltanschauung*:

> *A little while of Terra Paradise*
> *I dreamed, of autumn rivers, silvas green,*
> *Of sanctimonious mountains high in snow,*
>
> *But in that dream a heavy difference*
> *Kept waking and a mournful sense sought out,*
> *In vain, life's season or death's element.*
>
> ("Montrachet-le-Jardin")

One last aspect of metamorphosis in its relation to life is the way in which it functions during wartime. The soldier and the poet need each other. The poet elucidates for the soldier what is happening to him. "Gigantomachia" summarizes the principal metamorphoses war causes among its participants in a single line—"Each man himself became a giant"—implying that war is, truly, as the title states, a battle of giants. "Repetitions of a Young Captain" describes the mutations thus:

> *Millions of major men against their like*
> *Make more than thunder's rural rumbling. They make*
> *The giants that each one of them becomes*
>
> *In a calculated chaos: he that takes form*
> *From the others, being larger than he was.*

The captain and his men are one, as are the sailor and the sea. Heroes (the major men) are "characters beyond / Reality, composed thereof. They are / The fictive man created out of men." ("Paisant Chronicle") The lengthiest analysis of this view is "Examination of the Hero in a Time of War," a poem in ten sections of fourteen lines each, with which Stevens concludes *Parts of a World*. In it he defines the hero as his nation, "In him made one," an actor who cannot help being anonymous. The soldier becomes an abstraction: he is all courage, drawing a heroism from each of his companions. When he returns to civilian life, it will not be in the same form as when he departed.

As to the disorders which war causes, consciousness and fact during such a time replace imagination and fiction. War's tremendous impacts, just like the forces of Crispin's sea, cannot be managed:

> We are confronting, therefore, a set of events, not only beyond our power to tranquillize them in the mind, beyond our power to reduce them and metamorphose them, but events that stir the emotions to violence, that engage us in what is direct and immediate and real, and events that involve the concepts and sanctions that are the order of our lives and may involve our very lives; and these events are occurring persistently, with increasing omen, in what may be called our presence.*

* *Ibid.*, p. 22.

Metamorphosis, then, at least in times of peace, rebuilds our universe. Man is indeed the captain of his soul, the master of his fate, though he seldom acts as if he were. If he did, he would achieve freedom, Stevens declares in "The Latest Freed Man" and "On the Road Home," two poems which are placed side by side in *Parts of a World*. The freed man is tired of metaphysics, of trying to explore essences. His desired emancipation is presented thus:

> *For a moment on rising, at the edge of the bed,*
> > *to be,*
> *To have the ant of the self changed to an ox*
> *With its organic boomings, to be changed*
> *From a doctor into an ox, before standing up,*
> *To know that the change and that the ox-like struggle*
>
> *Come from the strength that is the strength of the sun.*
>
> *It was how he was free.*

"On the Road Home" accentuates Stevens's relativism in epistemology by its annunciation that freedom comes only after man discovers there is no absolute truth. After the denials of the speaker and his companion, the grapes grow fatter, the tree changes from green to blue ("Then the tree, at night, began to change, / Smoking through green and smoking blue,"), the night becomes warmer, closer. Everything takes on a new plentitude of being, as the six superlative adjectives in the last four lines indicate: *largest, longest, roundest, warmest, closest, strongest.*

Set against the imagination as shaping spirit is the desire of Stevens, expressed with equal vividness, to face things as they are. It may be that these two contradictory views are merely another instance of the opposites which fuse into a third and perfect singular—but on the other hand their incompatibility may constitute a crucial lack of clarity in his aesthetic, though perhaps the clash might better be described as a sign of countries of the mind yet to be explored. Subtle as Stevens's propositions are and admirable as is the

intricacy with which he has devised them in over a quarter
of a century, there appear to be basic difficulties in his position, which suggest that the center which he seeks is still in
the future tense. His devotion to things as they are is hard
to reconcile with his wish to remold them to what they
should be; the first point of view is summarized thus in
"Credences of Summer":

> *Let's see the very thing and nothing else.*
> *Let's see it with the hottest fire of sight.*
> *Burn everything not part of it to ash.*
> *Trace the gold sun about the whitened sky*
> *Without evasion by a single metaphor.*

Actually, such a dream may be unattainable; *gold* as applied to sun is already a metaphor. To the age in which Wallace Stevens finds himself, however, the sun is not what it
formerly was. Man uses nature now instead of revering it;
what science has taught him about the sun has destroyed
forever the bright-haired charioteer or the fiery eye among
the clouds. Susanne Langer has intelligently condensed the
change of attitude in this passage:

> With his [man's] new outlook on the world, of course the
> old symbolism of human values has collapsed. The sun is
> too interesting as an object, a source of transformable
> energies, to be interpreted as a god, a hero, or a symbol
> of passion: since we know that it is really the ultimate
> source of what we call "power," transformable energy
> measurable by units, we take a realistic, not a mystical,
> attitude toward it; its image is no longer "distanced" in
> a perspective of non-discursive thought; our literal con-
> cepts have caught up with it.*

The poetry of Wallace Stevens from "Sunday Morning" on
contains instances of sun-worship, but these refer to worship
of thing, not symbol; of matter, not spirit.

Stevens advocates a complete acceptance of the present,

* *Philosophy in a New Key.* New American Library.

not an evasion such as that practiced by the "metamorphorid" Lady Lowzen of "Oak Leaves Are Hands":

> *In Hydaspia, by Howzen*
> *Lived a lady, Lady Lowzen,*
> *For whom what is was other things.*
>
> *Flora she was once. She was florid*
> *A bachelor of feen masquerie,*
> *Evasive and metamorphorid.*
>
> *Mac Mort she had been, ago,*
> *Twelve-legged in her ancestral hells,*
> *Weaving and weaving many arms . . .*
>
> *So she in Hydaspia created*
> *Out of the movement of few words*
> *Flora Lowzen invigorated*
>
> *Archaic and future happenings,*
> *In glittering seven-clored changes,*
> *By Howzen, the chromatic Lowzen.*

Under the witty treatment is serious criticism: nothing but
the past and the future exist for this lady who is adept at
making these come alive, take on shimmering iridescence,
but who has no distinctive character of her own and no belief in the reality of her Indian (Hydaspia, Howzen) environment. Stevens shows her metamorphorid nature by dis-
torting *Flora* to *florid,* by using the word *bachelor* to keep
even her sex from definiteness, by parodying *ancestral halls*
to *hells.* As Miss Mac Mort, Flora had waited, spider-like,
preoccupied with the splendid past of her family as symbolized in heraldic designs. A subtle overtone here is the ety-
mology of Flora's maiden name: Mac Mort, the son (daughter) of death. Now, unsatisfied with being Lady Lowzen,
she still dreams of the romantic past and the exciting future,
her imagination a prism through which these two tenses
pass. In the present she has no interest; her metamorphic
powers do not touch it.

The problems raised by conflicting aspects of Stevens's theory of the imagination are not minor ones, though since their solution is "work in progress" one cannot at the present time criticize the theory with any conclusiveness. It would appear to be indisputable, however, that Stevens is a meliorist in the sense that he optimistically considers the human race to be moving forward toward a time when the faculties which comprise the psyche will be understood fully and will be used to the maximum of their powers. Then statements about the "change immenser than / A poet's metaphors in which being would / Come true" ("Description without Place") can be made in the indicative rather than in the subjunctive. All false conceptions of the imagination will be destroyed; as Stevens prophesies in "The Noble Rider and the Sound of Words," imagination will be seen for what it is, the sum of all other faculties:

> Like light, it adds nothing, except itself. What light requires a day to do, and by day I mean a kind of Biblical revolution of time, the imagination does in a twinkling of an eye. It colors, increases, brings to a beginning and end, invents languages, crushes men and, for that matter, gods in its hands, it says to women more than it is possible to say, it rescues all of us from what we have called absolute fact and while it does these things, and more, it makes sure that
>
> > . . . la mandoline jase,
> > Parmi les frissons de brise.*

Is such a Utopian position tenable? The philosopher by profession would probably answer that one cannot and never will be able to think by imagining, since nothing is more unsuccessful in philosophy than an attempt to obliterate the distinctions between the abstract and the concrete. Poetry, he would say, deals with the concrete, the particular; philosophy, with the abstract, the universal—to which Stevens might reply by quoting from his description of the

* *The Necessary Angel,* pp. 61–62.

primitive man, held up as a paragon, who "Imagines, and it is true, as if he thought / By imagining, anti-logician, quick / With a logic of transforming certitudes." ("Sombre Figuration") And perhaps the philosopher in refutation might then point to the description of heaven in "Sunday Morning"—an oriental paradise characterized by suspended motion except for the plucking of lutes—as an example of what happens when one demands that the suprasensible be clothed in sensory images. Despite Plato, Lucretius, Santayana, the marriage of poetry and philosophy is not ordinarily a happy one.

But that Stevens's thinking is tentative in nature is evident in "Effects of Analogy." The passage revelant to the confusion resulting from the necessity of transforming reality, when all that is requisite for felicity is its acceptance, runs thus:

> Take the case of a man for whom reality is enough, as, at the end of his life, he returns to it like a man returning from Nowhere to his village and to everything there that is tangible and visible, which he has come to cherish and wants to be near. He sees without images.*

Surely the intention here is that it is better to see the world without images. Yet the same paragraph defines poetry as an analogue composed of "the particulars of reality, created by the poet's sense of the world, that is to say, his attitude, as he intervenes and interposes the appearance of that sense." Intervention is a meddling with things as they are which might be permitted to ephebes, to weaker travelers in the journey toward summer, but not to those strong enough to look steadily at the green world. It agrees poorly with the definition of the imagination, elsewhere in the essay, as the power to see into reality to such a degree that one can be a poet in the very center of consciousness.

* *Ibid.,* p. 129.

But the spirit of Wallace Stevens is the spirit described in the tenth section of "An Ordinary Evening in New Haven": "It resides / In a permanence composed of impermanence." This is as it should be in one whose thought has metamorphosis at its heart—metamorphosis as it is operative in the effect of the senses and language on extra-mental reality, as it reproduces in poetry the resemblances found in nature. A mosaic of a man, even a major artist, is like a mosaic of the weather; in the very fluidity of both there is permanence of a sort:

> *See how*
> *On a day still full of summer, when the leaves*
> *Appear to sleep within a sleeping air,*
> *They suddenly fall and the leafless sound of the wind*
>
> *Is no longer a sound of summer. So great a change*
> *Is constant.*
>   ("The Statue at the World's End")

Yet, like the weather, a man can only be described from day to day.

☆

CHAPTER THREE

WILLIAM CARLOS WILLIAMS:

A Testament of Perpetual Change

FEW poems have ever been priced as high as William Carlos Williams's *Paterson,* if one may borrow the central metaphor of the third book in order to suggest the enormous cost in concentration which must be met before any adequate evaluation can be made. If this work were built around a consistently presented hero – the Paterson of the title – that cost might not be so prohibitive as many readers will find it; but when Williams asserts in the introduction to Book Three ("The Library") that Paterson is not only the hero but also the heroine, not only a city but also cliffs and a waterfall, one cries out for a critic to assist him, as the sea-god did Peleus, in conquering the metamorphic problem. Before judging the total merit of *Paterson,* however, one must weather a preliminary season of understanding, of looking hard and often at aim and structure – in brief, of giving the poem the creative reading that such an undertaking deserves. The poet, realizing the difficulty of meeting this high cost, has given some measure of help in the headnote to the entire poem, and also in the list of topics which he places immediately after the words "Book One," as if in apposition; the latter consists of eighteen phrases separated by semicolons, each phrase a possible definition of *Paterson.* The last of these phrases is "a dispersal and a metamorphosis."

This metamorphic emphasis is particularly prominent in the methods Williams uses to interchange man and certain aspects of his environment in order to compel a new awareness in citizens of the Waste Land:

> Truthfully pleading his inability to handle traditional coin traditionally, Williams improvises, issues a fluid currency of his own; in *Paterson,* a set of protean, imagist-symbolist centers of force which polarize his loose, fragmentary material. (R. W. Flint, *Kenyon Review,* XII, 538.)

Like Hart Crane, he has searched the world about him for a focal symbol, hitting upon one even more fitted to his poetic intentions than was Brooklyn Bridge to Crane's. He has seen in Paterson, New Jersey, neighbor to his own Rutherford, a point suitable for the intersection of several themes obsessing the modern artist. The very name, Paterson, with its Latin and Germanic components, unites the generating principle with the result of generation: man is both subject and object in the design of reality, since through perception, according to Williams, he creates what lies about him. In the Preface to the poem Williams, echoing Eliot, says paradoxically: "For the beginning is assuredly / the end – since we know nothing, pure / and simple, beyond / our own complexities." If Wordsworth's child was father to the man, Williams's father is also son. When considered as combining Latin and French roots, *Paterson* may also imply the father of sound; again, its connotations include the homonym of *son* (*sun*):

> It [Paterson] is the ignorant sun
> rising in the slot of
> hollow suns risen, so that never in this
> world will a man live well in his body
> save dying. . . .*

* All quotations from *Paterson,* copyright 1946, 1948, by New Directions, reprinted by permission of the publisher.

But the significance of Paterson as locale is far more than verbal, as Williams reveals in the first book, "The Delineaments of the Giants."

In establishing the elemental character of the place, the poet describes two titanic figures: masculine (Paterson the city) and feminine (Garrett Mountain). The first lies on his right side, sleeping on the bank of the Passaic River, head near the Great Falls, facing the woman, who is also asleep. Only the dreams of Paterson are stirring; they walk about the city as its citizens—unaware of the mighty mind which is their source and hence unable to realize their destinies. Of all American cities Paterson was indeed an excellent choice for such a concept, with its falls which Hamilton hoped would furnish water power enough to supply manufactured goods for the whole country, falls which even today make it the largest single silk-producing center in the United States. Besides, close to the coast, it is connected with the sea by the Passaic River and with inland waterways by canal, two facts making it desirable for the elucidation of Williams's "dispersal" motif, referred to in the headnote.

The setting for this drama of giants is given in a spirit of local pride. Largely through prose links, Williams as the poem progresses sketches in several places which any good map of the district will render easy to visualize: Notch Brook, the Valley of the Rocks, Ramapos Valley, Pompton, New Barbadoes Neck, Manchester, Singac, Morris Mountain, Hohokus, the Goffle. Williams feels very keenly about place, a concept which anchors his philosophy of "no ideas but in things." He disagrees with Eliot's rather glib assertion in the *Quartets* that place is only place, and that what is actual is actual only for one place. On the contrary, he believes that only in some one place does the universal ever become actual, and that therefore place is the only universal. He has been criticized for living out his lifetime in one fairly small city of a small Eastern state. Williams gives his apologia in these words:

We live only in one place at a time but far from being
bound by it, only through it do we realize our freedom.
Place then ceases to be a restriction, we do not have to
abandon our familiar and known to achieve distinction
but far from constricting ourselves, not searching for
some release in some particular place, rather in that
place, if we only make ourselves sufficiently aware of it,
do join with others in other places. ("The Fatal Blunder," *Quarterly Review of Literature,* II, 126.)

Paterson, however, is his supreme apologia. In view of
Williams's cardinal principle (no ideas but in things) one
can see how tremendously important setting is for his purposes. Paterson's ideas, his thoughts, are all things, such as
the "blank faces of houses" or "cylindrical trees." The inhabitants, ignorant of the forces motivating them, are
thoughts that are also things, a "thousand automatons."

Williams throughout his poem has given the city a life
organic as a man's life. In the prose passages he has taken
actual names and places in order to ground the experiment
in actuality. It is a matter of record that the Revolutionary
period considered the Falls a "wonder" along with other
freaks of nature such as Peter Van Winkle, the dwarf; that
sturgeon as large as that described in Book One were formerly caught in the Passaic; that Cornelius Doremus left an
estate of $419.58½; that Paterson had a noted German
Singing Society; that Dean William McNulty of Saint
Joseph's Catholic Church was a greatly admired leader in
the city; that Jack Reed, Bill Haywood, and "Gurley" Flynn
helped in the 1913 I.W.W. strike, in connection with which
the Paterson Pageant was staged in Madison Square Garden; that William Kieft, Governor General of New Amster-
dam, persecuted the Indians in 1643; that three weeks after
the big fire of February, 1902, the worst of four bad floods
ravaged Paterson, with a tornado occurring the same year;
that the Van Giesens and the Van Houtens were prominent
among early Paterson families. But Williams does not al-

ways feel bound to conform to the precise details of history; for instance, the tornado of 1902 is given as preceding the fire and flood though actually it was several months later. In several instances, Williams's prose links dealing with Paterson's past are not original at all but are merely taken verbatim from William Nelson's *History of the City of Paterson and the County of Passaic*. Examples are the description of an Indian sacrifice ceremony (37–38); the artesian-well passage (11); Peter Van Winkle, the dwarf (100); the Van Giesen witch story (269); the Hopper incident (345–346). Since this mosaic technique has been used five times in the poem, it is probable that thorough-going research in libraries of the region would yield the sources for other historical interludes. The famous Dutch lullaby used in *Paterson* is quoted in the history of Paterson by Nelson and Shriner (Vol. I, 156), which also gives an account of the Garrett Mountain riot of 1880, in which John J. Van Houten was killed (Vol. II, 499–500), an account which opens with the same words as the one in *Paterson*.

Some readers have grown impatient with these prose insertions, failing to see the reasons for their inclusion other than as contrast or as illustrations of the break-down of language. Perhaps they can best be understood as a study in sources, an ignorance of which is one of the main causes why citizens of Paterson walk around asleep, desires locked in their minds, inarticulate. Williams has earlier condemned his countrymen for not knowing their roots, from which their bones, thought, and action have sprung. (*In the American Grain*, 113.) Among these sources are the Puritans, represented in the poem by the witch-hunting Merselis Van Giesen; Revolutionary politicians such as Hamilton; Indians, to whom five different episodes are devoted; Negroes, both West Indian and American-born, such as D. J. B. in Book Three; Irish (McGuckin), German (Spangermacher), Dutch (Kieft, Van Houten), Scandinavian (Ferguson), French (Jan de la Montagne), English (Lambert). Special attention is called to Paterson's heterogeneous population in "The Delineaments of the Giants" by a listing of 1870 statistics: native-born, 20,711; French, 237; German, 1,420; English, 3,343; Irish, 5,124; Scotch, 879; Hollanders, 1,360; Swiss, 170. It is no wonder that in June of each year Paterson holds a Festival of Nations. Some prose links are harder to justify as sources, as biography of a region, than others are; for example, it is difficult to see just how the thumbnail sketch of "Billy" (Book One) or the anecdote about the dog Musty (Book Two) fits into the design, except as "modern replicas," degenerations of a worthier past. It is safe, however, to assume that they are not irrelevancies. One way of regarding them might be as manifestations of the irrational, so large a part of every life though impregnable to explication.

By returning to the sources of Paterson as city, Williams means to explain, in terms of a traditional microcosm-macrocosm analogy, the intricacies of twentieth-century Paterson as man, who differs from Oliver in Santayana's novel, *The Last Puritan*, a paragraph from which forms the headnote to Book Three:

> Cities, for Oliver, were not a part of nature. He could hardly feel, he could hardly admit even when it was pointed out to him, that cities are a second body for the human mind, a second organism, more rational, permanent and decorative than the animal organism of flesh and bone: a work of natural yet moral art, where the soul sets up her trophies of action and instruments of pleasure.

Williams feels, not only that the mind animates Paterson the city, but that the city contains within it the life of any individual citizen, concretized, since a man is what he experiences. This metaphor is pushed even further in Book Four, with the earth itself becoming a macrocosm of the human Paterson and including both sexes:

Woman is the weaker vessel, but
the mind is neutral, a bead linking
continents, brow and toe

The Passaic River is used in the poem to represent the
giant Paterson's stream-of-consciousness; this requires a
leap from the city where the citizen-dreams walk about to
the place where the river "crashes from the edge of the
gorge / in a recoil of spray and rainbow mists—." The parallel between the currents of the Passaic and Paterson's
thoughts (their interlacing, repulsion, advance, eddying,
coalescence, leap and fall, retaking of the course) is worked
out with a clarity of invention that brings the vehicle of the
metaphor sharply before the eyes and into the ears in the
best objectivist manner. A subsidiary meaning concerns the
river as a figure of the seminal fluid: ("The multiple seed, /
packed tight with detail, soured, / is lost in the flux. . . .")
Love between man and woman must beget marriage, not
death, as in the old plays—but how can it when divorce, not
union, is the sign of the times? "Divorce is / the sign of
knowledge in our time, / divorce! divorce!"

Louis Martz, reviewing Paterson One and Two, explains
the river's import thus:

> The basic image of Book I was the Passaic River, meta-
> morphosed into a symbol of the flow of all human mind,
> including the mind's half-conscious sense of powers be-
> yond itself; the falls of the Passaic seemed to represent
> the power of the poet to interrupt, refract, and coalesce
> this flow into a quivering and terrifying scene of beauty.
> (*Yale Review*, XXXVIII, 149.)

Such an interpretation assumes that the problem which
Williams poses reaches solution, but is it so solved in the
poem itself? Allied to Martz's view, yet distinct from it and
perhaps more accurate, is the view based on still another
level of reference, the identification of the waterfall with
language, a language not understood or at best misunder-

stood, which drives Paterson to shaken intensity as he tries to comprehend its cataract. The unheeded harangue of the Evangelist in Book Two is called a falls; often the Passaic is termed a voice. None but the poet can furnish the lexicon whereby this torrent may become meaningful, and no poet has come—at least, no poet able to comb out the language that pours from the rafter of a rock's lip. Yet one further stratum of the Falls image is its designation, at the end of the third book, as the present connecting the past and future:

> *The past above, the future below*
> *and the present pouring down: the roar,*
> *the roar of the present, a speech—*
> *is, of necessity, my sole concern.*

Williams is alert to every possibility of his pivotal metaphor, water, in illustrating the metamorphosis announced in his headnote. From time to time he adverts to the various phases water undergoes: the process of evaporation by which it is "lifted as air"; its polychromatic glory as a rainbow (a phenomenon particularly impressive at the Falls, in the season of melting snows or heavy rains); reduction to waterdrops again, when it is "divided as the dew"; "the clouds resolved into a sandy sluice"; "floating mists, to be rained down and / regathered into a river that flows / and encircles." He sees it as "clear ice," as the ice-cake in which Sam Patch, the daredevil jumper, was frozen after the fatal plunge into the Genesee River at Rochester. He uses the parable of the sower to show how crystals of snow can be wasted, lost in the flux:

> *the snow falling into the water,*
> *part upon the rock, part in the dry weeds*
> *and part into the water where it*
> *vanishes—its form no longer what it was:*

And he pictures in remarkably vivid detail the effects of the flood after the winter's snow has metamorphosed into trickling rivulets which gather for destruction.

A prose item about David Hower's 1857 discovery of pearls in the mussels of Notch Brook separates the initial appearance of Paterson as giant from his first metamorphosis: a conversion into Mr. Paterson the poet, whose "works / have been done into French / and Portuguese." He has gone away to rest and write, leaving his thoughts to sit and stand in the city bus, to alight and scatter. Immediately after equating the poet Paterson's thoughts with the citizens, Williams shifts in protean fashion to "the regularly ordered plateglass of / his thoughts," again fusing the subject and object – the reflected is also the reflector. He underscores the unifying character of the metaphor by using, at the conclusion of the stanza, the singular noun *thought:* "his thought is listed in the Telephone Directory." At this point the pronoun *I* is introduced as distinct from Paterson, evidently only one of the ideas mirrored in his thoughts; such a technique is bound to result in confusion for the reader unless he can preserve extreme agility in the following of images.

Set up as a complement of the city-man Paterson, the mountain-woman symbol changes throughout the work in equally protean manner. In Book One she lies:

> *facing him, his*
> *arm supporting her, by the Valley of the Rocks,*
> *asleep.*
> *Pearls at her ankles, her monstrous hair*
> *spangled with apple-blossoms is scattered about into*
> *the back country. . . .*

The Park is her head, the features of which have been carved by the Passaic out of the colored rocks. A few pages later this image is blended with that of a flower to which Williams has previously in the poem compared the woman. But no bee carries fertilizing pollen to the heart of this flower; instead it sinks back into the ground, wilting, disappearing, destined for sterility instead of fruitful marriage. This desecration of the feminine principle is emphasized in

the prose link immediately following, an account of how
Jackson sold English girls and West Indian Negresses during the American Revolution, and of how Cromwell shipped
thousands of Irish women to the Barbadoes for the slave-
market.

Next, the mountain-flower-woman becomes the first wife
of an African chief (photographed for the *National Geographic* with her eight successors), scowling, worn out, yet
elemental as a tree-trunk from which the other wives grow
like branches, a parallel of the tree-metaphor used for Paterson himself in Book Two. The various semantic threads are
twisted tightly together (flower, rock, and wife united) as
Williams elucidates his symbolism:

> *Which is to say, though it be poorly*
> *said, there is a first wife*
> *and a first beauty, complex, ovate —*
> *the woody sepals standing back under*
> *the stress to hold it there, innate*
>
> *a flower within a flower whose history*
> *(within the mind) crouching*
> *among the ferny rocks, laughs at the names*
> *by which they think to trap it.*

The first section of Book I (each of the four large divisions of the poem is broken up into three parts) finishes with
a prose link developing the third metamorphosis: N. F. Paterson, the old time Jersey Patriot, otherwise known as Sam
Patch (c. 1807–1829), who astonished crowds all over
America by diving from "cliffs and masts, rocks and
bridges." Williams explains that the initials N. F. stand for
Noah (the Biblical victor over water) and Faitoute ("Some
things can be done as well as others"), the latter a name
which Paterson is to assume intermittently for the rest of
the poem, its sense suggesting action in opposition to the
passive nature of his feminine partner. *The Dictionary of
American Biography* relates how Sam "in his cups would

parrot his two apothegms: 'There's no mistake in Sam Patch' and 'Some things can be done as well as others.' " He is finally overcome by the failure of language, falling sideways in his 125-foot leap into the falls of the Genesee River to hit the water and disappear until the breaking up of the ice the following spring. It is interesting to note that the plunge took place on Friday the thirteenth.

Williams does not tell us what Patch said in the inadequate little speech which preceded his jump, but Jenny Marsh Parker has preserved it in her history of Rochester:

> Napoleon was a great man and a great general. He conquered armies and he conquered nations. But he couldn't jump the Genesee Falls. Wellington was a great man and a great soldier. He conquered armies and he conquered nations, and he conquered Napoleon, but he couldn't jump the Genesee Falls. That was left for me to do, and I can do it, and will! (188)

Enormous interest and a strangely high emotional pitch of public recrimination surrounded the Patch incident, including a persistent expectation of his "resurrection," an interest recorded in the plays and poems on his fate written soon after the disaster. Even in his own day the victim was a symbol, as he is in *Paterson;* the fact that his death occurred not at the Passaic but at the Genesee Falls, a region where he was cut off from his sources, is of special symbolic importance, and the name of the Falls with its resemblance to *genesis* ironic.

To universalize his statement, Williams introduces Mrs. Hopper Cumming as a complement for Sam Patch; Mrs. Cumming, bride of a few months, mysteriously falls to her death from the cliff, in what is perhaps as intentional a plunge as Patch's professional jumps. William Nelson, the standard historian of the Paterson region, calls this the "most romantically tragic incident in the history of the Passaic Falls." William Carlos Williams gives the story in florid, sentimental, overwritten prose.

But Williams's style is conservative when compared to some of the contemporary versions. One Peter Archdeacon, prominent Paterson citizen, after telling of a blackbird which, like a supernatural warning, hovered around the Reverend Mr. Cumming's head during his sermon on Sunday, June 21, 1812, concludes his eulogy of the minister and his wife thus: "The next day alas! before the sun had veiled his head beyond yon western hill, the flush was nipped, and the lovely seraph's spirit fled to the regions of the blessed!" (Quoted in *History of the Old Dutch Church at Totowa, Paterson, New Jersey, 1755–1827,* 40.)

The language ("Stale as a whale's breath") in the relation of the tragedy, both in this account and in *Paterson,* indicates how wide the chasm between words and events has become. Since Mrs. Cumming had been standing twenty feet from the edge for half an hour or more, her fall is inexplicable other than as a result of the magnetic power of the waters roaring down in their untranslatable beauty or as an escape from a life in which falsity has superseded the truth of ideas located in things. One senses that Williams does not consider the drowning accidental, from these lines in Book Two: "leaped (or fell) without a / language, tongue-tied / the language worn out."

After the story of Patch, Williams shifts his central personality back to the sleeping giant:

> *with the roar of the river*
> *forever in our ears (arrears)*
> *inducing sleep and silence, the roar*
> *of eternal sleep . . . challenging*
> *our waking—*

With the thunder of the Passaic in his ears, he dreams of the "I" in whom he has, after all, no real interest. That *I,* however, goes on speculating, considering how "the ground has undergone / a subtle transformation, its identity altered" since the days of the Indians. The problem, he muses, is to interrelate details on the new ground, a difficult task possible only if the disparate can be pulled together "to clarify / and compress"; an assonance must be set up, a homologue. One of Williams's ways of doing this has been referred to by Vivienne Koch (in her book on the poet) as an echo device, a practice different from the tissue of repetitions which gives *Paterson* its orchestral quality (126). Over a hundred times he juxtaposes identical words or phrases, enriching the musical development (as Randall Jarrell has strikingly pointed out in his *Partisan Review* comments on the red bird's song (xiii, 494), suggesting the echo usually connected with the scene of a waterfall, even hinting at the narcissistic theory which the very word *Paterson* crystallizes, perhaps also paralleling that stutter which is descriptive of contemporary effort to use the language.

Replacing the third person singular with *you,* Williams in Book One, section two, separates the giants from their human replicas as he writes of a conversation between two lovers, against the background of the Falls. The couple is isolated in the stream of Faitoute's thoughts. Then, at the beginning of the next section, he nimbly turns the symbol of woman back into a flower, stressing again the permanence of art, which will outlast the artist.

He starts by alluding to woman in her character of rose carved out of the red rock, destined to remain after that nine-months' wonder, Paterson the man, or even the city itself, has vanished:

> *So you think because the rose*
> *is red that you shall have the mastery?*
> *The rose is green and will bloom,*
> *overtopping you, green, livid*
> *green when you shall no more speak, or*
> *taste, or even be.*

But whatever the future triumph of the rock, its present is a degradation, daily raped as it is by the "great beast." Paterson sees this debasement; he broods over the woman's fate: "What can he think else – along / the gravel of the ravished park, torn by / the wild workers' children tearing up the grass, / kicking, screaming." Just as the university has corrupted the language ("knowledgeable idiots" blocking genuine communication) so have the dyeworks corrupted the river into which their waste products are spewed; since man and the city are one, an interpenetration, what defiles the mind of one defiles the other. Miss Koch calls this section of the poem "a powerful attack on 'learning' in which the persistent change and metamorphosis of natural forms is used as counterfoil to 'the whole din of fracturing thought.' " (128–129)

Moreover, man's bride, the imagination, figured by the Park, cannot avoid this corruption. In commenting on Shapiro's *Essay on Rime,* Williams has used the analogy of a composite woman as representing rime; he says: "We express ourselves there (men) as we might on the whole body of the various female could we ever gain access to her (which we cannot and never shall)." Yet we should not, he goes on, feel thwarted as artists, since "We do the best we can – as much as the females of our souls permit." (*Kenyon Review,* VIII, 123.) We cannot attain the composite woman, but there are always two women, three women, "Innumerable women, each like a flower," though "only one man – like a city." Throughout the course of the whole poem these representative women appear, "each like a flower." One is reminded of Thomas Hardy's search for the ideal woman in *The Well Beloved.* Paterson's problem, as he finally summarizes it in Book Four is:

> *To bring himself in,*
> *hold together wives in one wife and*
> *at the same time scatter it,*
> *the one in all of them*

Another meaning of this composite female is society itself, apart from which the poet cannot write immortally or even validly, since he needs the nourishment which she alone can give him. This is a Whitmanesque idea, denied on one hand by Pound and apostolically affirmed on the other by Williams, with poor Hart Crane in the middle, torn between the extremes as he struggled to build his *Bridge*. Williams has made the identification of woman and society explicit in a letter to an Australian editor; speaking of the poet, he says:

> He will continue to produce only if his attachments to society continue adequate. If a man in his fatuous dreams cuts himself off from that supplying female, he dries up his sources—as Pound did in the end heading straight for literary sterility. (*Briarcliff Quarterly*, III, 208.)

The poet's function, then, becomes a metamorphic one: "Let me insist, the poet's very life, but also his forms originate in the political, social and economic maelstrom on which he rides. At his best he transmutes them to new values fed from the society of which he is a part if he will continue fertile."

The rock Williams has chosen for his woman is indeed a most appropriate symbol by which to express metamorphosis, since the geological sense of that term is the one which comes first to many minds; in geology, metamorphosis means a change of forms without essential change of the ingredients of a rock. Thus it is fully as important a symbol as water, and united to it in that water is the chief agent of metamorphosis; *metamorphism* and *metamorphosis* are used interchangeably. Taken from a large-scale view, the very world we live in is a natural result of metamorphosis; when that view is reduced, the circulation of water on, in, and above our earth becomes merely a figure of the human blood stream, the blood of Paterson. Again, water as the scientist regards it is the active principle as against the passive rock that endures the changes which water brings about.

As the book proceeds, Paterson's thoughts are again the city-dwellers: the two lovers who sit talking, a mental defective who writes a letter signed T., a mysterious person afraid of being murdered, a shopper for groceries who shows off a new set of teeth. Williams comes back to the tenet that his thought, though multiple, is also one, "his whole concept"—composed of "the divisions and imbalances" of the facts that constitute Paterson as city. By adding up particulars, he hopes to arrive at the general, an idea expressed figuratively by the Society for Useful Manufactures (S. U. M.) whose factories cluster below the Passaic Falls. All opposites (and the Preface alone contains many: beginning, end; drunk, sober; illustrious, gross; ignorance, knowledge; up, down; addition, subtraction; Pater, son) are reducible somehow to one—"by multiplication a reduction to one." This idea is not new in Williams: in 1934 he addresses scientists thus:

> And you poor fishes haven't yet understood that one plus one plus one plus one plus one equals not five but one. A thing every artist has known from the beginning of time, so thoroughly inescapable that even science is beginning at last to catch on to it. ("Reply to a Young Scientist," *Direction*, I, 28.)

The second section of Book One closes with a letter from a literary man who signs himself T. J., warning Paterson the poet about the impossibility of dividing book and man. It is just this separation which the poet has been trying to bridge, in his effort to show the interpenetration of the two Patersons, the external with the internal:

> *Yet there is*
> *no return: rolling up out of chaos,*
> *a nine months' wonder, the city*
> *the man, an identity—it can't be*
> *otherwise—an*
> *interpenetration, both ways.*

Another correspondent, a woman initialed C., also accuses him of dividing art and life, of keeping them strictly apart.

One feels sympathy with the recipient of the two letters, together with an awareness that he cannot be completely exonerated from the charge, as his own frequent admissions of ineffectuality show.

The third part of Book One begins with a picture of Paterson the man, standing in a room outside which snow melts at a regular rate and dreaming of imagined delights. His thoughts become trees, the leaves of which stream rain, a metaphor Williams is to return to later. Throughout seven stanzas the tree-figure is elaborated, ending in the simple statement, "Everybody has roots," reminiscent of Pound's praise of William Carlos Williams as "rooted." Since there are no ideas but in things, Paterson thinks of mouths eating, kissing, spitting, sucking, speaking; of eyes; of silk-producing machines; of pathetic souvenirs such as a comb and nail-file in an imitation leather case, or a photograph holder. He fluctuates between the city-man and the city, the man: "Such is the mystery of his one two, one two."

Continuing his metamorphosis, he becomes one of the crowd; getting into his car as he drives with the rest out past the rhubarb farm in the suburbs, to the convent of the Little Sisters of Saint Ann, which he pictures minutely. Then he "shifts his change," reverie turning into narrative as the 1737 earthquake is described. The first book closes with Thought, personified, climbing up like a snail on the wet rocks of the cavern behind the Falls. Earth is not only our mother, but the father of all speech (Pater*son*), the chatterer (Paterson is often spelled Patterson), a chamber private as a skull to which the world has no access and from which man cannot truly know the world. The torrent (the language) pours down before it, hiding it from sun and sight. In the cavern resides the force that gives reality to all external phenomena:

> *And the myth*
> *that holds up the rock,*
> *that holds up the water thrives there—*

> *in that cavern, that profound cleft,*
> *a flickering green*
> *inspiring terror, watching.* . . .

Time, in the traditional symbol of the serpent, is the fact that makes real the physical universe.

One sees quite clearly, at this stage of the poem, what metaphysical premises Williams prefers, an idealism which involves a curious ambivalence of beliefs for one to whom the importance of red wheelbarrows, plums, and white chickens (representative sensory detail) looms so large. As far back as the early years of *Poetry,* he was propounding a similar doctrine: "The world of the senses lies unintelligible on all sides. It is only interpretable by the emotions. It only exists when its emotion is fastened to it." (XIV, 213.) The emotion with which the first book closes is one of terror— terror at the sight of the father of all speech (Paterson) standing shrouded amid the din of the Falls, locked away from the secret of salvation. In the Word alone is life, and the contemporary Paterson feels that Word to be inaccessible.

The second book relates the events connected with Paterson's walk on a Sunday afternoon in late May, among the citizen-thoughts seeking pleasure on the rocks outside the city:

> Paterson, now signifying both the poet and the historic shade of "the place," strolls in the Park, "female to the city," and like a lover "instructs his thoughts" upon her body. (Koch, 135.)

On the first page of Book Two occurs the most direct definition of the mountain's role:

> *The scene's the Park*
> *upon the rock,*
> *female to the city*
>
> —*upon whose body Paterson instructs his thoughts*
> (*concretely*)

Paterson refers to the ground as passive-possessive, in contrast to himself as the positive term, the active principle, with the pronoun slipping easily from *he* to *I* in the fusion of the focal persons in the poem. Here the second letter from the woman-writer C. is inserted, a complaint that the union she had hoped for and which is essential to her has been unreasonably blocked off by Paterson—a cry of abandonment to be often repeated as the work progresses.

With the others he climbs the footpath to the top of the cliff (meditating as he does so), walks through the thickets of sand-pine and cedar, "finds hard going / across-field," is led forward by intermittent flights of grasshoppers. Next follow images that are protean indeed; uniting stasis and motion, his mind is shown metamorphosing into a carved red stone in flight (which also incorporates the woman in her role as the red rock of the Park), then into a live grasshopper.

> *—his mind a red stone carved to be*
> *endless flight.*
> *Love that is a stone endlessly in flight,*
> *so long as stone shall last bearing*
> *the chisel's stroke.*
> *.   .   and is lost and covered*
> *with ash, falls from an undermined bank*
> *and—begins churring!*
> *AND DOES, the stone after the life!*

Love, another meaning attributed to the stone, is the only force strong enough to break the power of that sleep which prevents wholeness, the creative act here being identified with love as one of its manifestations.

In the poetic statement, "The stone lives, the flesh dies," Williams wishes to indicate how art outlives man, the same idea that appears in his *Kenyon Review* tribute to Karl Shapiro referred to earlier:

Anyone who has seen 2,000 infants born as I have and pulled them one way or another into the world must

know that man, as such, is doomed to disappear in not
too many thousand years. He just can't go on. No
woman will stand for it. Why should she?

We'll have to look to something else. Who are we any-
how? Just man? What the hell's that? Rime is more.

A red stone in this passage, later a bottle tried by fire—the
artifact surpasses and survives the artist.

Before the "great beast" the rock-woman, Garrett Mountain Park, stretches out passively:

> *Thus she finds what peace there is, reclines,*
> *before his approach, stroked*
> *by their clambering feet—for pleasure*

In a more specific presentation of the feminine principle, the
old Italian woman Mary as she lifts her skirts and dances to
the sound of a guitar played by a boy incarnates "the female
of it, facing the male." Then the symbol switches back to C.
again, still trying to explain her maladjustments, the disas-
trous effects of her failure. The second section of BookTwo
closes with more of her letter, in which she speaks of the
metamorphosis of her thoughts into dry sand by Paterson's
note requesting her to stop corresponding with him, a mutation appropriate in view of the pivotal rock-metaphor:

> . . . I have been feeling (with that feeling increasingly
> stronger) that I shall never again be able to recapture
> any sense of my own personal identity (without which
> I cannot write, of course—but in itself far more impor-
> tant than the writing) until I can recapture some faith in
> the reality of my own thoughts and ideas and problems
> which were turned into dry sand by your attitude to-
> ward those letters and by that note of yours later.

Paterson continues his walk through the Park, noticing
things others never notice: three laughing colored girls, a
white couple in bathing suits, a line of Indian alders, a
chipmunk. This gift of observation is a precious one, and

characteristic of Williams. In writing about him, Marianne Moore says: "The 'ability to be drunk with a sudden realization of value in things others never notice' can metamorphose our detestable reasonableness and offset a whole planetary system of deadness." (*Poetry*, XLIV, 105.) He ascends a treeless knoll to where a man in tweeds combs a new-washed collie—one beautiful thing amidst the unbeautiful manifestations of the "great beast" (as Hamilton called the people) come to sun itself on the mountain. He listens to his own voice, the thunderous voice of the Falls, moving under the various voices of the picnickers. He sees a sixteen-year-old guitar player, back to the ferny rock; an old woman named Mary, from Paterson's "Little Italy," dancing to express her joy in the flower of a day; two drunken lovers in a grassy den, peered at by boys; a cop directing traffic; the variety of trees—oak, chokecherry, dogwood, ironwood, sassafras.

Again, Paterson becomes Faitoute, as he stands with his back towards the pit where the two lovers, now sleeping, lie. Listening to the grotesque attempt of an old evangelist, Klaus Ehrens, to convert the "great beast," he is not sure if he should consider the display as "the beauty of holiness," the only beauty visible here besides the view and a budding tree. Inadequate as it is, the sermon leads Paterson's mind to God, Who is the Addressee in the last lyrical passage of Book Two, section two, according to the title given this section in a microfilmed version of the Williams manuscript at the Lockwood Memorial Library of the University of Buffalo. The metamorphic theme is here employed with a sober loveliness:

> *The world spreads*
> *for me like a flower opening—and*
> *will close for me as might a rose—*
>
> *wither and fall to the ground*
> *and rot and be drawn up*

> *into a flower again. But you*
> *never wither—but blossom*
> *all about me. In that I forget*
> *myself perpetually—in your*
> *composition and decomposition*
> *I find my   .   .*
>   *despair!*

This is not the only place in his work where Williams calls the world a flower; writing of the Jesuit, Father Sebastian Rasles, he says: "The world is parcel of the Church so that every leaf, every vein in every leaf, the throbbing of the temples is of that mysterious flower." (*In the American Grain*, 120.)

The ambiguity of the word "decomposition" makes this passage from Paterson a difficult one. The prayer of praise seems to be directed toward an unchangeable Beauty amidst the constantly shifting loveliness of the natural world as it goes through its cycles of bloom and decay, day and night, life and death. But the praise rises from a heart unsure of itself, tortured by the fear of illusion—not necessarily identifiable as the author's, yet infected by such a credo as Williams voices in the essay about Shapiro:

> Where then will you find the only true belief in our day? Only in science. That is the realm of the incomplete, the convinced hypothesis—the frightening embodiment of mysteries, of transmutations from force to body and from body to—nothingness. Light.

This statement, however, is not as positivistic as it sounds, if one considers that the man writing it has elsewere classified science as an emotion. (*Poetry*, XIV, 215.)

The next part begins with an economical lyric on the negative character of woman, the rock; this concept is picked up again later when Williams says that stones cannot invent, "only a man invents." Yet woman is the antithesis which in union with Paterson (thesis) will produce the synthesis (integrity, wholeness) so lacking among today's dichotomies. The "archaic persons of the drama" (He and She) argue, She begging for marriage, reproaching him for having forsaken her, He fleeing, "pursued by the roar." Williams has once before identified poetry and marriage, in his review of Kenneth Rexroth's *The Phoenix and the Tortoise.* (*Quarterly Review of Literature,* II, 149.)

At nine o'clock, closing time for the Park, Faitoute strolls off, noticing the flowers strewn upon the path, the broken tree-branches. He pauses once more to look down at the Falls, trembling with the strain of trying to decipher the language of the torrent. The moment is perilous. Like Patch at the Genesee Falls, Paterson is drawn towards destruction by the terrifying plunge of the waters, loses his humanity, metamorphosing into a tree uncorrupted by the frantic longing to translate:

> he sees squirming roots trampled
> under the foliage of his mind by the holiday
> crowds as by the feet of the straining
> minister. From his eyes sparrows start and
> sing. His ears are toadstools, his fingers
> have begun to sprout leaves (his voice is drowned
> under the falls.)

Now, as poet, he must sing his song quickly, if he is to escape the impinging disaster, if he is not to know fellowship with the weeds of the river-bottom.

This character of poet is retained as he flees from the demands for marriage made by the imagination (feminine principle of the universe), answering her call with anger rather than love: "Faitoute ground his heel / hard down upon the stone." Then comes the longest exposition of C.'s woes, her final appearance in the prose passages of *Paterson.* She is still referring to the atrophy of her literary powers in terms of metamorphosis, this time of water, the central non-human metamorphosis in the whole poem:

The anger and the indignation which I feel towards
you now has served to pierce through the rough ice
of that congealment which my creative faculties
began to suffer from as a result of that last note
from you.

The whole letter is a verbose confession in letter form of the failure of any satisfactory relationship between man and woman, between the artist and the imagination. Here, for the first time, the mask of physician is added to the multiple Paterson personality, whom the correspondent twice refers to as Dr. P. If, as Louis Martz thinks in the review mentioned above, the theme of this second book is love, its metamorphic nature is made meaningful by reference to an earlier belief of Williams as set down in *Kora in Hell: Improvisations:* "It is in the continual and violent refreshing of the idea that love and good writing have their security." (24) *Paterson* is truly, from start to finish, his testament of perpetual change. (*The Clouds, Aigeltinger, Russia, etc.,* 41.)

The next book begins with a new setting, the Library— probably the Danforth Memorial Library at the corner of SE Broadway and Auburn in Paterson. Driven by heat and futility Paterson seeks for beauty in the cool of books. Spring has drifted into summer, but "the roar in his mind is / unabated." He must find some way out of the staleness which suffocates him, examples of which litter the entire poem: stale lyrics from minds like beds always made up, a whale's breath, the Library itself, a back-house stench, rotten beams, old furrows, grey beds of dead grass, withered weed stalks, black sumac. Against these Paterson opposes earthquake, cyclone, flood, fire—the locust tree and the sea. Twenty-two times he cries out for the Beautiful Thing which men strive to destroy: this destruction of beauty is another constant theme, providing some of the poem's most fascinating complexities.

The modern world fears beauty more than death—and. since beauty exists only in the particular, tries ceaselessly to

kill, or at least mutilate, beautiful things. The first example
of this occurs in Book One when pearls are ruined through
being boiled; others are: the brutal capture of huge sturgeon; the wholesale killing of eels from the bottom of the
drained lake; the chase of the mink in Clark's hardware
store; the shooting of the last wolf; the burning of Sappho's
poems; the battle against the great 1902 fire; the death of
the little dog who never harmed anyone; the treatment of
the girl in the white lace dress; the murder of six-months-old
Nancy Goodell by her father. As a matter of fact, the ugliness of the crime of murder is heavily underscored throughout the entire poem. Besides Nancy Goodell, Williams presents the discovery of a corpse in 1875 by Leonard San-
ford; the shooting of John Joseph Van Houten; the fate of
the woman in love with a Fort Bragg soldier (though this is
only hinted to be a case of homicide); Kieft's massacre of
the two Indians; the murdered woman whose killer had
served four years of his sentence; Jonathan Hopper, Revolutionary hero slaughtered in bed by ruffians; the slaying
of the elderly Van Winkles.

Beauty is spoiled by severance from the springs of its life
—the bud upon the pavement, divorced from its fellows,
symbol of all those who revolt against wholeness, who refuse to embrace what would save them. In lines vividly suggestive of the problems of Dr. Williams himself, an interior
voice offers objection after objection to deter Paterson from
the search for beauty:

> Give it up. Quit it. Stop writing.
> "Saintlike" you will never
> separate that stain of sense,
> an offense
> to love, the mind's worm eating
> out the core, unappeased
>
> —never separate that stain
> of sense from the inert mass. Never.
> Never that radiance

This is a foreshadowing of the Madame Curie story which will be given considerable space in Book Four. Like the French woman-physicist, Williams is looking for the radiant gist. The taunting voice goes on, urging him to give up his political faith as well:

> *Doctor, do you believe in*
> *"the people," the Democracy? Do*
> *you still believe—in this*
> *swill-hole of corrupt cities?*
> *Do you, Doctor? Now?*

At this point Paterson metamorphoses from Faitoute back into the city, struck by a tornado: "It pours / over the roofs of Paterson, ripping, / twisting, tortuous," moving one of its churches, blowing the flame over its entire area in an integration of violence, after which the work of the artist still survives in an old bottle, emblem of how the poet can beat fire at its own game. This spreading fire is one variety of the "dispersal" motif mentioned in the head-note, a motif crucial to the design.

In the last two sections of Book Three, the character of Paterson as poet again takes precedence over other aspects of the symbol; section two begins with an autobiographical passage which stresses the inability of an *avant-garde* writer like Dr. Paterson to communicate with his townspeople.

> *A wonderful gift! How do*
> *you find the time for it in*
>
> *your busy life? It must be a great*
> *thing to have such a pastime.*
>
> *But you were always a strange*
> *boy. How's your mother?*
>
> *—the cyclonic fury, the fire,*
> *the leaden flood and finally*
> *the cost—*
>
> *Your father was such a nice man.*
> *I remember him well.*

Or, Geeze, Doc, I guess it's all right
but what the hell does it mean?

Williams confesses that it is not entirely their fault, since he finds himself along with the rest, squirting little hoses of objection at the fire which twines about the Beautiful Thing as its lover. But the dispersal—hallmark of contemporary poetry—goes on. This property Williams long ago called attention to in *Poetry* (xIV, 215): "But the particular characteristic of modern poetry has been its dispersive quality."

Williams has set up in several places throughout the poem an antithesis between the man and the book, one which he realizes ought not to exist. Perhaps the best expression of this is the following:

> *What more clear than that of all things*
> *nothing is so unclear, between man and*
> *his writing, as to which is the man and*
> *which the thing and of them both which is*
> *the more to be valued.*

It is for the second leading metamorphic agency—fire—to obliterate the distance separating them. As he says in Book Three, section two: "To write / is a fire and not only of the blood." The final amalgamation comes as a climax to the devastating fire of 1902:

> *Rising with a whirling motion, the person*
> *passed into the flame, becomes the flame—*
> *the flame taking over the person*

But Williams goes on to make the metamorphosis even more wonderful; like Dante's men turning into serpents and serpents into men of *Inferno* xxv, this exceeds anything in Ovid. For not only does the person become fire, but the fire is transformed into the person: "The person submerged / in wonder, the fire become the person."

The flames that consume Paterson are like a cataract reversed, and just as uncontrollable; no poet has as yet come upon the invention powerful enough to transform the fire into an image of the hero at Iwo Jima or to translate the roaring of the Falls into a white replica which will mean physical and spiritual salvation for Paterson. Until such comes, the external world or its inhabitants does not even exist: "Until your artists have conceived you in your unique and supreme form you can never conceive yourselves and have not, in fact, existed," Williams told the members of the English Institute in 1948. To make the material universe come true, a new mind and a new metrical line are required:

> *without invention*
> *nothing lies under the witch-hazel*
> *bush, the alder does not grow from among*
> *the hummocks margining the all*
> *but spent channel of the old swale,*
> *the small foot-prints*
> *of the mice under the over-hanging*
> *tufts of the bunch-grass will not*
> *appear. . . .*

The woman-symbol in the third book is consistently designated as Beautiful Thing, undergoing transformations from a dove to "a dark flame, / a wind, a flood" to a girl in a white lace dress to a young Negress (possibly the same person) back to "you! / – in your white lace dress" to the opening metaphor of the rock. She is set against a background of destruction, which Williams believes to be a necessary prelude to creation, since it frees the present from the stale forms of the past. ("Letters to an Australian Editor," 207.) Now that the flood water of 1902 has laid waste the region, only through metamorphosis can any new beauty come forth. The leaf must be torn from the calendar, the past forgotten:

> *Give*
> *it over to the woman, let her*
> *begin again—with insects*
> *and decay, decay and then insects:*

the leaves—that were varnished
with sediment, fallen, the clutter
made piecemeal by decay, a
digestion takes place.

—of this, make it of this, *this,*
this, this, this, this   .

Paterson now composes a love song to her, all about the
winter birds and the summer flowers that rejoice her and
about the sorrow (Love), her secret over which she cries by
the hour.

In the next to last prose link of Book Three Williams
goes back to Africa and the wives of chieftains, telling how
"Only married women, who have felt the fertility of men in
their bodies, can know the secret of life," on the guarding of
which the strength of the tribe depends. It is not by accident
that the final lyric of this book mentions the Chapel of Saint
Rock rather than that of some other saint, and the shrine of
Montpellier.

In the last lines of *Paterson* III, the sleeping giant struggles to awake, to break the spell laid upon him by the eternal roar of the Falls. All that has happened in the poem has
happened in his subconscious, just as the events involving
H. C. Earwicker occur in the course of a night's sleep. The
comparison with Joyce is one which naturally suggests itself: about the resemblance Parker Tyler writes:

> Dr. Williams' situation is Finnegan's situation. It is that
> of the epic, or myth, hero who *dreams his action* to the
> extent that it ceases to be individually his and becomes
> also that of others. (*Briarcliff Quarterly,* III, 171.)

The central pronoun, the fluidity of which Vivienne Koch
has remarked on in her study of Williams, shifts from third
to first person, and the book ends with the urgency of a
man beating on a bolted door. Paterson has defined his task,
but it is not Williams's intention to permit him success in his

efforts to complete it, since he says in the introduction to Book Three:

> Book IV shows the perverse confusions that come of a failure to untangle the language and make it our own as both man and woman are carried helplessly toward the sea (of blood) which, by their failure of speech, awaits them.

Earlier, in the headnote, he has described this last book as the conclusion of life, corresponding to the Passaic River below the Falls as it runs toward the sea: a section in which the episodes of a man's lifetime will come back to him.

Book Four introduces Paterson not in his elemental character but as a married man who is also the city, commented on by the poet as observer:

> *Oh Paterson! Oh married man!*
> *He is the city of cheap hotels and private*
> *entrances . of taxis at the door, the car*
> *standing in the rain hour after hour by*
> *the roadhouse entrance.*

This last book is indeed full of perverse confusions and separations. By using the pastoral technique in the opening section, Williams obtains a garishness, an incongruity, which, however disagreeable, hammer home his theme of divorce, sterility. The failure of language is neatly summarized in the first line by the adjective *silly* ("Two silly women!") which no longer communicates its former meaning and yet is inadequate to describe Phyllis, the new mask assumed by the rock-woman, or her odd wealthy employer, who wants to be called Corydon. The relationship between the two goes quickly from Miss to Phyllis to darling. In accordance with the rock analogy, Phyllis's hands as she massages Corydon are compared to stone (diamonds). The book's first division consists entirely of an idyl—a disgusting travesty of the pastoral genre—which is built around three triangles: Phyllis, Corydon and Paterson; Phyllis, her boyfriend, and Paterson; Phyllis, Mrs. Paterson, and Paterson. The last two triangles do not actually figure in the poem but are there marginally as factors the reader is aware of in the background.

The relationships are further complicated by Phyllis's attachment to her drunkard father, constantly stressed by means of letters. The point of the section is the impossibility of union in modern life: Phyllis and her father are kept apart by his alcoholism, which forces her to live in New York instead of in Ramapo, her home town; the infatuation of Corydon, as her employer insists on being called, illustrates the frustration of homosexuality; Paterson himself has to be content with partial satisfaction, as he had to in the case of the Beautiful Thing in the previous book. There is a suggestion that the Paterson of these opening pages is Dr. Paterson, an autobiographical aspect which becomes definite in the second section.

It is hard to evaluate a poem which has as subject the failure of language, since the author may always claim its defects intentional as illustrative of his theme. This difficulty is especially relevant in appraising the incredible combination of poet and soft-headed old maid that Williams has created in Corydon, who insists upon reading Phyllis lyrics of her own composition which are quite out of key with her character.

One of the best of these passages concerns all that is left of the elemental: the three rocks off Blackwell's Island, now covered with gulls' excrement. Describing the attack of the gulls upon a floating corpse, that of a Hindu princess, Corydon says:

> *The gulls, vortices of despair, circle and give*
> *voice to their wild responses until the thing*
> *is gone   .   then ravening, having scattered*
> *to survive, close again upon the focus,*
> *the bare stones, three harbor stones, except*
> *for that   .   useless*

Earlier, she has called these stones her sheep; now she goes on to equate them with love, "begrimed, befouled," which

> *begrimed*
> *yet lifts its head, having suffered a sea-change!*
> *shorn of its eyes and its hair*
> *its teeth kicked out   .   a bitter submersion*
> *in darkness   .*

Corydon's poem then goes backward to trace, in the living hell of New York, the reasons for such a suicide, which has made "The flesh a / flesh of tears and fighting gulls." Unable to unite herself with the imagination, as personified by Phyllis, she can only exclaim:

> *Oh I could cry!*
> *cry upon your young shoulder for what I know.*
> *I feel so alone.*

The second section does not directly mention Phyllis, though it quotes her once. However, she is there right at the edge of consciousness as one reads, the pejoration of the feminine principle. Williams reiterates this idea in two other ways: (1) by the analogy "As Carrie Nation / to Artemis / so is our life today" and (2) by the contrast between the Abbess Hildegard, who composed the choral for her own funeral in 1179, and a woman who went out west (ostensibly on a photographing expedition but really to have her marriage annulled) and who upon her return shocked people by taking her baby to all her girls' parties. Then he gives the supreme example of what woman might be: Madame Curie, woman of genius.

Here, as was promised in the headnote, episodes from Paterson's life are given: taking his son of high-school age to the Solarium for a lecture on atomic fission; seeing the Madame Curie moving picture; hearing Billy Sunday preach; getting a letter from a young poet, initialed A. P.; reading a case history of a nurse with intestinal disease. The

analogy between the poet's business and the physicist's is
treated at length, Madame Curie's discovery—and by im-
plication the poet's also—being compared to that of Columbus. Both Madame Curie and Paterson were seeking the
radiant gist, the luminous stain:

> *A dissonance*
> *in the valence of Uranium*
> *led to the discovery*
>
> *Where dissonance*
> *(if you are interested)*
> *leads to discovery*

Through the experience of twentieth-century scientists
like the Curies, a man's old dream of transmuting the elements, which lasted even as late as Strindberg, has indeed
come true. (As a matter of fact, in natural radioactivity this
element-mutation had been occurring all along.) Basic to
such metamorphoses is the conversion of mass into energy,
as predicted by Einstein, whose work revised the traditional
concept of the indestructibility of matter to the present law
of conservation of mass and energy. Because of physical research in this direction, scientists can now go through the
Mendelief molecular weight table, explicitly referred to by
Williams, changing one element into another—for instance,
mercury to gold—by capturing into a nucleus such extra
particles as protons, neutrons, deuterons, and alpha particles. Another aspect of artificial transmutation is the splitting of the uranium 235 atom. Man-made devices, such as
the cyclotron, can today achieve a metamorphosis which
will set up chain reactions of incredible power.

By the inevitable laws of nature itself, uranium transmutes into radium and finally to the stable substance of
lead: "Uranium (bound to be lead) / throws out the
fire . " The important part of this process, however, is
not the lead, its conclusion, but the enormous forces for
good or evil which the giving off of radioactive emanations

(Gamma rays) means for the human race. All these implications Williams weaves into his poem. For an understanding of the second part of *Paterson Three,* only an elementary
knowledge of physics is necessary, yet that minimum is indispensable because the pivotal metaphor here not only
interprets Williams's view of Paterson as city and man but
also redefines his whole attitude toward language as used in
poetry.

The poem continues:

> *—to dissect away*
> *the block and leave*
> *a separate metal:*
>
> *hydrogen*
> *the flame, helium   the*
> *pregnant ash   .*

Here, Williams shows physicists in action, changing helium
to hydrogen (the first element in the Mendelief chart) by
reducing the atomic number of the former through the emis-
sion of a proton. The "block" he speaks of is the proton,
nucleus of the hydrogen atom. By his overtones of an image from sculpture he sets in motion a fresh way of visualiz-
ing the mutation.

Uranium, the basic material, is later called a city:

> *Uranium, the complex atom, breaking*
> *down, a city in itself, that complex*
> *atom, always breaking down   .*
> *to lead*

The idea of radium as separated from this uranium is a fertile one indeed for Williams's symbolic intentions. The element is destined to cure cancer, just as the effective use of
language, if ever arrived at, will cure the large-scale cancer
eating humanity. Considered from this point of view, Madame Curie is like Sappho, the great lyric poet of ancient
Greece, rather than like Elektra, its equally great destroyer

("Sappho vs Elektra!") Williams does not let us entirely forget the sleeping giant or the married citizen as he propounds his analyses of modern evils and their remedies: he reiterates the words of Phyllis, "A man like you should have everything he wants," and then presents as contrast a few lines suggesting Faitoute drowsing near the Falls:

> . . . *half asleep*
> *waiting for the sun to part the labia*
> *of shabby clouds* .

What follows is a vehement attack on the cancer of usury worthy of Ezra Pound, one worked out through an extension of the radium metaphor: radium is to uranium what credit is to money. Radium or credit corresponds to fire, to the tornado driving out staleness, to the trade winds blowing the *Santa Maria* forward on its way to discovering a new continent. Credit, Williams says, is the Parthenon, incapable of being stolen; money is the gold meant for a statue of Athena but pilfered by Phideas. If man can but split the atom, fracture the basic thought (Paterson as city, money, uranium) he can achieve the radiant gist; this is all the "Difference between squalor of spreading slums / and splendor of renaissance cities." The debt to Pound is obvious, and welcome. Not only does Williams quote directly from what are undoubtedly communications to him from Pound but he poeticizes Pound's fiery economic theses in a most successful manner.

The final section goes back to the giant asleep, now old:

> *Shh! the old man's asleep*
>
> *—all but for the tides, there is no river,*
> *silent now, twists and turns*
> *in his dreams* .

More episodes out of a lifetime are presented, not only the lifetime of one man (the funeral of a girl he used to love, the gift of an ash-tray inscribed *La Vertue est toute dans l'effort,*

the President of Haiti at the Paterson pageant) but also that
of the city itself (newspaper accounts of the murder of
Jonathan Hopper in 1779, the uncovering of Peter Van
Winkle's skeleton in 1885, the Van Winkle double slaying;
in addition, excellently written poetic passages recreating
Paterson's past).

In the last section the woman too has grown old: "–and
did you ever know of a sixty year / woman with child
. . . ?" She is again the giantess, sprawled out against the
river, with her hair flung over the back country. In this web
struggle the flies of all the women Paterson has ever known:
Margaret–proud, stupid, but graceful and daring; the
golden-haired, blue-eyed Lucille who married a saloon-
keeper; calm, loving, self-sufficient Alma; cold, exciting,
silent Nancy:

> *There were*
> *others–half-hearted, the over-eager*
> *the dull, pity for all of them, staring*
> *out of dirty windows, hopeless, indifferent,*
> *come too late and a few, too drunk*
> *with it–or anything–to be awake to*
> *receive it. All these*
> *and more–shining, struggling flies*
> *caught in the meshes of Her hair, of whom*
> *there can be no complaint, fast in*
> *the invisible net–from the back country,*
> *half awakened–all desiring. Not one*
> *to escape, not one .   a fragrance*
> *of mown hay, facing the rapacious,*
> *the "great" .*

The river as microcosm is again emphasized in these concluding pages:

> *My serpent, my river! genius of the fields,*
> *Kra, my adored one, unspoiled by the mind,*
> *observer of pigeons, rememberer of*
> *cataracts, voluptuary of gulls! Knower*

> *of tides, counter of hours, wanings and*
> *waxings, enumerator of snowflakes, starer*
> *through thin ice, whose corpuscles are*
> *minnows, whose drink, sand   .*

The role of the serpent, conventional figure of time, is pointed up by Williams's references to tides, counting, the moon's cycle. This passage is followed by one again presenting the Falls as the seminal fluid: "And here's to the peak / from which the seed was hurled!" Just as the river will go on after Paterson the man has given himself up to the sea of death, so will humanity itself continue; Williams makes provision for this through the letters of the neophyte poet, A. P.

A. P. is preoccupied with the technical problems to which Paterson the poet has given his life. He shows more sympathy for the older man than his other two literary correspondents, T. J. and C., have done. When he first writes to Paterson he is twenty-three, recently released from a mental hospital and trying to get a newspaper job. As a poet he wants

> . . . to perfect, renew, transfigure, and make contemporarily real an old style or lyric machinery, which I use to record the struggle with imagination of the clouds, with which I have been concerned. . . . All that I have done has a program, consciously or not, running on from phase to phase, from the beginnings of emotional breakdown, to momentary raindrops from the clouds become corporeal, to a renewal of human objectivity which I take to be ultimately identical with no ideas but in things. But this last development I have yet to turn into poetic reality.

Here is not only an accent on poetry as metamorphosis, but also one on the central metamorphosis, water. A. P. disclaims any direct copying of Paterson's achievements though he admires them greatly; the look is clearly toward the future. He will go on where Paterson has left off, seeking the radium of true poetry.

It is easy to see, as the poem approaches its end, what is one meaning at least of the sea of blood referred to earlier in this chapter: it is the total war threatened by the Korean conflict begun in 1950. There is no more sense to war as a solution of difficulties than there is to outright murder, as in the Van Winkle case with which *Paterson* closes: both are "a poverty of resource." Invention must replace murder: mathematics powerful as a waterfall for Madame Curie, poetry based on things as in the dreams of Williams. The mind "will best take out / its spate in mathematics / replacing murder."

The pathos of man's struggle against death is crystallized by means of a debate, one voice urging that "the sea is not our home," a second insisting "You must come to it." In spite of the exquisite imagery with which the second speaker clothes the sea ("nicked by the light alone, diamonded / by the light from which the sun / alone lifts undamped his wings / of fire!"), the first speaker has the last word: "It is NOT / our home." This may be understood as an affirmation of immortality, a theory documented by the final scene in which a man swims in from the sea to the shore where his dog has been guarding his clothes and after a rest in the sun goes off up the bank, sampling beach plums as he climbs and heads inland. Human life is, after all, a somersault; like water (drawn up, formed into clouds, rained down, gathered into water-bodies on earth, drawn up again) it goes on endlessly. Paterson has many guises, but contains within an abiding core of identity impervious to that which would destroy him.

The woman in her human nature meets her death as Mrs. John S. Van Winkle, murdered with her husband by John Johnson, with whose hanging close to Garrett Mountain the book concludes; he does not even know why he committed this crime, is overcome by pity at the sight of his butchery.

Death to Paterson and his feminine counterpart, as to Sam Patch and Mrs. Cumming, is a useless thing, something which might well have been prevented, a disaster due to the break-down of language. The river has flowed into a sea of blood—but even as water is sucked upward into the clouds this end is but a beginning.

The two leading characters of *Paterson* (the river-city-man and the rock-woman), are in the last analysis only one, yet the division was needed if the work was to be truly universal. Williams has asserted as much in his introduction to Book Three (The Library):

> *Paterson* is a man (since I am a man) who dives from cliffs and the edges of waterfalls, to his death—finally. But for all that he is a woman (since I am not a woman) who *is* the cliff and the waterfall. She spreads protecting fingers about him as he plummets to his conclusions to keep the winds from blowing him out of his path. But he escapes, in the end, as I have said.
>
> As he dies the rocks fission gradually into wild flowers the better to voice their sorrow, a language that would have liberated them both from their distresses had they but known it in time to prevent catastrophe.

What is this language which could have forestalled the tragedy of Paterson and his mate? It is the wild flowers themselves, breaking up from the rock of the imagination, but still things, no ideas but in things. "The poet alone in this world holds the key to their [the man's and the woman's] final rescue."

Williams believes, first of all, that the poet causes the world to exist for eternity: "No world can exist for more than the consuming of a match or the eating of an apple without a poet to breathe into it an immortality." (*Quarterly Review of Literature*, II, 348.) But more than that, he believes, as does Wallace Stevens, that the poet makes a new world. In the essay just quoted from he goes on to say of Byron Vazakas:

> He seems more the artist, the poet in the full sense of a transformer by work of the imagination, than anyone I know. . . . Like the newspaper that takes things as it finds them—mutilated and deformed, but drops what it finds as it was, unchanged in all its deformity and mutilation—the poet, challenging the event, recreates it as of whence it sprang from among men and women, and makes a new world of it.

In a 1926 lyric, "Struggle of Wings," Williams had declared it was for the poet, "Out of such drab trash as this / by a metamorphosis," to release the radiations of being from common objects and let man's earthly garden shine forth as it did to the dazzled eyes of Adam in Eden. To such a task has Williams dedicated his life. From the beginning he knew that the cost would be high—high in self-abandonment, high in spending out of sympathy even to the point of empathy. The bargain, however, is an anti-Faustian one, since it concerns the saving, not the losing, of a soul.

The whole progress of this bargain is related in "The Wanderer," a poem significantly given the same title as Alain-Fournier's novel depicting the pursuit of the ideal. "The Wanderer" ends with a metamorphosis—the poet becomes the Passaic River, after an initiation into the high quest of supreme poetry by a constantly changing woman who symbolizes the imagination:

> *Then she, leaping up with a fierce cry:*
> *"Enter, youth, into this bulk!*
> *Enter, river, into this young man!"*
> *Then the river began to enter my heart,*
> *Eddying back cool and limpid*
> *Into the crystal beginning of its days.*
> *But with the rebound it leaped forward:*
> *Muddy, then black and shrunken*

Till I felt the utter depth of its rottenness
The vile breadth of its degradation
And dropped down knowing this was me now.
But she lifted me and the water took a new tide
Again into the older experiences,
And so, backward and forward,
It tortured itself within me
Until time had been washed finally under,
And the river had found its level
And its last motion had ceased
*And I knew all—it became me.**

These lines could never have been written by Wallace Stevens or Ezra Pound, eager as they are to make the world new. They are lines that arise from the deeply compassionate heart of a man who has passed his life easing the sufferings of his fellows. They arise from the heart of a man who is not afraid to identify himself with his environment even to the point of metamorphosis. And in *Paterson,* this man's testament of perpetual change is evidence of the ancient truth that he who shall lose his soul shall find it, though the soul in this case extends beyond the man, beyond the city, to the soul of a future generation for whom Williams has striven to prepare the world.

* From *Complete Collected Poems, 1906–1938,* copyright 1938 by New Directions. Reprinted by permission of the publisher.

☆

CHAPTER FOUR

ELIOT AND CRANE:

Protean Techniques

CERTAINLY the two most important American poems of the first fifty years of our century are *The Waste Land* and *The Bridge*. They are linked together not only by their preoccupation with the theme of modern civilization—though each presents a different side of that coin—but also by the cinema technique in which one character or scene is merged into another, a technique which is really the contemporary artist's approximation of Ovid's metamorphoses.

As early as 1917, T. S. Eliot revealed his concept of the poetic process as a metamorphic one. In a now very familiar if inaccurate analogy, "Tradition and the Individual Talent" goes to chemistry for an illustration of this view:

> When the two gases previously mentioned [oxygen, sulphur dioxide] are mixed in the presence of a filament of platinum, they form sulphurous acid. This combination takes place only if the platinum is present; nevertheless the newly formed acid contains no trace of platinum, and the platinum itself is apparently unaffected; has remained inert, neutral, and unchanged. The mind of the poet is the shred of platinum. It may partly or exclusively operate upon the experience of the man himself; but, the more perfect the artist, the more completely separate in him will be the man who suffers and the mind which creates; the more perfectly will the mind digest and transmute the passions which are its material.*

* *Selected Essays*, 1917–1932 by T. S. Eliot, copyright, 1932, by Harcourt, Brace and Company, Inc.

In this example it is almost as if Prospero, from the Shakespearian play which forms the background of *The Waste Land,* were to command the palm trees and sea wind of his island to fuse into new beings—a miracle which they perform obediently in his unchanging presence.

Indeed, Eliot's Shakespeare essay points to *The Tempest* with its burden of sea-change, in the critic's attempt to describe the act of creation:

> Shakespeare, too, was occupied with the struggle which alone constitutes life for a poet—to transmute his personal and private agonies into something rich and strange, something universal and impersonal. The rage of Dante against Florence, or Pistoia, or what not, the deep surge of Shakespeare's general cynicism and disillusionment, are merely gigantic attempts to metamorphose private failings and disappointments.*

That the chemical metaphor is completely applicable, however, is dubious, for what is there in the human organism static enough to compare to Eliot's shred of platinum? The poet himself does not know when he begins to write a poem just what that poem will say, and after he has undergone the intense experience of composition, he (or his mind) will not, certainly, remain unchanged. Nor will the mind be *inert* and *neutral* in the process itself, unless one is to conceive of that process as automatic writing; and however favorably disposed Yeats may have been to this procedure, Eliot is too much of a classicist to uphold it. But the exaggeration of the analogy may be accounted for by the poet's eagerness to preserve the division between subjective and objective, between in other words the person and the poem.

De-personalization, then, is the keynote of the above aesthetic, and descriptive of Eliot's role as cultural hero in that he himself seems to have been replaced by the various masks created in his poems, while the meditative man that

* *Ibid.,* p. 117.

Eliot himself is, suffering through very real personal sorrows, remains largely unknown to his public. This, however, is what he has always wanted: the disappearance of the accidents of personality in the permanence of the work, the transmutation in a drama of author's life into character's life. "The creation of a work of art, we will say the creation of a character in a drama, consists in the process of transfusion of the personality, or, in a deeper sense, the life, of the author into the character," remarks Eliot in "The Comedy of Humours," an article in *The Athenaeum*. (November 14, 1919, 1180.)

Elizabeth Drew in the introduction to her book on Eliot underlines one important aspect of the poetic act regarded as metamorphosis:

> Poetry, using the medium of language, seeks to give a living verbal substance and outline to the unorganized feelings, perceptions, ideas and sensations afloat in the personal consciousness of the poet. But any attempt at the elucidation of this process of metamorphosis by which shapeless, untidy, vagrant consciousness becomes what Yeats calls "proud, living, unwasted words," brings with it the further awareness that "a style, a rhythm, to be significant, must embody a significant mind." *

The metamorphic agent, then, must be truly first-rate, comparable to platinum, if the catalysis is going to occur. Otherwise a new substance may result, but it will be denied the breath of life.

Such remarks as these apply to the poem as it exists in the writer's mind, as it comes together out of his three degrees of consciousness. But Eliot also follows the principles of metamorphosis in the very patterning of the artifact itself, in a manner that comes close to dream construction as that will be explicated in the chapter on Randall Jarrell. In fact, Maud Bodkin defines phantasmagoria as "the shifting play

* *T. S. Eliot: The Design of His Poetry.* Charles Scribner's Sons.

of figures, as in dream delirium, or the half-discerned under-
currents of consciousness" and then calls this characteristic
of Eliot's poetry. (*Archetypal Patterns in Poetry,* 308.) The
way in which the Waste Land images merge one into another is apparently based upon dream phenomena, which in
turn universally anticipated the montages of today's moving
pictures, as Parker Tyler notes in his excellent study of the
cinema as an art form, *Magic and Myth of the Movies*
(xiii). He goes on to show how the film world is at present
the equivalent of classical mythology:

> I do not claim any absolute value for the myth and magic
> of Hollywood or for those modern vestiges of the old
> Greek divinities I have dubbed "the gods and goddesses
> of Hollywood." On the contrary the principle I mean is
> one of relativity and metamorphosis rather than absolut-
> ism and changelessness: just as a word has synonyms—
> and antonyms—so has a myth. . . . Even as the gods
> do, they [Hollywood actors and actresses] undergo con-
> tinual metamorphosis never losing their identities, being
> Rita Hayworth or Glen Ford no matter what their movie
> aliases. (xvii–xviii) *

It will be useful to examine at this point just how the
Waste Land scenes and characters melt into one another;
as C. M. Bowra in *The Creative Experiment* says, "Scene
fades into scene and character into character, because ulti-
mately there is only one scene and not more than three characters." (164) Such an examination is not meant to be another in the already all but interminable series of explica-
tions of *The Waste Land;* it is intended merely as an attempt
to draw together the metamorphic threads so that the relation of these scenes and characters one to another may be
revealed.

The reader is aware immediately, from the epigraph out
of Petronius, that the Waste Land landscape may be that of

* Reprinted by permission of Henry Holt and Company.

Hell, since the Cumaean Sibyl quoted there from the Satiri-
con is the same personage who provided Aeneas with the
golden bough for his descent through the underworld. Then,
too, the very title of the poem suggests the third division of
the seventh circle of Dante's *Inferno*. "The Burial of the
Dead" opens with an April vignette—lilacs and spring rain,
contrasted with the memory of winter. The first setting to
be enlarged upon, however, is summer at the edge of the
Starnbergersee, where an aristocratic lady, Marie, describes
her childhood and her present recreations. Against such
vanity the voice of the prophet Ezechiel rises, evoking a
stony desert, sun-baked, scattered with broken images; from
the shadow of the red rock he stretches out his handful of
dust to terrify by its unequivocal prophecy empty souls who
think of the past and future only as shadows. Then the spot-
light moves to the ship from Act I of Wagner's *Tristan and
Isolde* and a snatch of poignant song calls forth the first
moment of illumination, coming to us not directly but related as if by a modern Tristan; this moment concerns
woman as the hyacinth girl, the initial (though oblique)
reference to the dying fertility god—in this case, Hyacinth—
who is to assume several disguises in *The Waste Land*.

Next, Eliot transports us to the salon of Madame Sosostris
(a name perhaps suggested by Tristan, in the fashion of free
association as it operates throughout the poem), where the
protagonist has his fortune read. The central character is
now established by his card as the drowned Phoenician
Sailor, with pearls for eyes, a role foreshadowed, as Eliot
indicates in the notes, by the words "My eyes failed" (which
the poet relates to "Those are pearls that were his eyes") to
be repeated in the final lines of "The Burial of the Dead,"
where the Phoenician Sailor cries out to his co-seaman in
the ships at Mylae. Among other *personae* presented
through the Tarot pack are the man with the three staves
(Eliot in the notes calls him the Fisher King; the triad of
staves may possibly symbolize the tenses, or even the

Trinity), and, although he does not appear in the fortune, the Hanged Man (again the fertility god).

From the fortune-teller's room the poem moves to London Bridge at dawn—in a sense, the fortune itself has been a bridge between present and future, and has alluded to the walking crowds now seen to be souls of the dead. The closing lines of the first section dramatize both the sacrificed god and the theme of burial itself, as the protagonist asks one of the damned, Stetson (the man who stands for all of us) about the condition of a corpse he had planted the year before in his garden. That question ("Has it begun to sprout? Will it bloom this year? / "Or has the sudden frost disturbed its bed?") is paraphrased thus by Elizabeth Drew: "Will the metamorphosis from death to life take place or has the chill of cowardice blighted its growth?" (74)

The original superstition underlying the Waste Land sacrifice referred to in the above lines is a very ancient one. Edith Hamilton in *Mythology* describes it thus:

> Long before there were any stories told in Greece or any poems sung which have come down to us, perhaps even before there were storytellers and poets, it might happen, if the fields around a village were not fruitful, if the corn did not spring up as it should, that one of the villagers would be killed and his—or her—blood sprinkled over the barren land. There was no idea as yet of the radiant gods of Olympus who would have loathed the hateful sacrifice. Mankind had only a dim feeling that as their own life depended utterly on seedtime and harvest, there must be a deep connection between themselves and the earth and that their blood, which was nourished by the corn, could in turn nourish it at need. (116–117) *

And in antiquity as the seasons progressed, when narcissus and hyacinth grew up where a beautiful youth had been oblated, men easily linked the two things by believing that the flowers were his very self. Thus Eliot, by his Hyacinth-garden section preceding the inquisition on the corpse, has

* Reprinted by permission of Little, Brown & Company.

prepared for the fertility figure whose solemn presence will continue to be felt throughout the poem.

Yet since Eliot in his notes has revealed the Frazer volumes on Adonis, Atthis, and Osiris as sources for *The Waste Land,* we must consider the fertility symbol as representing more than a human being. Adonis, born of a myrrh tree, went back to the vegetable kingdom by metamorphosing into the flower of Venus after he had been slain by a wild boar. The blood of Atthis, too, turned to violets after his death. About Osiris, the mythologist H. G. Baynes says: "In the temple of Isis at Philae there is a wall-painting representing the dead body of Osiris with stalks of corn springing from it, while a priest waters the corn with a pitcher." (*Mythology of the Soul,* 692.) The Dog, against which the protagonist warns Stetson, at least implies the devil, as in Randall Jarrell's "A Conversation with the Devil" ("A Dog in a tub, who was the Morning Star!"); through diabolic intervention even the buried fertility god may fail to save the Waste Land.

As the dawn-scene on the Bridge fades out, it is replaced by the boudoir of a twentieth-century Cleopatra, the luxury of which intensifies the horror of the Waste Land, just as the richly emblemed money bags tied to the necks of the usurers in Dante's seventh circle accentuate their misery. The room belongs to a woman whose name means not only *beautiful lady,* but also *poison.* And here occurs the most striking and direct instance of metamorphosis in the entire poem, a borrowing from Ovid's Book VI, which describes the mutation of Philomela. The transformation is indeed an excellent one to illustrate Eliot as myth-maker, or, more appropriately, as myth-remaker. The idea underlying the Philomel lines in "A Game of Chess" is that out of suffering art is born, as eternal and inviolable as suffering is temporary and violable. Cleanth Brooks regards the passage in this way:

> If it is a commentary on how the waste land became waste, it also repeats the theme of the death which is the

door to life, the theme of the dying god. The raped woman becomes transformed through suffering into the nightingale; through the violation comes the inviolable voice. The thesis that suffering is action, and that out of suffering comes poetry is a favorite one of Eliot's.*

The Ovidian story is here combined with Milton's Eden and with a glimpse of the mutilated heroine of Titus Andronicus until the living picture burns green and orange like the sea-wood in the fireplace transformed by copper dust and flames. But the nightingale's melodious singing is in the past tense. After calling the central theme of *The Waste Land* metamorphosis, Miss Drew points up this songlessness: *"There,* in that world where the physical and temporal is transcended by the spiritual and the eternal, her song gave meaning to her mortal pain. But she does not sing in the desert places of the present." (76) The nightingale's modern counterpart utters only harsh syllables that fall upon Sweeney's dirty ears. Lloyd Frankenberg in *Pleasure Dome* calls this deterioration metamorphosis in reverse: "By a shift of focus—a reverse metamorphosis—the nightingale of mythology has been transformed into a raucous bird. Keats' urn of beauty is a jug of ugliness." (68)

Two other contemporary poets who have seen the nightingale as a figure of poetry are John Crowe Ransom ("Philomel") and Peter Viereck ("Birth of Song"). Ransom's is a brittle, meticulous lyric in his best satiric manner on the impossibility of Philomel's singing in our urbanized world. Viereck's, which in 1950 he called his best poem to date, "photographs the ego in the fleeting moment of metamorphosis from owl, the bird of wisdom, into philomel, the bird of song," as he phrases his intention in John Ciardi's *Mid-Century American Poets* (26). But neither has found in the tale of Ovid a metaphor that will function with the vivid allusiveness of Eliot's in the second part of *The Waste*

* *Modern Poetry and the Tradition* by Cleanth Brooks. University of North Carolina Press.

Land, or in the two later passages where he returns to this myth with its piercing contrasts and tragic insight.

In the midst of a futile dialogue (interspersed with reverie) between Belladonna and the Phoenician Sailor, the setting shifts to the island of *The Tempest.* The protagonist lets his mind rest upon art as an escape from the dreadful present. Miss Drew considers this as a temptation:

> . . . the temptation to drown out the moral and spiritual problems of the personal life by the creative activity of art alone. This is borne out by the quotation from *The Tempest,* which follows the introduction of the sailor symbol '(Those are pearls that were his eyes).' We know that that quotation and the lines that follow it in Ariel's song, are associated in Eliot's mind with the transmuting of life into art. But the quotation stands for much more than that. It is the central symbol in the poem for the whole process of metamorphosis in both its destructive and creative aspects. (172) *

She goes on to remind us that after all the pearl is a disease in the oyster, and here, a degeneration from living tissue to inorganic matter, although at the same time Ariel's song epitomizes that sea change which was "a metamorphosis from blindness to new vision." (71–72)

The phrase leading into the next scene (an English pub) is "a knock on the door," symbol of the bartender's eagerness to clear his establishment of Bill, May, Lou, and the rest of the sterile crowd whose gossip reveals the failure of love. The little monologue following, carried on by Lil's nameless friend, only serves to highlight the sad truth that, as Helen Gardner phrases it in *The Art of T. S. Eliot,* "all wars are the same war, all love-making is the same love-making, all homecoming the same homecoming. . . ." (88–89) At the end the speaker changes into Ophelia, who has been crazed by Hamlet's murder of her father. Belladonna and Lil stand out starkly in this section against the

* Drew, *op. cit.*

vision of three women from the heights of literary art—Dido, Cleopatra, Ophelia—three women who loved completely, though each paid for her passion with her own destruction.

Ophelia's death by drowning suggests the fate of the protagonist, immediately after which section III, "The Fire Sermon," fittingly opens with a river scene. The Fisher King now becomes Ferdinand, Prince of Naples, though the macabre context contrasts ruefully with the exquisite lyricism of *The Tempest*. Beauty tries to break through the Fisher King's sordid environment (the Grail legend as revealed by the children *chantant dans la coupole* and the nightingale); but postwar London resists too strongly, and Ferdinand assumes the ironic mask of the merchant Mr. Eugenides, whose very name means son of a noble race.

In the person of Ferdinand, the Phoenician sailor and the Fisher King appear to converge, a puzzling development in that they have separate cards in Madame Sosostris's fortune. But then the Hanged Man, whose card (though evidently a member of the Tarot pack) is missing from the fortune, is clearly identified with the Fisher King, not only because of the early-Christian fish symbol for Christ but also because of the respective missions of deliverance of the pagan and Christian divinities. That this overlapping, though a source of confusion, is intentional is plain from Eliot's statement in the note to line 218: "Just as the one-eyed merchant, seller of currants, melts into the Phoenician Sailor, and the latter is not wholly distinct from Ferdinand Prince of Naples, so all the women are one woman, and the two sexes meet in Tiresias." Thus is Everyman given artistic rebirth in the twentieth century. Eliot has thereby done the two things he accused Blake of not doing when he reviewed Charles Gardner's *William Blake the Man:* "You cannot create a very large poem without introducing a more impersonal point of view [Tiresias] or splitting it up into various personalities." (*The Athenaeum,* February 13, 1920, 209.)

Section III brings forward Tiresias who, Eliot announces

in his note to line 218, is the most important personage in the poem, though spectator rather than character. No other could ever serve so perfectly as an agent for understanding modern love (or its absence), since the Theban seer had spent seven years metamorphosed to a woman before his second encounter with copulating snakes in a forest, at which he was turned back again into a man. Eliot in the Notes quotes this myth of transformation, as told by Ovid, and also the incident where Tiresias, to settle an argument between the king and queen of Olympus, decided that women enjoy love more than men, for which he is blinded by Juno though recompensed with prophetic gifts by Jove.

The prophet of Thebes is the only person in the poem who explicitly identifies himself; why, George Williamson in "The Structure of *The Waste Land*," explains thus: "He is not a character in the fortune; but he is the supreme metamorphosis that brings together all the metamorphic transformations and thus is qualified to summarize their experience." (*Modern Philology*, XLVII, 202.) Although Tiresias does not appear until the middle of the poem, he retains his crucial position in that he has been prefigured in Madame Sosostris, and seems to be present, though unnamed, in section IV, where some controlling intelligence observes the skeleton of Phlebas, the drowned sailor, as the waves pick its bones, an intelligence that sends forth a warning to all sailors, Gentile or Jew, who yet are privileged to sail the ocean of life. This omnipresence fits in with Eliot's note to line 218: "What Tiresias *sees,* in fact, is the substance of the poem." Another way of looking at this omnipresence is proffered by R. P. Blackmur: "In other words, for the purposes of the poem, Eliot and Tiresias are identified, and are the sensibility of the poem." (*The Hound and Horn,* I, 192.) And what Tiresias sees is surely not merely the seduction of the typist by the young man carbuncular, but the unwisdom of all the world, from antiquity to the present.

The last section, "What the Thunder Said," exchanges the

peace of the "deep sea swell" for Jerusalem immediately after the Crucifixion; then in succession the road to Emmaus, the sites of falling cities throughout the history of western civilization, the Chapel Perilous, India in time of drought, the ninth circle of the *Inferno,* the Elizabethan Thames, and finally the edge of the sea where the Fisher King sits fishing, having crossed the Waste Land. Concerning the allusions from five languages with which the poem ends, one can only agree with Elizabeth Drew: "Material from the past is amalgamated into the poem, becomes part of its organization and issues in a metamorphosis." (24) Taking what he can salvage from the beauty of the past, the poet will exercise his powers as catalyst to build his brave new world, though such a reclamation of the Waste Land must wait for future days and poetry to be realized.

Until now, this chapter has been largely preoccupied with the technique of working out the theme of the *Waste Land.* What is that theme? It is the same motif, actually, which underlies all of Eliot's poetry since the early twenties: metamorphosis considered as rebirth. Nothing is more central to the Christian life, or even to the gropings after spiritual truth antecedent to Christ, for instance, the regenerative aspects of initiation rites in pagan cults. H. G. Baynes, to clarify this idea in *Mythology of the Soul,* uses an example from biology:

> The three stages of initiation in the pagan mystery cults were sometimes symbolized by three concentric rings. The outer ring represented the rite of purification or lustration; the middle ring, the ordeals and the sacrifice; and the inner ring, the identification with the god. The same symbol could express the three stages of realization —experience, reflection and understanding. These again correspond with the three stages of insect metamorphosis—the larva, the pupa and the imago. (749)

The preceding analysis has shown how Eliot associates the protagonist as Phoenician Sailor with the fertility god himself regarded as Fisher King. Miss Weston, in her essay, "The Grail and the Rites of Adonis" (*Folk-Lore,* XVIII, 295), further connects the Fisher King's quest with the ritual of the Greek fertility god Adonis by showing that these myths possess in common (a) a waste land, (b) a slain youth, (c) mourning, especially by women, and (d) the restoration of fertility. As for the two other circles mentioned by Baynes, those of ordeal and purification, it is easy to see how these are concretized in the water and fire imagery pivotal to the poem.

Elizabeth Drew's book on Eliot constantly interprets the poetry in terms of Jung, a quite understandable if overworked theory. Carl Jung in *Modern Man in Search of a Soul* develops the concept of baptism as a means of symbolic transformation thus:

> Baptism endows the human being with a unique soul. I do not mean, of course, the baptismal rite in itself as a magical act that is effective at one performance. I mean that the idea of baptism lifts a man out of his archaic identification with the world and changes him into a being who stands above it. The fact that mankind has risen to the level of this idea is baptism in the deepest sense, for it means the birth of spiritual man who transcends nature. (167)

If water is symbolic of the unconscious, it is also symbolic of the origin of all life. Christ's metaphor of the seed, His insistence that man be re-born of water and the Holy Ghost, represent for Eliot the full glory uniting the broken lights furnished by Tammuz, Adonis, Attis, Hyacinth, Osiris, and all the other antique types of burial and resurrection. The Golden Bough itself crystallizes such a renewal, as Bodkin's book on archetypes shows: "The bough whose significance Frazer and others have pursued through so many obscure places of myth and ritual, appears as representing the tree-spirit, or, more generally, the power of renewal in vegetation and in other forms of life." (130)

In devoting so much space in *Four Quartets* to this end-beginning, rebirth view of Christian life, Eliot is in close accord with innumerable writers, ancient and present-day, on spiritual progress. For metamorphosis, after all, is but another term to express Saint Paul's admonition that man should put on the new man, Christ. Dietrich von Hildebrand, a distinguished Catholic lay-educator, summarizes the doctrine thus in his *Transformation in Christ:*

> At the beginning and at the end of the road we travel in the process of our transformation in Christ, we hear Our Lord speak these mysterious words: "He that shall lose his life for me shall find it" (Matt. 10:39). . . . It is the holy paradox of Death and Resurrection that flares up in these words – the mystery of dying with Christ, and awakening to life again with Him. (390)

In another place in this volume von Hildebrand explains how the nearer we come to transformation in Christ, the more we are free, paradoxically, from the law of mutability affecting Nature, since we are approaching participation in the unchangeableness of God Himself. (9) It is this eternal and invariable state at which Eliot hints in the timeless moments which he intersperses among the philosophical speculations of his long poem.

Mystical contemplation, too, with which Eliot is specifically concerned in the *Quartets* – particularly as represented by Saint John of the Cross and Blessed Juliana of Norwich – has long used the language of transmutation to explain its mysterious processes and effects:

> In more than one passage St. Bernard gives expression to the idea of transformation (Cant. xxv. 5, lvii. 11, lxii. 5, lxix. 7); but all these passages are based on St. Paul, 2 Cor. iii. 18: 'We all, beholding the glory of the Lord with face unveiled, are transformed into the same image from glory to glory, as by the Spirit of the Lord.' In each case, however, the passage is applied to the result of

mystical contemplation in this life, and gives a lead to the idea of mystical transformation as found in later mystics.*

The iron in the fire, air transformed by light to light, drop of water indistinguishable from wine into which it is dropped, are only some of the images used by spiritual writers and taken over by the emblemists of the sixteenth and seventeenth centuries. Eliot is especially fond of the symbol of fire used in this sense: "We only live, only suspire / Consumed by either fire or fire." ("Little Gidding") In fact, he concludes the *Quartets* by uniting a quotation from Blessed Juliana with this transfiguration concept:

> *And all shall be well and*
> *All manner of thing shall be well*
> *When the tongues of flame are in-folded*
> *Into the crowned knot of fire*
> *And the fire and the rose are one.*†

The truth that the end and beginning are one, that death is also the point at which real life commences (as Catholic liturgy demonstrates when the feasts of saints are celebrated on the days of their deaths) finds consummate development in *Four Quartets*. After John M. Bradbury's perceptive examination, *"Four Quartets:* The Structural Symbolism," published in the *Sewanee Review* for Spring, 1951, there is little new that criticism can say of the way in which Eliot transmutes one element to another as a means of showing that second birth essential to the life of the spirit. Bradbury bases his explication on Heraclitus, though he stresses Eliot's selectivity in taking over Heraclitan philosophy:

> What largely appeals to Eliot, evidently, is Heraclitus's accent on transmutation. Each element lives in the death

---

* From *Western Mysticism* by Dom Cuthbert Butler. E. P. Dutton and Co., Inc.
† From *Four Quartets,* copyright, 1943, by T. S. Eliot. Reprinted by permission of Harcourt, Brace and Company, Inc.

of the others, so that each carries within it the nature of all the others which appear in successive rebirths. The process suggests the Christian death-resurrection cycle —"my end is my beginning"—and therefore the major chord which Eliot wishes to sound. (256)

Each *Quartet* concentrates upon a particular element, points out Bradbury: "Burnt Norton," air; "East Coker," earth; "The Dry Salvages," water; "Little Gidding," fire— one converting easily into another and the final one subsuming the other three. The beginning of "East Coker" is illustrative of this method:

> Old stone to new building, old timber to new fires,
> Old fires to ashes, and ashes to the earth
> Which is already flesh, fur and faeces,
> Bone of man and beast, cornstalk and leaf.*

Using as a focal point a house that rises, falls, and is replaced by another, the poet makes concrete the Heraclitan propositions and at the same time carries over from the first *Quartet*, "Burnt Norton," the connotations which its title (based on the name of an ancestral mansion) has aroused.

At the conclusion of the world—the General Judgment— the four elements as they meet in man are to be united by "the Love that moves the sun and the other stars"; this fusion, however, is but the natural period to that process begun when created things were drawn out of nothingness. Eliot's concentration on the elements is really a modern variant of the Ovidian ordering by Love of the warring elements, expressed thus by the seventeenth-century translator of the *Metamorphoses*, George Sandys: *"Fire, aire, Earth, Water, all the Opposites that strove in Chaos, powerfull Love unites."* Truly can creation say, "In my beginning is my end," as well as "In my end is my beginning."

Even some of the incidental *Quartet* images (the tree, the

* *Ibid.*

hidden children, the roses) are reduced in the end to an
elemental form, as Wallace Fowlie's *The Clown's Grail*
brilliantly brings out in the chapter paralleling the painter
Tchelitchew's *Cache-Cache* and Eliot's *Four Quartets:* "The
leaves of Tchelitchew's tree which gradually change colour
until they burst into the tiny flames of the final fire resemble
the roses of Eliot's poem which are, at the end, converted
into tongues of flames." (153) The external resemblance
between canvas and lyric is, of course, the children hidden
among the leaves of the tree: but deeper meditation upon
this use of the child as symbol (one of the most familiar of
archetypes) links it as specialist in metamorphosis with the
poet himself:

> Tchelitchew and Eliot have both composed works which
> are simultaneously a cycle and a drama. Their memory
> of pure childhood provides the cycle, and the memory of
> the agonized search for the world in childhood and the
> subsequent desperate search for the child in adulthood
> provide the drama. Both the poet and the painter have
> been guided by the children, and in each case the artist
> is depicted against the background of the awful lucidity
> of children. The inner landscapes of the children, which
> are their dream and their horror, are recast by the artist
> who, alone in the society of man, remains the child in his
> power of metamorphosis and symbolism. (152) *

The artist, then, stands isolated among the world of adults,
able to furnish new understandings of reality through his
power of metamorphosis. Eliot was hinting at such a concept as far back as 1919, when he reviewed W. B. Yeats's
The Cutting of an Agate. He quotes from that book:

> The end of art is the ecstasy awakened by the presence
> before an ever-changing mind of what is permanent in
> the world, or by the arousing of that mind itself into the
> very delicate and fastidious mood habitual with it when
> it is seeking those permanent and recurring things.
> (*The Athenaeum*, 4653, 553.)

* By permission of Fowlie's publisher in the United States, Alan
Swallow.

This is not enough for Eliot. He wants the emphasis put upon the objective, not the subjective, components of the aesthetic experience. He objects in these words to Yeats's formulation: "Why introduce the mind? Why not say—the recognition of the permanent in the changing, and the recognition of the protean identity of the permanent with the changing?" What is this but an assertion that there exists an invariable substratum which may have manifold concretizations, guises that art is lucky enough to make visible or audible, but which in the "deep heart's core" of the universe are mysteriously one? Like Pound, Eliot is an absolutist in his insistence upon perfection underlying the imperfections of ordinary life, and capable of being summoned forth at the bidding of the greatest masters.

In technique, Hart Crane's *The Bridge* resembles quite closely *The Waste Land,* with eight instead of five sections connected by imagery and rhythms which result from free association, or what has been termed progression by logic of feeling. Both find their anchoring symbol in place, a symbol which undergoes perpetual metamorphoses throughout the poem. Both, too, combine passages in the fashion of montages; in fact, Crane uses the film as one of the ways of expressing his vision in the "Proem" to *The Bridge:*

> *I think of cinemas, panoramic sleights*
> *With multitudes bent toward some flashing scene*
> *Never disclosed, but hastened to again,*
> *Foretold to other eyes on the same screen;* *

Just as one episode in a newsreel is broken off sharply before any conclusive disclosure, only to be repeated for another audience at the next show, so are the vivid passages of such poems put together, with the readers never able to arrive at an end, any more than the watchers of sea-gulls can complete the arc of the birds' flight.

* From *Collected Poems of Hart Crane,* published by Liveright Publishing Corporation, copyright Liveright Inc. 1933. All quotations from the poetry of Hart Crane reprinted by permission of Liveright Publishing Corporation.

We have seen how T. S. Eliot turned his Waste Land at will into Dante's Inferno, modern London, ancient Jerusalem, India in drouth. Crane's Bridge is equally protean. At its first appearance it is capitalized: "And Thee, across the harbor, silver-paced / As though the sun took step of thee. . . ." Only after a study of the entire poem does the full reason for this become clear. Whether consciously or not, Crane presents his Bridge as a concretization of God considered in terms of the Incarnation—an idea at least as old as the thirteenth century when Saint Catherine of Siena used it as the focal symbol in her Dialogues.

I am indebted to Caroline Gordon Tate for this suggestion of a likeness between Crane's imagery and that of Saint Catherine. In a letter of December 4, 1950, Mrs. Tate wrote:

> I have been reading Saint Catherine of Siena's Dialogues and I am much struck by the resemblances between her images of the Bridge (Christ) and Hart's images of his Bridge. I used to think when he was writing the poem that Roebling's bridge was almost too frail to stand up under the imagery he loaded on it. I see now that he had got hold of an archetypal symbol, or image, or rather that it had got hold of him.

The dissatisfaction which Crane felt with the poem, towards the end of its composition, is well-known; this inadequacy of reference was no doubt in part accountable.

"Proem" really provides a synopsis of most later uses in Crane's work of the Bridge as a Christ-symbol. In "Thy cables breathe the North Atlantic still" the Bridge is personified; the next two lines compare it to a heavenly reward ("And obscure as that heaven of the Jews, / Thy guerdon . . ."); and the following ones turn it into a king in the act of knighting vassals ("Accolade thou dost bestow / Of anonymity time cannot raise:"), a figure easily extended to Christ the King. The stanza concludes with the Bridge

pardoning and reprieving ("Vibrant reprieve and pardon
thou dost show"), certainly a divine prerogative.

The fervent invocation with which the next stanza begins
—"O harp and altar, of the fury fused, / (How could mere
toil align thy choiring strings!)"—unites the themes of art
and religion, with even the symbol for the former having
religious overtones. The fury spoken of is allied to the
Romantic theory of inspiration conceived of as ecstasy,
madness. Crane welds the harp and altar references in the
adjective describing the strings (*choiring*), a marvelous
economy typical of his verse. The next title given the Bridge
("Terrific threshold of the prophet's pledge") is the equivalent of this sentence from the Revelations to Saint Catherine:

> Wherefore, those who follow this road are the sons of
> the Truth, because they follow the Truth, and pass
> through the door of Truth and find themselves united to
> Me, who am the Door and the Road and at the same
> time Infinite Peace. (Thorold, Algar [tr.], *The Dialogue
> of the Seraphic Virgin Catherine of Siena,* 82.)

Christ is the Door, inspiring terror only to the damned, a
class with whom the rest of the poem will be preoccupied.
The closing line of this quatrain might almost have come
from Saint John of the Cross addressing his God: "Prayer
of pariah, and the lover's cry,—." Immediately afterward,
Crane calls the Bridge a "swift / Unfractured idiom"; what
is this but the Word? Then he refers to it as a path, and one
thinks of Him Who is the Way, the Truth, and the Life.
"Proem" ends with a petition: "Unto us lowliest sometime
sweep, descend / And of the curveship lend a myth to God."

All this is not to say that in "Proem" Crane deliberately
selected Jesus Christ as the tenor of his metaphor, or (what
is far less likely) that he had read Saint Catherine of Siena,
but rather that his mind, hungry for the Absolute, reached
out to Roebling's triumph of engineering as one way of expressing the means to union with His Creator, so passion-
ately and blindly desired under all his excesses.

It would be difficult indeed to read "Ave Maria" without identifying the Bridge as described therein with Christ. The most relevant lines are:

> *O Thou who sleepest on Thyself, apart*
> *Like ocean athwart lanes of death and birth,*
> *And all the eddying breath between dost search*
> *Cruelly with love thy parable of man,—*
> *Inquisitor! incognizable Word*
> *Of Eden and the enchained Sepulchre,*
> *Into thy steep savannahs, burning blue,*
> *Utter to loneliness the sail is true.*
>
> *Who grindest oar, and arguing the mast*
> *Subscribest holocaust of ships, O Thou*
> *Within whose primal scan consummately*
> *The glistening seignories of Ganges swim;—*
> *Who sendest greeting by the corposant,*
> *And Teneriffe's garnet—flamed it in a cloud,*
> *Urging through night our passage to the Chan;—*
> *Te Deum laudamus, for thy teeming span!*

Here Crane dramatizes Columbus's apostrophe to God, with a particularly Christian emphasis in the allusions to the Word and to the Sepulchre.

Saint Catherine of Siena has worded the Bridge figure thus, reporting a message she received from God in a mystical experience: "And so, wishing to remedy your great evils, I have given you the Bridge of My Son, in order that, passing across the flood, you may not be drowned, which flood is the tempestuous sea of this dark life." (74) This passage might be taken as an exegesis on Crane's conception of the Bridge as God, made explicit in his phrase, "Te Deum laudamus, for thy teeming span!" He goes on in "Ave Maria" to celebrate the victory of Elohim (Hebrew name for God) over science, the discoveries of Columbus and later heroes only adding to the Creator's glory. He finishes with a jubilant "Te Deum laudamus, / O Thou Hand of Fire,"

the last phrase to come back in far other circumstances at
the end of the "Tunnel" section.

The first glimpse we have of the woman-principle in the
poem is of an Indian girl turned into a human wheel, clearly
a human replica of the Bridge. The quotation presenting
this picture (from William Strachey's history of colonial
Virginia, taken at second hand from William Carlos Williams) is used to preface the five divisions of "Powhatan's
Daughter," which Crane intends as parts of the body of this
Indian princess, New World version of the fertility deity
whose masculine type informs *The Waste Land.* Writing to
his patron, Otto Kahn, on September 12, 1927, Crane explains his aims thus:

> Powatan's daughter, or Pocahontas, is the mythological
> nature-symbol chosen to represent the physical body of
> the continent, or the soil. She here takes on much the
> same role as the traditional Herthe of ancient teutonic
> mythology. The five sub-sections of Part II are mainly
> concerned with a gradual exploration of this "body,"
> whose first possessor was the Indian. (*Hound and Horn,*
> VII, 679.)

Not only is this exploration geographical (Manhattan, the
Catskills, the Mississippi valley, the West); it is also chrono-
logical, throughout time as lived in by an individual man as
well as time as it contains the history of the American continent. For, as Crane says in the same letter, each of the five
sections corresponds to a stage in the story of man: the
sowing of the seed ("Harbor Dawn"), childhood ("Van
Winkle"), youth ("The River"), manhood ("The Dance"),
age ("Indiana"). This symbolic odyssey is unified by the
title-image of the poem, metamorphosing through the gamut
of vehicles and avenues of transportation man has devised in
his technological advance across the ages.

The arch formed by the cartwheeling of the Indian girl, if
it is reflected upon, will permit the addressee in "The Harbor

Dawn" to be interpreted as the Bridge itself. While Crane
was working on the poem, he lived in the same room that
the engineer Roebling had occupied, a room having a fine
view of Brooklyn Bridge. The actual Bridge may be a
materialization of the love, here called "blessed" in harmony
with the theistic connotations already noted, that wakes out
of dream: "Serenely now, before day claims our eyes / Your
cool arms murmurously about me lay." Wallace Fowlie's
provocative reading of this poem supplies an insight into
Crane's use of woman as Bridge-symbol:

> In a sense, then, the bridge is the intercessor and media-
> tor for Hart Crane, the modern mechanistic counterpart
> of the Virgin who, like Brooklyn Bridge—contemplated
> by the poet as the statue was contemplated by the Jug-
> gler in the Medieval poem—is "sleepless" and "con-
> denses eternity." (*The Clown's Grail,* 130.)

Prepared for by the phrase "goes to sleep," the next division, "Van Winkle," metamorphoses the Bridge into a
macadam road between Far Rockaway in Long Island and
the Golden Gate. It is also a road through time (Memory),
through the life of the nation and the life of the poet, a high-
way involving not only Pizarro, Cortez, Priscilla, and Captain Smith but also Crane's childhood friends and parents.
The link between early America and the twentieth century
of "The River" is old Rip of Sleepy Hollow, whose long
slumber obliterated time. As Crane tells Kahn, he means the
historical characters drawn from America's childhood to be
united in "the figure of Rip Van Winkle who finally becomes
identified with the protagonist, as you will notice, and who
really boards the subway with the reader. He becomes the
'guardian angel' of the journey into the past." (*Hound and
Horn,* VII, 680.) The object of the journey, as suggested
before, is to make familiar to her modern lover the body of
Pocahontas, land of his origin and loyalties.
      In a fantastic extension of the subway line, the protago-

nist is transported to the Middle West. The most obvious
mutation of the Bridge in this section ("The River") is the
Mississippi river, which connects north and south, and even
east and west through its tributaries. As Howard Moss says,
"The river which begins as the railroad tracks (seen in terms
of moving water) ends as the Mississippi River." ("Disorder
as Myth," *Poetry*, LXII, 34.) A secondary one is the tele-
graph:

> *The last bear, shot drinking in the Dakotas*
> *Loped under wires that span the mountain stream.*
> *Keen instruments, strung to a vast precision*
> *Bind town to town and dream to ticking dream.*

A third is the railroad itself – a bridge "From pole to pole
across the hills, the states." Throughout this division, as in
the two just before it, the figure of Pocahontas as America
is hinted at in preparation for the next, "The Dance," which
is largely devoted to her; in the last section of "Powhatan's
Daughter," she appears as the mother of a ranger in Indiana,
accompanying her son to the banks of the Mississippi.

The actual Brooklyn Bridge is mentioned again in Section III, "Cutty Sark," as the protagonist crosses it at dawn
after his talk with a sailor in a South Street bar ("I started
walking home across the Bridge . . ."). Lines in italics, suggested by the nickelodeon's music, foreshadow the Bridge
of the final section, conceived of as the sunken continent of
Platonic myth, Atlantis. The two bridges – the material one
and the transcendental one – alternate, as in a dialogue of
voices out of time and eternity. This loosening of the strict
bonds of place and time, this sublimation of the ordinary, is
facilitated by the rum of the tavern. Such a view of liquor
occurs elsewhere in Crane's verse: about his "Wine Menag-
erie" R. P. Blackmur says:

> The principle of association which controls this stanza
> [the first] resembles the notion of wine as escape, release,
> father of insight and seed of metamorphosis, which con-

trols the poem; and in its turn, the notion of extra-logical, intoxicated metamorphosis of the senses controls and innervates Crane's whole sensibility. (*The Double Agent,* 134–135.)

"Cape Hatteras" is dedicated to Walt Whitman in a frenzy of admiration which contrasts strangely with Crane's tempered evaluation of the Camden writer in his essay, "Modern Poetry":

> The most typical and valid expression of the American *psychosis* seems to me still to be found in Whitman. His faults as a technician and his clumsy and indiscriminate enthusiasm are somewhat beside the point. He, better than any other, was able to coordinate those forces in America which seem most intractable, fusing them into a universal vision which takes on additional significance as time goes on.

It is only fair to mention here, however, that Crane wrote "Cape Hatteras" under frantic pressure, in response to demands of the Black Sun Press, a circumstance which goes far towards explaining its forced exultations. The Open Road of Whitman has become a skyway traveled by planes of every variety, planes that "course that span of consciousness thou'st named / The Open Road—" The *Panis Angelicus* reference used twice here (ridiculous as applied to Whitman) strengthens the interpretation of the Bridge as Christ the Way, a metaphor expressed thus by Saint Catherine: "Therefore He says of Himself that He is the Road, and this is the truth, and I have already shown thee that He is a Road in the form of the Bridge." (82) The Bridge also becomes "the rainbow's arch," a metaphor given fourfold presentation in the poem.

Critics are always blaming Hart Crane for faulty organization in his great paean to America, and are particularly severe in writing of the "Three Songs" that follow the Whitman section. It is true that he appears to abandon any direct reference to the Bridge as a central image. But the cross-references of these lyrics knit them firmly into the fabric of the whole. They are united, too, through their revelations of different facets of the woman-symbol. From the priestess of love, Hero, suggested by the headnote from Marloe, to Cathedral Mary, the guise Virginia's Indian princess has taken in the twentieth century, the verse portrays a Woman who is mother of us all ("Venus, homeless Eve"), yet at the same time daughter ("wraith of my unloved seed!") "Quaker Hill," the next section, adds the artists Isidora Duncan and Emily Dickinson to this composite woman. Then Crane returns to the metamorphoses of his chosen subject.

A new major transformation of the Bridge is its re-conversion to the subway in the following division, "The Tunnel." The protagonist journeys from Manhattan to Brooklyn via the East River tunnel, while within his brain is reproduced a miniature subway, labyrinth more terrifying than the Cretan one. Earlier, "Cape Hatteras" has alluded to this interior labyrinth, "Where each sees only his dim past reversed. . . ." As Crane brings out in his prefacing quotation from Blake, the subway is "the Western path / Right thro' the Gates of Wrath." The setting is clearly a terrestrial (or sub-terrestrial) Hell, despite Crane's earlier intention, written to Kahn, that he meant to present it as purgatory. The subway itself is a monstrous Daemon whose Hand of Fire (no longer the hand of a benign Providence as in "Ave Maria") gathers the kiss of man's agony. Yet at the end of "The Tunnel," after a shift of tone to exultation and hope, the Hand of Fire again becomes the Hand of God Himself.

In the conclusion, "Atlantis," Crane returns to the Bridge-as-harp of "Proem" and to the Bridge-as-telegraph of "The River":

> *Through the bound cable strands, the arching path*
> *Upward, veering with light, the flight of strings,—*

> *Taut miles of shuttling moonlight syncopate*
> *The whispered rush, telepathy of wires.*
> *Up the index of night, granite and steel—*
> *Transparent meshes—fleckless the gleaming staves—*
> *Sibylline voices flicker, waveringly stream*
> *As though a god were issue of the strings. . . .*

The arc of the Bridge becomes "synoptic of all tides below," assuming into its symbolic identity the oceans and rivers later to be commented on in an analysis of time and space as these appear in the poem. In a blinding glory of architectural vision (magnificent vanished cities such as Atlantis, Tyre, Troy) Crane increases the splendor of his verse until it reaches the summit where the Bridge becomes Love itself:

> *O Choir, translating time*
> *Into what multitudinous Verb the suns*
> *And synergy of waters ever fuse, recast*
> *In myriad syllables,—Psalm of Cathay!*
> *O Love, thy white, pervasive Paradigm. . . .*

The imagery of light is overwhelming in this section: *veering with light, moonlight, gleaming staves, bright carrier bars, crystal-flooded aisle, silver terraces, palladium helm of stars, glistening fins of light, planet-sequined heights, glimmer, silvery.* This emotional radiance is a lyric expression of Saint Catherine's more tranquil description:

> For those who cross by the Bridge, being still in the darkness of the body, find light, and, being mortal, find immortal life, tasting, through love, the light of Eternal Truth which promises refreshment to him who wearies himself for Me, who am grateful and just, and render to every man according as he deserves. (84)

Light, from the earliest Christian eras, even before the Incarnation, has been the leading symbol of God.

Crane then retreats from his organ peals of divine praise to the Bridge as microcosm, turning it into the blood-stream:

"iridescently upborne / Through the bright drench and fabric of our veins," and ends with an apostrophe to the Bridge under a new title, "whitest flower . . . Anemone." He blends this reference with that of the coral queen, the skeleton city Atlantis, beyond time, where the perplexing multiplicities of this life will be "One Song, one Bridge of Fire!" But this is all ahead, a Cathay of the future, a psalm unsung. The present can only whisper its antiphon: "Whispers antiphonal in azure swing."

One must not suppose that the Bridge is the only symbol to assume "deliberate disguises" in Crane's poem. Perhaps the most important of the subsidiary symbols so manipulated are those of the serpent and eagle as figures of time and space. Again, it is only after one has read the whole that he can return to the initial signs of symbolic patterning and see them as meaningful. Such a foreshadowing is the incident in "Van Winkle" relating a boyhood experience:

> Remember, remember
> The cinder pile at the end of the backyard
> Where we stoned the family of young
> Garter snakes under . . .
> Recall—recall the rapid tongues
> That flittered from under the ash heap day
> After day whenever your stick discovered
> Some sunning inch of unsuspecting fibre—
> It flashed back at your thrust, as clean as fire.

A few lines further on, Crane pictures his mother's smile, on her return from church, with almost the same verb as was used for the serpent: "It flickered through the snow screen. . . ." And surely in the closing lines of this section, it is not by accident that the protagonist asks Van Winkle, as they enter the subway, if he has his *Times.*

The next section, "The River," makes clear the figurative significance of the serpent. Speaking of Pocahontas as a type of America, the poet says:

But I knew her body there,
Time like a serpent down her shoulder, dark,
And space, an eaglet's wing, laid on her hair.

Down the vast shoulder of America runs the river. The vision of the Mississippi as serpent appears as if in technicolor in "The basalt surface drags a jungle grace / Ochreous and lynx-barred in lengthening might."

Not until "The Dance," however, are the metamorphic aspects of this symbol completely realized. Maquokeeta, an Indian chief whose name means Big River, is apotheosized after a snake dance that involves the whole firmament. Even then the river-imagery is not entirely relinquished: "And every tendon scurries toward the twangs / Of lightning deltaed down your saber hair." But here the impression is definitely a serpentine one:

Now snaps the flint in every tooth; red fangs
And splay tongues thinly busy the blue air. . . .

Dance, Maquokeeta! snake that lives before,
That casts his pelt, and lives beyond!

Crane in these lines is going back to the aboriginal superstition that snakes are immortal, a delusion described by Alexander Krappe in *The Science of Folk-lore:*

Men in widely separated countries observed that snakes throw off their skin, which led to the belief that snakes are immortal, the change of skin being really a process of rejuvenation. So the question arose: Why are snakes able to do this whilst man is not? And the answer given was that the snake tricked man out of his immortality, acquiring it for himself. (61)

This basic image appears in a different key in the two words that follow the command to Maquokeeta; Crane goes on, "Sprout, horn!" summoning up a vision of blossoming antlers, and the reader recalls how antlers, like the sloughed-away snake skins, are also cast off as a sign of rejuvenation.

The other participants in the ritual dance are spoken of as *flickering*, the adjective used with serpent-undertones in the Van Winkle section. The stag teeth encircle the Indian's neck like a snake.

The incantatory ecstasy with which Crane leads up to the metamorphosis is intended to reproduce a hallucinatory experience similar to that undergone by the Indians themselves in colonial or pre-colonial days: "Hallucination might be a potent factor in aiding belief in transformations. Savages have often declared that they have witnessed such a change of shape." (Hastings' *Encyclopaedia*, VIII, 594.) Several ruses of the medicine-man, who is asked in this poem to "Lie to us," helped in fostering such illusion:

> The custom of dressing in an animal skin at sacred dances, or before a bear-hunt, or of wearing animal-masks in war, would also aid the belief in metamorphosis. The frenzy of the dance would suggest self-transformation to the dancer, while the onlookers or the enemy would imagine that they saw human animals. There is no doubt also that medicine-men have often strengthened the belief by exploiting it — e.g., dressing as an animal, imitating its howls and its actions. (*Ibid.*)

The illusion in this case has a slight beginning — the protagonist's imaginative concept of the storm he encounters in his search for dogwood along the Hudson — but the poet works it up into a whirlpool of primitive madness making himself co-dancer and co-victim with Maquokeeta:

> —*I, too, was liege*
> *To rainbows currying each pulsant bone:*
> *Surpassed the circumstance, danced out the siege!*

The transition of Maquokeeta from death to immortality unites the Indian hero, burning at the stake, with time itself as "pure serpent," and finally with a tribal god:

> *O, like the lizard in the furious noon,*
> *That drops his legs and colors in the sun,*

> *—And laughs, pure serpent, Time itself, and moon*
> *Of his own fate, I saw thy change begun!*
>
> *And saw thee dive to kiss that destiny*
> *Like one white meteor, sacrosanct and blent*
> *At last with all that's consummate and free*
> *There, where the first and last gods keep thy tent.*

Here the snake as symbol is given the human attribute of laughter, a transference related to Lord Raglan's theory in his book on comparative mythology, *The Hero: A Study in Tradition, Myth, and Drama:* "And since men disguised as animals can speak, it may well come to be believed that magic animals can speak." (262–263) Stanley K. Coffman, Jr., in an excellent study of imagery in *The Bridge,* suggests that this change is a fusion of man and nature: "Crane has used 'The Dance,' which presents the ecstasy of union between the protagonist as Maquokeeta and Pocahontas, the earth of America. Man and nature here become one, and the preparation for union, the tribal dance, in itself suggests an abandon like that expressed in the eulogy of flight." (*PMLA,* LXVI, 67.)

Immediately after the apotheosis, the "swift red flesh" of the "winter king," grown to cosmic proportions, is opposed to the "bride immortal in the maize!" Crane proceeds to turn this Corn Queen (still, of course, Pocahontas and by extension America) into a torrent, then a singing tree, then the whole continent. The presentation of Pocahontas as tree is reminiscent of Crane's "Garden Abstract," in which the unnamed heroine becomes so emotionally identified with a brilliant autumn landscape as actually to feel if she were the apple tree beneath which she stands:

> *The apple on its bough is her desire,—*
> *Shining suspension, mimic of the sun.*
> *The bough has caught her breath up, and her voice,*
> *Dumbly articulate in the slant and rise*
> *Of branch on branch above her, blurs her eyes.*
> *She is prisoner of the tree and its green fingers.*

And so she comes to dream herself the tree,
The wind possessing her, weaving her young veins,
Holding her to the sky and its quick blue,
Drowning the fever of her hands in sunlight.
She has no memory, nor fear, nor hope
Beyond the grass and shadows at her feet.

Like Eve in Paradise, the girl gazes, fascinated, at the glittering fruit, a suggestion underlined by the title of the poem. The tree itself is established as human (with "green fingers"), desiring the sun even as the girl desires its image, the apple, turned gold by the strong light. The first stanza makes it evident that here is no realistic world, confusing auditory with visual imagery; the girl's voice, described in the paradoxical "Dumbly articulate" is credited with blurring her eyes which look upward into the lifting boughs. In reverie she metamorphoses into the tree, sweetheart of the wind that weaves and interweaves the purple veins branching through her young flesh; that holds her against the blue sky, also animate, *quick;* that drives waves of sunlight over her fevered, reaching hands.

"Garden Abstract" gives that rare sense of peace, of resting in a setting wherein all factors seem satisfactory, which, fleeting as it is, is one of our best compensations for the ills of this life. Past and future do not exist for the girl; experience is concentrated in the present (*abstract* signifies *epitome*): "She has no memory, nor fear, nor hope / Beyond the grass and shadows at her feet." In this she resembles the eternal Pocahontas, a symbol once human but transfigured into a "singing tree," a creature not of time but of timelessness.

As "The Dance" finishes, the protagonist and Maquokeeta merge into a brave who clasps this perfect woman, Pocahontas, to his heart:

We danced, O Brave, we danced beyond their farms,
In cobalt desert closures made our vows . . .
Now is the strong prayer folded in thy arms,
The serpent with the eagle in the boughs.

It was Crane's belief that the only way a twentieth-century American could fully possess his cultural heritage was to identify himself imaginatively with the Indian. Such a resolution of the struggle between races is what he aims at in this section of *The Bridge,* about which he wrote to Otto Kahn:

> Not only do I describe the conflict between the two races in this dance—I also become identified with the Indian and his world before it is over, which is the only method possible of ever really possessing the Indian and his world as a cultural factor. I think I really succeed in getting under the skin of this glorious and dying animal, and in terms of expression, in symbols, which he, himself, would comprehend.

Of special interest in this passage is Hart Crane's unequivocal use of the first person singular pronoun, thus limiting his poem in a way exactly opposite to the practice and theory of Eliot. To Crane, however, as to all egotists, such a personalization would but confer additional value.

In the conclusion of "The Dance," for the first time, though not the last, time and space are symbolically united as snake and eagle resting in the boughs of the "singing tree," Pocahontas. The eagle as representing space has been introduced twice before in *The Bridge:* the "eaglet's wing" against the Indian maiden's hair, the eagle feathers swooping down Maquokeeta's back.

After the saccharine interlude of "Indiana," Maquokeeta is apparently reincarnated as a sailor in South Street, or at least so one might assume from several references which link the modern man to the chieftain. First, "a nervous shark tooth swung on his chain," like the stag teeth around the Indian's neck. Then, at "His eyes pressed through green grass" the reader's mind goes back to the "winter king" of "The Dance," whose "Mythical brows we saw retiring—loth, / Disturbed and destined, into denser green." Moreover, in the sailor's first speech he mentions time (the tenor of the serpent vehicle) five times. The title for this section, "Cutty Sark," besides being both the name of a whiskey Crane used and of a nineteenth-century clipper, recalls Burns' poem about a witches' dance, a choice connecting it not only with the Pocahontas passages but also with the infernal theme running throughout the entire poem.

The eagle-as-space recurs again in "Cape Hatteras": "Now the eagle dominates our days, is jurist / Of the ambiguous cloud." In this section, by a natural association, it becomes the airplane itself, "eagle-bright," that governs in "the strident rule / Of wings imperious. . . ." Howard Moss considers Crane to have abandoned the eagle as a figure of space in "Cape Hatteras," about which he says: "Space is no longer an eagle nor time a serpent; the radio and the camera become the new symbols for time and space." ("Disorder as Myth," 37.) The airplane, however, conquers not only space but also time and hence its various models are spoken of as the "dragon's covey."

In "Southern Cross" Crane goes back to that image he had evoked in "The River" of a woman whose hair fell like a serpent down her back. This time, however, it is not Pocahontas, but the nameless Woman of the South – Eve, Magdalen, Mary, Venus. The connotations of the name *Eve* inevitably include Lucifer in the guise of a serpent. An excerpt from Saint Catherine of Siena connects Eve with the Bridge as symbol: " 'And, with that Truth, He confounded and destroyed the lie that the Devil told to Eve, with which he broke up the road to Heaven, and the Truth brought the pieces together again and cemented them with His Blood.' " (82) The Fall, moreover, is explicitly referred to by Crane in the "Cape Hatteras" section: "Adam and Adam's answer in the forest / Left Hesperus mirrored in the lucid pool," lines reflecting hope in a Redeemer to come.

The snake of "Southern Cross" is pictured as a rattler: "Water rattled that stinging coil, your / Rehearsed hair – docile, alas, from many arms." Here the image is not a tranquil one as in "The River," but rather allied to the Medusan tradition.

The second of "Three Songs," which presents a burlesque dance (parodying real desire and the religious ritual of the Maquokeeta section), has one serpentine allusion: "Her silly snake rings begin to mount, surmount / Each other – turquoise fakes on tinselled hands," right after which Crane refers to the dancer as *writhing*. In the last song of the section, set in the native state of Pocahontas ("Virginia"), the hair-as-serpent undergoes a metamorphosis, as Cathedral Mary in the high wheat tower is asked to let down her golden hair – Crane's analogue of the Rapunzel story. There is no mention of time or space or their symbols in "Quaker Hill" – a singularly unrelated interlude – but "The Tunnel" speaks of "what time slays," the words recalling (in view of the whole poem) the poisoned fangs of the serpent.

"Atlantis," companion-piece to the "Proem," finishes the cycle which has included four hundred years and a continent; this conclusion makes it clear repeatedly that the Bridge has conquered time: its girders give "the timeless laugh of mythic spears"; it translates time into the Verb (in Latin *Verbum* is a noun used for Christ); it is located "at time's end"; "Sight, sound and flesh Thou leadest from time's realm / As love strikes clear direction for the helm"; and finally, "Thine Everpresence, beyond time."

Only in the last stanza of "Atlantis" does the permanent significance of the Maquokeeta transformation find expression. Crane in September of 1927 had told Kahn his intentions concerning it; referring to the union of protagonist and chieftain with which "The Dance" ends, he writes Kahn:

> Pocahontas (the continent) is the common basis of our meeting; she survives the extinction of the Indian, who finally, after being assumed into the elements of nature (as he understood them) persists only as a kind of an "eye" in the sky, or as a star that hangs between day and night – "the twilight's dim perpetual throne."

This star has been introduced as early as "Harbor Dawn," where as the lover and his mistress watch the day rise, a star "As though to join us at some distant hill— / Turns in the waking west and goes to sleep." It shines again in "The Dance":

I

Drifted how many hours I never knew,
But, watching, saw that fleet young crescent die,—

And one star, swinging, take its place, alone,
Cupped in the larches of the mountain pass—
Until, immortally, it bled into the dawn.

"Cape Hatteras" and "The Tunnel" have seven references to stars, but none seems to be the personified one of the passages just quoted. However, Maquokeeta (if we accept Crane's explication) returns in "Atlantis" in the same context as was used in "The Dance." Addressing the Bridge itself, the poet cries:

So to thine Everpresence, beyond time,
Like spears ensanguined of one tolling star
That bleeds infinity - - - the orphic strings,
Sidereal phalanxes, leap and converge:
—One Song, one Bridge of Fire!

The idea of time is retained in that concentrated adjective *tolling,* but the stellar Maquokeeta is immortal, infinite—a source of divine blood to anoint the cables of the Bridge that move toward heaven like spears in the hands of troops of star-bright warriors.

The last stanza returns the time-symbol to its serpentine form and repeats with only one change (boughs to leaves) the closing line of "The Dance":

Is it Cathay,
Now pity steeps the grass and rainbows ring
The serpent with the eagle in the leaves . . . ?

The Bridge itself, multiplied into rainbows, binds together
time and space in this singing tree that is America, or Cathay, or Atlantis—the kingdom of perfection, promised to
men by the rainbow as "Deity's glittering Pledge," but also
by the star of Hope several times alluded to in the poem.
This kingdom of perfection, here called Cathay, is of course
much more than the fabulously treasured land toward which
Crane's forerunner, Columbus, sailed. In his letter to Otto
Kahn, dated March 18, 1926, the poet explains its significance thus: "The theme of "Cathay" (its riches, etc.) ulti-
mately is transmuted into a symbol of consciousness, knowledge, spiritual unity. A rather religious motivation, albeit
not Presbyterian." It would hardly strain this definition to
consider Cathay as Crane here employs it as a synonym for
salvation. The same letter goes on to state Crane's plan of
finishing his great poem with the Bridge itself used as a
symbol for Cathay; the conclusion was to be a "sweeping
dithyramb in which the Bridge becomes the symbol of consciousness spanning time and space."

It is not surprising, after all, to find metamorphosis in
both Crane and Eliot, since these writers proceed in their
major works according to the logic of the imagination—akin
to that of dreams and hence of metamorphosis. In neither of
them, however, is metamorphosis so much a habit of the
mind that it informs a large share of their briefer poems, as
is true, for instance, of Wallace Stevens and Randall Jarrell,
who appear to be unconscious specialists in the technique,
like butterflies, so thoroughly is it a part of the way in which
they view their worlds. On the contrary, the transformation
motif is almost entirely absent from the minor lyrics of
Crane and Eliot. They use metamorphosis rather as a means
of unifying their difficult insights into modern reality,
through constantly shifting *personae* and images. Both poets
demand much of their readers, among other things (certainly, in Crane's case) a relinquishing of common sense,
if by that is understood what we perceive in the coldest,

clearest light of a winter day. They give in return, however, accretions of meaning that may be described on their lowest level as variations on a theme, but at their peak, as protean disguises of the human spirit itself.

✩

CHAPTER FIVE

RANDALL JARRELL:

His Metamorphoses

PERHAPS the most likely candidate among younger writers for a permanent place in American letters, Randall Jarrell avails himself of the transformation device in order to secure emphases somewhat different from those of the poets already discussed. Between Ovid and Jarrell have come nineteenth-century scholarship and interest in folklore, the rise of dream psychology, particularly as popularized by the work of Jung and of Freud; technological warfare, with its tremendous effect upon the psyche; and important changes in philosophical thought concerning reality.

Like Ransom, Jarrell has been attracted to *Märchen* as a means of objectifying modern man's psychological position, since these continue to be part of a common heritage, at least during the brief space of childhood. Indeed, for an understanding of his preoccupation with folklore, some orientation in that field is almost a requisite. Grimm's tales abound in metamorphoses: prince to flounder ("The Fisherman and his Wife"), fox to prince ("The Fox's Brush"), elf to raven ("The Elfin Grove"), straw to gold ("Rumpelstiltskin"), fairy to owl to cat and maiden to bird ("Jorinda and Joringel"), frog to prince ("The Frog-Prince"), young man to ant ("Giant Golden-beard"), boy to lake to fawn and girl to rose to daisy ("Hänsel and Gretel"), people to asses ("Donkeywort"), princess to white snake ("Heads Off"), seven brothers to ravens ("The Seven Ravens"). In the minds of their youthful readers, these irrationalities occasion no surprise; they belong to the universe the stories create.

Such a world is in many ways a far more satisfactory one than that of real life. Though it does not exclude evil, it permits supernatural help to man in his eternal struggle against it, help which inevitably leads to happiness if the rules of the game are observed. It is hardly strange, indeed, that psychoanalysts early seized upon the *Märchen* as objectifications of the wish-fulfillment principle. In these, merit in the strict sense does not determine reward.

Another striking feature of this world of fairy tale is absence of death. Spenser, in his Mutability Cantos, gets around the fact of dissolution through metamorphosis. M. C. Bradbrook and M. G. Lloyd Thomas have noted this device in the sixteenth-century poet:

> Metamorphosis is for Spenser and the Spenserians the poetical answer to the problem of Time and the decay of beauty. Spenser was not being a fanciful poet when he wrote the Mutabilitie Cantoes, but he was drawing upon modes of thought and experience not readily accessible in the twentieth century. ("Marvell and the Concept of Metamorphosis," *The Criterion*, xviii, 243.)

Even so, fairy tales contrive even for their villains euphemisms for death: petrifaction and other types of transformation. There is eternal truth beneath this escape-mechanism in both Spenser and the younger art-form; to appreciate either, however, we must become as little children.

Irrationalities of folk stories, moreover, give evidence of a time when metamorphosis was considered a natural occurrence—a necessary corollary to the animism which characterized primitive thinking. This conviction that all created objects had life was strengthened by the ordinary facts of man's day-to-day existence:

> If every man, animal, and plant, every rock and stone, every star, river, and wind, is animated by a spirit, there

is nothing to prevent such spirits passing from one object into another, especially when to dream of an absent friend suggests the ability of one spirit to visit another, or when the resemblance of a child to his grandfather postulates a fresh incarnation of the spirit of the latter into the body of the former. Consequently, since our fairy-tales embody the original or modified forms of ancestral beliefs, we find transformations and transmigrations abundantly represented in them; indeed, no incident in fairy-tale is better known.*

One need not, in fact, go back to prehistoric times in order to justify the logic of metamorphosis; as the chapter on Ezra Pound has already indicated, Nature abounds in such apparently marvelous changes: egg to chicken, caterpillar to chrysalis to butterfly, larva to dragon-fly, acorn to oak. One ought not to wonder, then, if poets, ancient or modern, are drawn in their search for poetic techniques to this fascinating process, involved as it is in explanations of the origins of the human race and of the metaphysics of the universe.

The *Märchen* themselves undergo perpetual transformations, a phenomenon which has aroused the interest of innumerable scholars from the days of the Grimm brothers. Yet always there seems to be a primal entity, recognizable under racial and geographic disguises. Present-day theorists have focused attention upon these variations of a few central plots as basic to narration—heroes of folklore appear over and over in the literature of the twentieth century. Even more interesting is the connection between this protean folklore and our adventures in dreaming. Susanne Langer remarks, in *Philosophy in a New Key,* on how strongly mythological figures and the *dramatis personae* of legends resemble dream-images, and calls such tales the great dreams of mankind, like the dreams of individual men in that they are "so embarrassed with the riches of symbolic conception that every fantasy is apt to have a hundred versions." (159)

* *The Folklore of Fairy-Tale* by Macleod Yearsley. Watts and Co., London.

Randall Jarrell has clearly been influenced by Germanic popular stories, as he himself acknowledges in *Mid-Century American Poets,* an anthology edited by John Ciardi, where he lists them as furnishing subjects for some of his poems. (219–221) In his collection entitled *Losses,* "The Märchen" appears, with "Grimm's Tales" as a subtitle; again in "Deutsch durch Freud" he pictures himself as sitting on a sofa reading Grimm. In the first poem allusions occur to many of the best-known tales, such as "Hänsel and Gretel" in which Hänsel is startlingly identified with Christ; as a matter of fact the Hänsel story figures conspicuously in two other Jarrell poems, "The Night before the Night before Christmas" and "A Quilt-Pattern." Other tales referred to in "The Märchen" include "The Peasant and the Devil," "The Valiant Little Tailor," "The Mouse, the Bird, and the Sausage," "Little Snow-White," "The Louse and the Flea," "Godfather Death," and "The Blue Light." Metaphor rather than metamorphosis dominates the introduction of the poem, the forest pictured as a sea which stands for life as a whole, considered as the kingdom of Necessity. But in the final lines Jarrell sums up the metamorphic lesson we ought to have learned from the *Märchen:*

> *Had you not learned—have we not learned from tales*
> *Neither of beasts nor kingdoms nor their Lord,*
> *But of our own hearts, the realm of death—*
> *Neither to rule nor die? to change, to change!* *

Again, in "The Island," he mentions German folk literature—"the dawn's out-speaking smile / Curled through my lashes, felled the Märchen's wood"—in order to show how daylight destroys this modern Robinson Crusoe's dream in his desert solitude, a further linking of dream and folk tale. In still another poem, "The Carnegie Library, Juvenile Division," from an earlier book, *Little Friend, Little Friend,*

---

* From *Losses* by Randall Jarrell, copyright, 1948, by Harcourt, Brace and Company, Inc.

Jarrell describes the child's world of make-believe, "where the beasts loom in the green / Firred darkness of the marchen," alluding in the same stanza to Aladdin, of all transformers perhaps the most famous. This lyric concludes on a note less optimistic than the finish of "The Märchen"; the speaker says that he and his contemporaries have learned many things from these children's books in the Carnegie Library; they have learned how to understand their lives, but they have not found here the will to put this knowledge into action: "We learned from you to understand, but not to change."

Not only Grimm among folklorists but also Hans Christian Andersen is a source for Jarrell's poems. "A Soul" is based on that exquisite Danish folk tale, "The Little Mermaid," a story in which the youngest mermaid forsakes the certainty of three hundred years of perfect happiness on the chance that a mortal may love her well enough to obtain for her a human soul; this dream failing, she is changed to a bright, translucent spirit wandering through thin air. The dénouement in Jarrell's lyric varies from that in Andersen, where the prince never offers his love to his beautiful companion, risen from the sea through enchantment, but rather marries someone else. If this love had been freely given, the mermaid's desire for a soul would have been fulfilled, for in Andersen's tale the witch responsible for her transformation instructs the mermaid thus:

> "No," said the old lady, "only if a human being held you so dear that you were to him more than father or mother, and if with all his thoughts and affections he clung to you and made the priest lay his right hand in yours with the promise to be faithful to you here and for ever, then his soul would flow over into your body, and you too would have a share in the destiny of men. He would give you a soul and still keep his own."

There is a suggestion of what-might-have-been in Jarrell's treatment, though various aspects of the tale are amalgamated into a new whole. After setting a most picturesque scene, the poet reports the dialogue of mortal and undine:

"Thou art here once more."

In the castle someone is singing.
"Thou art warm and dry as the sun,"
You whisper, and laugh with joy.
"Yes, here is one,

Here is the other . . . Legs . . .
And they move so?"
I stroke the scales of your breast, and answer:
"Yes, as you know."

But you murmur, "How many years
Thou hast wandered there above!
Many times I had thought thee lost
Forever, my poor love.

"How many years, how many years
Thou hast wandered in air, thin air!
Many times I had thought thee lost,
My poor soul, forever." *

The use of the pronouns *thee, thou* charmingly differentiates the mermaid from her human lover who has brought his soul to share with her. That Andersen and his tales are of interest to Jarrell is suggested by his comment on Kafka's *The Castle* in a review of that novelist's *Amerika:* "It is a charming and often extremely funny story, a sort of Candide *a la* Hans Christian Andersen, with extraordinary over-tones." (*The Kenyon Review,* III, 116.) Indeed, the deep knowledge of Kafka revealed by this review is an aspect of Jarrell's literary preferences which ought not to go unmentioned in such a study as the present, in view of Kafka's short novel, *Metamorphosis,* as well as his experiments in a fiction which approximates the dream.

Imagery from the fairy tales helps too in an explanation

of the poetic process as Jarrell sees it. In discussing *What Are Years* by one of his favorite writers, Marianne Moore, he makes the following comparison, reminiscent of Grimm's "Rumpelstiltskin":

> She not only can, but has to, make poetry out of every-thing and anything: she is like Midas, or Mozart pur-posely choosing unpromising themes, or the princess whom a wizard forces to manufacture sheets out of net-tles—if the princess were herself the wizard. (*The Kenyon Review,* IV, 408.)

Any examination of his own use of colloquial material, both in his verse and as illustration in his critical prose, reveals that Jarrell too possesses this magic power of conversion.

The most ambitious and complete handling by Jarrell of the metamorphosis theme as it appears in popular tales is "Hohensalzburg: Fantastic Variations on a Theme of Romantic Character." All during the summer of 1948 Jarrell lived under the shadow of this famous castle, supposed to be haunted by ghosts who, like the wizards of folklore, have power to change whomever they meet into something else. This belief, frequent in the *Märchen,* is summarized in the section about the chandelier with china roses, the swan floating beside its shepherd, the star set in the antlers of an iron deer, all of which were once human—a passage reminiscent of Grimm's Fundevogel tale, in which a woodman rescues a little boy from a bird of prey, only to leave him in the charge of a cruel old cook who plans to boil him alive but is prevented from doing so by the magic of the woodman's daughter Lina. Lina changes Fundevogel to a rose bush and herself to the rose upon it; when this trick is discovered, she turns the boy to a church, with herself as the chandelier in it; finally, in order to escape the enraged cook, who has penetrated their disguises, Lina transforms Fundevogel to a fishpond and herself to the duck upon it. The last metamorphosis (the stars in the antlers of the iron deer) has no antecedent in the *Märchen,* but rather refers to an actual iron deer with gilt stars in its antlers (an emblem frequently seen in Austrian decoration) which stood at the entrance to the park of Leopoldschloss where Jarrell stayed during the time that he taught at the Salzburg Institute.

Jarrell sets the Hohensalzburg scene carefully: the little people singing from the river, moving from the wood, calling from the rushes; the ancient woman spinning; the offer of a wish to be granted; the Briar Rose story from Grimm. In sketching the background of the ghost whose visit forms the heart of the poem Jarrell touches delicately on one form of metamorphosis of great anthropological interest, petrifaction. He represents a stone maid who was once a young girl of exceptional loveliness, now sunk in the waters of the earth and whispering to the child who has run all evening on the beach. Transformation into stone is as catholic a belief as that into animal shape. Here the stone maid symbolizes the skeletal future of man. The child's wish for invisibility which immediately follows the allusion to petrifaction is of course a reference to another variety of metamorphosis and is a skillful foreshadowing of the final passage in the poem.

Waking at night in a house near the castle, the protagonist is first aware of a strange visitor by a touch, swallowlight, on his hand. Next, he hears her speak. At first he sees only the moonlight, but she assures him that she is behind the moonlight. From moonlight, the "ghost" changes, at least in the way he talks about her, into the enchanted princess of the Grimm story, lying asleep "in the last, least room"; this passage has echoes of "The Garden of Eden" in Andersen's fairy tales. The Briar Rose story, a favorite with Jarrell, appears in at least five of his other poems: "La Belle au Bois Dormant," "When You and I Were All," "Head of Wisdom," "For an Emigrant," and "The Sleeping Beauty: Variation of the Prince." The protagonist here is merely one drop of Sleeping Beauty's blood, one drop of the immense quantities that death has sucked. Then follows a most effective creation of suspense, fright; in a breathless dialogue, the princess describes to her victim how, some day, she will come to him and

> I shall take you and . . .
> *Tell me.*
> No, no, I shall never.
> *Tell me.*
> You must not know.
> *Tell me.*
> I—I shall kiss your throat.
> *My* throat?
> There, it is only a dream.
> I shall not so—I shall never so.

Then, even as he kisses her, she takes on the taste of the lime tree, flower and fruit, and finally—horrible fulfillment of her prophecy—turns to a vampire who fixes her teeth into his throat and sucks all his blood into herself. The victim's dreadful predicament is dramatized through a crucifixion image; the moonlight pierces his extended arms as if with nails. Just as Christ's Body and Blood are separated on Calvary, so are the speaker's here:

> *When I saw that it was my blood,*
> *I used my last strength and, slowly,*
> *Slowly, opened my eyes*
> *And pushed my arms out, that the moonlight*
> *pierced and held—* *

The terror recedes, and his guest is a girl again. The speaker, too, grows backwards until he reaches his own childhood. In a passage included in the *Poetry* first publication of the poem but omitted in *The Seven-League Crutches*, the whole meaning of the experience is now clarified: "The past is a child that sucks our blood / Back into the earth." Here the man grows tender toward his "Little Sister," for he sees that

* *Ibid.*

she is really his life; somberly, she adds to his voicing of this truth that she is also his death.

Economically, Jarrell has selected effective fragments from the vast body of vampire superstition current in Europe until very recently (and probably not yet entirely vanished), a superstition allied to the belief in werewolves. The idea that by stealing blood the dead can sap the strength of the living is an ancient one, and even now not obsolete, one manifestation of a primitive conviction that the dead savagely hate the living. (Theda Kenyon, *Witches Still Live,* 56.) The word *vampire,* of Slavonic derivation, refers to a blood-sucking ghost, capable of leaving its grave at night in order to suck the blood from the necks of the living. A vampire might be very beautiful, as here, or in the third story of the Grimm collection, where there is at least an intimation that the Virgin's taking of the Queen's children may be the result of blood-sucking. It differs from an ordinary ghost in that its appearance is purely physical, requiring a means of entrance (in the Hohensalzburg episode, the open window) and demanding physical labor to "lay" it; unlike a ghost it fears a second death. (Alexander Krappe, *The Science of Folk-lore,* 225.) The means of destroying such a creature must be drastic ones indeed. Its detection is often accomplished by craft, as in "Hohensalzburg"—generally by recourse to a sacramental or some other strategy of a religious nature, since: "As all other demoniacal monsters the Vampire fears and shrinks from holy things." (Montague Summers, *The Vampire His Kith and Kin,* 208.) According to tradition, the name of God, as is seen in the poem under consideration, is effective protection against sorcery (cf. the Sign of the Cross in *Hamlet*).

Another commonplace of vampire lore which Jarrell has utilized is the magic sleep which drugs the victim during the operation. One more resemblance to widely circulated details of the vampire legend ought to be noted: the transference to the victim of the dreadful passion for sucking blood.

In the twenty-three lines which conclude "Hohensalzburg," Jarrell uses *we* seven times, indicating that the destinies of the Being of the Earth and the protagonist are now forever linked. This union accords with what Theda Kenyon reports in *Witches Still Live:*

> The werewolf is the result of the supernatural fusing of human and animal elements; the vampire is a human ghost, which rises from its grave to suck the blood of living human beings, who are thereupon infected with the awful disease, and in their turn become vampires. (25)

This theme of the living mortal as having turned into a ghost after being bitten by a vampire has been anticipated in the protagonist's speech to the girl:

> *Before I was a ghost*
> *I was only a—*
>
> *A ghost wants blood . . .*

Towards the conclusion of the poem it is explicitly stated, by the spectral visitor herself:

> *Many a star*
> *Has fallen, many a ghost*
> *Has met, at the path to the wood, a ghost*
> *That has changed at last, in love, to a ghost.**

Towards the end of "Hohensalzburg," Jarrell speaks again of the "harsh clumsy things"—no longer ghosts but now villagers and farmers in tunics, quite possibly wearing *Lederhosen* and with badges stuck in their Tyrolese hats—who when they find him without his blood, will search for the "child" all night, for the ghost whose identity is much more complicated than that of the famous composite one in the *Quartets;* the poet has the pursuers invoke God in order to trap the girl, the "dweller of the Earth," as he now calls her. Although the conclusion of the vampire-hunt in Jarrell's poem sounds incredibly bizarre, like a macabre

* *Ibid.*

fantasy, actually it varies only slightly from the account of one of the measures frequently used, as related by Montague Summers, authority in demonology: "Sometimes the body was hacked to pieces before it was cast into the fire; very often the heart was torn from the breast and boiled to shreds in oil or vinegar." The similarity to the Procne-Philomel tale is striking.

It would seem as if this stratified interpretation of death were rich enough, without further deepening. Yet to understand Jarrell's lyric, one must take under examination a final metamorphosis. The moonlight > princess > vampire > girl ("Little Sister") > life > death becomes next a star. Foreshadowing of this last change has occurred in the line "Your cold flesh, faint with star-light"; the process is again suggested in the earlier version of the poem by "as all my blood / Flows from your starry limbs into your heart—"; it is at the end defined thus:

> *We shall change; we shall change; but at last, their stars,*
> *We shall rest in the branches of the antlers*
> *Of the iron deer.**

German ghosts, one remembers from earlier in the poem, have power to enchant. The fact of decay, a familiar theme of literature, was next described in the *Poetry* version as the turning of the "great limbs" of the protagonist and his murderess to lime trees, though Jarrell has seen fit to omit this mutation in revising for book publication.

The poem closes with a declaration that there is something more, something unexplained in the above account of reality, something best represented by the Christian concept of the Word. All these things which appear to be so different —"at the last, all these are one, / We also are forever one: / A dweller of the Earth, invisible." In these lines the two chief characters in the poem become one and achieve invisibility, the metamorphosis which is the consummation of the girl's childhood wish.

* *Ibid.*

In recent years, psychologists interested in anthropology, men such as Riklin, Abraham, Rank, Maeder, Silberer, have become increasingly convinced that these Germanic fictions, developing out of the wisdom of the common people, spring from universal mental experiences:

> Modern psychology treats the products of unconscious imagination as self-portraits of what is going on in the unconscious, or as statements of the unconscious psyche about itself. They fall into two categories. Firstly, fantasies (including dreams) of a personal character, which go back unquestionably to personal experiences, things forgotten or repressed, and can thus be completely explained by individual anamnesis. Secondly, fantasies (including dreams) of an impersonal character, which cannot be reduced to experiences as something individually acquired. These fantasy-pictures undoubtedly have their closest analogues in mythological types. We must therefore assume that they correspond to certain *collective* (and not personal) structural elements of the human psyche in general, and, like the morphological elements of the human body, are *inherited*. Although tradition and transmission by migration certainly play a part there are, as we have said, very many cases that cannot be accounted for in this way and drive us to the hypothesis of "autochthonous revival." These cases are so numerous that we cannot but assume the existence of a collective psychic substratum. I have called this the *collective* unconscious. (Carl G. Jung, *Essays on a Science of Mythology,* Bollingen Series, XXII.)

One should keep in mind always that such an explanation is assumption, not fact; the words *assume* and *hypothesis* are especially significant. Yet Jung and his theories have influenced many modern poets. And if they believe, as Jung believes, that a layer of the collective unconscious forms the foundation of the personal unconscious in every mind and is approximately the same in all Western men, then for them the myths and later the fairy tales (both of which are after all only the recorded thought of the race) codify the basic images of the collective unconscious. Myths thus represent the nature of the psyche, not an allegorization of nature; dreams take over the same archetypal symbols to voice the deepest needs of the ego.

A poetic way of voicing these needs—and here is the truly exciting feature of dream-imagery as used by Jarrell—is through a new language, one composed not of words but of pictures. These pictures, however, are not purely personal; they recur from dreamer to dreamer. What words figure in them have lost their character as conventional symbols and have become, like the name of Rumpelstiltskin, inseparable from their referents ("Deutsch durch Freud"). Jarrell has noted this traumatic approach in W. H. Auden, a writer who exerted tremendous influence upon the younger poet's first book of verse:

> They [the early poems] gain an uncommon plausibility from the terse understated matter-of-factness of their treatment, the insistence (such as that found in the speech of children, in Mother Goose, in folk or savage verse, in dreams) upon the thingness of the words themselves. (*Partisan Review*, XII, 438.)

In "Hohensalzburg" the two types of images, dream and folklore, are combined. As a matter of fact, no image, not even that of blood or of ghosts, is more integral to Jarrell's work than that of the dream, which appears in more than half of the lyrics published by him thus far in book form.

In the folk tale, the worlds of fantasy and of dream unite, a fact now generally recognized. Lightning metamorphoses in dreams are part of the experience of the ordinary person as well as the stuff that fairy-lore is made of. According to modern psychology, the heroes, heroines, and villains of both *Märchen* and myth serve to concretize the life of the psyche which goes on uninhibited during the time of dreaming. Outside space, time, and causality, the dream-elements give a picture of the individual unconscious, which Jung and others view as a microcosm of the collective unconscious. A more traditional interpretation, rooted in the fact that human nature remains always and everywhere the same, would account for the latter purely as the expected resemblance between one mind and another.

Borrowing from Saint Augustine, Jung refers to the recurrent symbols of dreams as archetypes, somewhat like Plato's ideas, except that they embody the imperfect as well as the perfect:

> Today we can hazard the formula that the *archetypes appear in myths and fairy-tales just as they do in dreams and in the products of psychotic fantasy.* The medium in which they are embedded is, in the former case, an ordered and for the most part immediately understandable context, but in the latter case a generally unintelligible, irrational, not to say delirious sequence of images which nonetheless does not lack a certain hidden coherence. (*Essays on a Science of Mythology,* 100.)

On the preceding page in this essay, Jung points out how standard motifs, the same all over the world and from age to age, run through the structure of dreams:

> In the dream, as in the products of psychoses, there are numberless combinations to which one can find parallels only in mythological associations of ideas (or perhaps in certain poetic creations which are often characterized by a borrowing, not always conscious, from myths).

Jarrell mentions Jung's archetypal images in his discussion of Auden's poetry quoted above, a circumstance which suggests that he is conscious of their pertinence to the poet's problems.

Appositely, Randall Jarrell in his poetry almost always identifies death with dreaming. The most extensive expression of this identification, "The Night before the Night before Christmas," is a poignant case-history of adolescent heartbreak. It begins with the simplicity and generality of a fairy tale, one set in an apartment house significantly called the Arden Apartment. Throughout its twelve pages, the principal character is referred to only as "the girl"; her mother has been dead for two years and she lives with her father, her invalid brother, and an aunt. Jarrell supplies obliquely the dreary intercourse of her daily life: her transferred love for the new high school teacher; the chapped hands with bitten nails, pressed together in a middy blouse; the unselfish efforts to amuse her brother with dominoes or books; the Christmas presents which she wraps, each one a gauge of her regard for the recipient; the bedroom with its babyish decorations; the Marxian propaganda she reads, straining to illuminate its abstractions by the various light of her imagination; the clanking radiator, like the voice of Martha in the dark; her pet squirrel, a "clawed / Dead rat with an Angora tail," symbol for her of all the injustice in the world, injustice which she cannot reconcile with the thought of God.

The girl's first dream, upon falling asleep the night before the night before Christmas, is a grotesque scene in which a big squirrel teaches lines from *Romeo and Juliet* to six others with radiator-steam-valve voices, an application of the Communist panacea of education which will at last destroy all evil. Then: "She whispers: 'I'm awake. / No, I'm not dreaming, I'm awake.'" The girl thinks of the vertiginous expanse of the universe; from her window she stares at the evergreens, stars, trees, the bushes covered with snow that stand like Hänsel and Gretel, sparkling as brightly as Lot's wife after her metamorphosis to salt. She sees herself and her brother look at the squirrel dead in the snow:

> She and her brother float up from the snow —
> The last crumbs of their tears
> Are caught by the birds that are falling
> To strew their leaves on the snow
> That is covering, that has covered

The play-mound under the snow . . .
The leaves are the snow, the birds are the snow,
The boy and girl in the leaves of their grave
Are the wings of the bird of the snow.
But her wings are mixed in her head with the Way
That streams from their shoulders, stars like snow:
They spread, at last, their great starry wings
And her brother sings, "I am dying."

The passage just following conveys in a brief dialogue, partly through manipulation of tenses, the children's bewilderment at this mixture of fantasy and truth. Then the dream goes on:

They are flying.

They look down over the earth.
There is not one crumb.
The rays of the stars of their wings
Strike the boughs of the wood, and the shadows
*Are caught up into the night. . . .**

The leaves and the birds—a skillful use of motor imagery —have become the snow; the boy and girl, buried in their graves of snow, are radiantly transformed to the wings of the bird of the snow. Such a mutation is grounded in primitive belief: "To the natural mind the soul is a bird, and at certain rare moments, when the issue of life or death hangs in the balance, or when the rational habit of the mind is humbled by the presence of death, the vision of a bird at the window touches a chord in the heart which will not be silenced by all our scientific scepticism." (H. G. Baynes, *Mythology of the Soul*, 707.) In *The Tree of Mythology, Its Growth and Fruitage,* the folklorist Charles De B. Mills points out another basis for Jarrell's image: "The comparison of snow-flakes to feathers is an ancient one, and is found in Greek history. Herodotos says the Scythians declared the regions north of them inaccessible, because they were filled with feathers." (123)

* *Ibid.*

The snow-birds increase in magnificence in the poem till their great starry wings spread like the Milky Way itself. As in "Hohensalzburg" and in the fifteenth book of Ovid, where Caesar is made a constellation, they have been changed after death into stars. Looking back to earth, both of the children whisper of the time when they were alive. The motto hanging in their father's office – *To Travel Hopefully Is a Better Thing Than to Arrive* – becomes *To End Hopefully Is a Better Thing – A Far, Far Better Thing*, the girl's memory of Sidney Carton from her English book. The motherless girl's crying, with which the poem ends, belongs not to the world of death and dream which she has created but to the problems that Christmas Eve will bring.

This poem, then, represents a retreat from reality into the glittering world of dreams; it is focused upon the normal way of escape from unpleasantness, but at the same time it serves as a parallel of the abnormal method of fleeing from the difficult. Freud has shown this symbolic connection in his *New Introductory Lectures on Psycho-Analysis:*

> The state of sleep represents a turning away from the real external world, and thus provides a necessary condition for the development of a psychosis. The most penetrating study of serious cases of psychosis will reveal no characteristic which is more typical of these pathological conditions. In psychosis, however, the turning away from reality is brought about in two ways; either because the repressed unconscious is too strong, so that it overwhelms the conscious which tries to cling on to reality, or because reality has become so unbearably painful that the threatened ego, in a despairing gesture of opposition, throws itself into the arms of the unconscious impulses. (27) *

What for the girl is only a brief respite, a tranquil and shimmering interlude, is for the psychotic a permanent if diseased release from suffering.

* Reprinted by permission of W. W. Norton and Company.

"The Black Swan" is another child's attempt to understand death by way of the hallucinatory imagination; its title is the name usually given to a *pas de deux* extracted from Tchaikowsky's ballet, *Swan Lake*. Instead of facing the fact that her sister is dead, the little girl in the poem makes up a fairy tale about her: the swans have turned her into a swan. At sunset, when chores are done, the girl goes in search of her transformed sister, down to the lake across which even the sun has become a swan with a red beak huge enough to contain the night:

> When the swans turned my sister into a swan
>   I would go to the lake, at night, from milking:
> The sun would look out through the reeds like a swan,
>   A swan's red beak; and the beak would open
> And inside there was darkness, the stars and the moon.

Jarrell understands the why and how of children's make-believe; he uses it to its fullest poetic possibilities. The reeds by the edge of the lake are not reeds, but clusters of little voices whispering an incantation intended to metamorphose the living girl into the same form as her dead sister:

> Out on the lake a girl would laugh.
>   "Sister, here is your porridge, sister,"
> I would call; and the reeds would whisper,
>   "Go to sleep, go to sleep, little swan."
> My legs were all hard and webbed, and the silky
>
> Hairs of my wings sank away like stars
>   In the ripples that ran in and out of the reeds:
> I heard through the lap and hiss of water
>   Someone's "Sister . . . sister," far away on the shore,
> And then as I opened my beak to answer
>
> I heard my harsh laugh go out to the shore
>   And saw—saw at last, swimming up from the green
> Low mounds of the lake, the white stone swans:
>   The white, named swans . . .

The pathetic child leaves her own body waiting with the bowl of porridge on the shore and finds herself a swan, at the center of the lake, where the laugh had come from: through the intensity of her longing and loneliness she becomes her sister. Across the lapping water–the very waves hissing like swans–comes her own voice, faintly calling; and now, from the other side of death, she learns the impossibility of any reconciliation. It is as if the white tombstones of the cemetery where they had laid her sister come swimming up from the lake's bottom–the low green mounds, the named white stones.

But all this hasn't happened, no, not really happened; in her dreams, the little girl has created even the trip to the lake; actually, she is home in bed, though the moon, stars, frogs, waves, swans are all about her in the darkness as her dead sister soothes her to rest (or calls her to death):

> "It is all a dream,"
> I whispered, and reached from the down of the pallet
>
> To the lap and hiss of the floor.
>   And "Sleep, little sister," the swans all sang
> From the moon and stars and frogs of the floor.
>   But the swan my sister called, "Sleep at last, little sister,"
> And stroked all night, with a black wing, my wings.*

There is a great tenderness here, and a willingness to present emotion without apology, unique among poets writing today. Sentimentality is avoided by the union of dream and fantasy, both of which refuse to be bound by the precepts of waking, practical life.

The concept informing "The Black Swan"–a girl's transformation into a swan–is part of an old and very extensive body of folklore centering around swan-maidens, folkstories which perhaps originated as dramatization of white fleecy clouds swimming through a sea of sky, even as in the beginning the werewolf may have been the night-wind.

* From *The Seven-League Crutches.*

(John Fiske, *Myths and Myth-Makers: Old Tales and Superstitions,* 102.) Traditionally these swan-maidens have been thought of as summoning mortals to their home in a far-away land, thus figuratively as beautiful omens of death.

The ballet upon which this lyric is based, Tschaikowsky's *Swan Lake,* is thoroughly in the metamorphic tradition. In the second act, Prince Siegfried and his followers come upon a crowned swan floating toward the shore of a moonlit lake. She is no ordinary bird, but a victim of sorcery:

> This is the hour when Odette—a Queen who has incurred the enmity of the enchanter Von Rothbart—may for a brief time resume the human form of which she has been deprived by her enemy's magic art. . . . With the arrival of dawn Odette and her ladies must change their human forms and again become swans. (314) *

Through the offer of the Prince to share Odette's doom, she and her companions are freed of the spell. To parallel this, Jarrell has the live sister share the enchanted fate of her swan-sister, though the poet permits no happy dénouement at sunrise to the girl of "The Black Swan."

Another metamorphic ballet used by Jarrell in his series of poems giving dream experiences is *Giselle,* by Jean Coralli. The plot is a graceful and melancholy fantasy: Giselle, gone mad, kills herself when she discovers deception in her fiancé, Loys, and after death is transformed into one of the Wilis, maidens enchanted by a fairy queen, Myrtha, who by night dance through the moonlit shadows of the wood. Act two opens thus:

> The scene is a clearing in the forest by the side of a lake. Giselle's lonely grave, surmounted by a cross, is on a rise to the left of the stage.
>
> It is night, and a shadowy form, veiled and mysterious, is seen. The moon rises and the veil disappears, dis-

---

* *The Borzoi Book of Ballets* by Grace Robert: copyright 1946 by Alfred A. Knopf, Inc. By permission of Alfred A. Knopf, Inc.

closing Myrtha, Queen of the Wilis. The Wilis are the
spirits of young girls who in life loved dancing too much.
They are condemned to haunt the forest, dancing nightly
as a punishment for their frivolity. Myrtha summons her
ghostly band to the tomb of Giselle, who is to become
one of them. At the Queen's command, Giselle rises
from her tomb. The veil that covers her dissolves. Slowly
she descends from the mound to stand before the Queen.
At a touch from the Queen's flowery scepter, she is possessed with ghostly animation.*

One commentator on the ballet, Cyril W. Beaumont, describes Myrtha as a pale vapour gradually become a young
girl, and also adds a colorful detail to the heroine's metamorphosis: "A glittering star is placed on Giselle's forehead
and from her shoulders spring a pair of wings." (*Complete
Book of Ballets,* 131–132.)

Again, as in *Swan Lake,* the spell is broken with the rising of the sun, signifying the end of the sway of diabolical
powers. Thus runs the story of *Giselle.*

Randall Jarrell might have written a dramatic monologue
on this theme, as he did, for instance, in "The Island,"
wherein Robinson Crusoe speaks. He prefers to present
Giselle, however, at one more remove from the real world,
and therefore calls his poem "The Girl Dreams that She Is
Giselle":

> *Beards of the grain, gray-green: the lances*
> *Shiver. I stare up into the dew.*
> *From her white court—enchantress—*
> *The black queen, shimmering with dew,*
>
> *Floats to me. In the enchainment*
> *Of a traveling and a working wing*
> *She comes shying, sidelong, settling*
> *On the bare grave by the grain.*
>
> *And I sleep, curled in my cold cave . . .*
> *Her wands quiver, as a nostril quivers:*

* *Ibid.,* p. 172.

> *The gray veilings of the grave*
> *Crumple, my limbs lock, reverse,*
>
> *And work me, jointed, to the glance*
> *That licks out to me in white fire*
> *And, piercing, whirrs* Remember
> *Till my limbs catch:*
>   *life, life! I dance.**

An examination of the verbs and verbals in this reveals in how remarkable a manner Jarrell has caught the exquisite nuances of faeryland, the glimmering motion and uncertain light of the realm of magic. In the end, Giselle is figuratively ignited by the white fire that flickers out to her from the Queen. As she dances, one might visualize a flame, leaping high and wildly under the supernal excitement.

All ballet might, as a matter of fact, be given a metamorphic interpretation, since the dance postures therein employed are used to create so strong an illusion that the spectator almost believes a *ballerina* has turned into a swan, a snake, a fountain, or whatever object the score demands. Indeed, it has been shown that even the psyche, partly through dream, partly through visual imagination, uses the dance to carry on its interior life. Jung has given us a graphic example of this:

> A magician is demonstrating his tricks to an Indian prince. He produces a beautiful young girl from under a cloth. She is a dancer, who has the power to change her shape or at least hold her audience spellbound by faultless illusion. During the dance she dissolves with the music into a swarm of bees. Then she changes into a leopard, then into a jet of water, then into a sea-polyp that has twined itself about a young pearl-fisher. Between times, she takes human form again at the dramatic moment. She appears as a she-ass bearing two baskets of wonderful fruits. Then she becomes a many-coloured peacock. The prince is beside himself with delight and

* Reprinted by permission of Harcourt, Brace and Company, Inc.

calls her to him. But she dances on, now naked, and even tears the skin from her body, and finally falls down —a naked skeleton. This is buried, but at night a lily grows out of the grave, and from its cup there rises the *white lady,* who floats slowly up to the sky.

This piece describes the successive transformations of the illusionist (artistry in illusion being a specifically feminine capacity) until she becomes a transfigured personality. The fantasy was not invented as an allegory; it was part dream, part spontaneous imagery. (*Essays on a Science of Mythology,* 238, Bollingen Series, XXII.)

The girl who dreams she is Giselle, then, is perhaps using her subconscious imagination to transform the undesirable in her waking life.

"A Rhapsody on Irish Themes" begins with a half-dream, half-waking experience in which the poet's great-grandmother appears at the porthole of his ship waiting to set sail from Ireland. In mocking rhetoric he shows her, even as she holds out to him a handkerchief made by the Little People, undergoing metamorphosis:

> *Then you turned into the greatest of gulls*
> *That brood on the seasaw green*
> *Swells of the nest of the harbor of Cobh.**

Later in the poem he playfully refers to the old woman as "old Circe," enchantress who will detain him on her island of Faith, lulled by the musical speech of her countrymen. "Great-grandmother, I've dreamed of you till I'm hoarse," he exclaims, but in the end the cold practical world conquers the dream.

In "The Venetian Blind" Jarrell again works the difficulty of separating dream from reality and again discovers that the true nightmare is the wide-awake one. Here also he utilizes the technique of metamorphosis. The person waking has the illusion that he is in Eden on the first day of the world. Falling in the shape of bars of a musical staff, the

* From *Seven-League Crutches.*

sunlight becomes his face. Then: "His dream / Has changed into this day, this dream. . . ." He cannot remember where he is—a common enough experience—and imagines that his limbs are curled about space:

> *He thinks that he is younger*
> *Than anything has ever been.*
> *He thinks that he is the world.*
> *But his soul and his body*
> *Call, as the bird calls, their one word—*
> *And he remembers.*
>
> *He is lost in himself forever.**

The implications of this attitude, as they affect the question of personal identity, are echoed in many of Jarrell's lyrics.

Another type of effect in dream-analysis is obtained in the final lines of "King's Hunt," wherein a child dreams a complete fairy story, one in which a tyrannical king is poisoned by a deaf-mute whose tongue has been cut out by a royal order; after the crime, the mute and a dwarf who has led the king to the trap prepared for him gaze through the window at the corpse until their two faces merge into the face of a child (the one dreaming the story) who knows that something is dreadfully wrong without understanding precisely what and is all the more fascinated on that account: "Their blurred faces, caught up in one wish, / Are blurred into one face: a child's set face." The murder by the mute and the dwarf in the dream represents the child's passionate wish to destroy some part of the grown-up world that oppresses him. About this type of dream Freud says:

> Very often pictures and situations appear in the manifest content of the dream which remind one of well-known themes from fairy stories, legends and myths. The interpretation of such dreams throws light on the original motives which created these themes, though naturally we must not forget the change of meaning which this ma-

* *Ibid.*

terial has undergone during the passage of time. (*New Introductory Lectures on Psycho-Analysis,* 39.)

"A Quilt-Pattern" is another dream of an unhappy child, an invalid whose subconsciousness tries to compensate for the agonies of his conscious life. The title is drawn from the actual quilt on his sick-bed; on it is blocked out the Tree of Life, gray as the light fades. On seven-league crutches the boy travels into "the oldest tale of all," sleep.

In his dream he sees his mother dead and transformed into a house; her "scaling face" is "square in the steam of a yard." He hates her demanding, possessive love that pursues him every moment of his waking life; only by such a stratagem can he evade it. At first the boy (divided into two selves, one good and one bad) is confined in the cages near the house, the cages for

> *All small furry things*
> *That are hurt, but that never cry at all —*
> *That are skinned, but that never die at all.*

Through the wire of the cages "Good me, bad me" gather black-berries, their only food. It is very likely that one may be the boy himself, the other an imaginary companion such as small children commonly construct. The house itself is deep in the forest, "here in the wood of the dream."

At this point, Jarrell makes it unmistakable that he is using, in a Freudian way, the Hänsel and Gretel tale (probably read by the child during the tedious day) as a basis for the boy's dream:

> *Here a thousand stones*
> *Of the trail home shine from their strings*
> *Like just-brushed, just-lost teeth.*
> *All the birds of the forest*
> *Sit brooding, stuffed with crumbs.*

He combines the two trips of the children into the forest, adding modern touches—the extracted teeth on strings, agleam from recent polishing. The lies little Hänsel told to

his mother to account for his backward glances are united
in "His white cat eats up his white pigeon." It seems as if no
deceit is strong enough to conquer the powers of evil working against him.

The next stanza divides the child again into separate
selves, existing in the boy's mind, though actually they are
only one, who "Sits wrapped in his coat of rabbit-skin—"
But this coat is more than coat:

> *—good me*
> *Sits twitching the rabbit's fur of his ears*
> *And says to himself, "My mother is basting*
> *Bad me in the bath-tub—"*

Back in the Hänsel and Gretel framework, the boy looks
into the house, which has a mouth, not a door, and hopes he
will find what he needs, but "there is nothing." Psycho-
analysis commonly interprets the house in dreams as a
symbol for woman. In hunger, he breaks off one of his
mother's fingers, and when the house asks who is eating her
he replies with her remembered pet name for him, "It is a
mouse." Just as his mother is accustomed to singing around
the house (the first reference to her is to "the humming stare
/ Of the woman—the good mother—") the house of bread
"Calls to him in its slow singing voice" to ask if he is fat,
demanding that he hold out his finger; instead, he extends
the bone of her own finger, which moves. She tells him that
he hasn't eaten enough to *know,* and one thinks of the Tree
of Life in Eden, which brought knowledge of death into the
world. Even in dreams, the little boy will not face the fact
that the house is the mother whom he has desired dead.

The dream itself, personified and blending into the house,
whispers:

> *"You are full now, mouse—*
> *Look, I have warmed the oven, kneaded the dough:*
> *Creep in—ah, ah, it is warm!—*
> *Quick, we can slip the bread in now,"* *

* *Ibid.*

The house, up to this point apparently representing the dead mother, is now clearly and horribly identified with the witch of Grimm's fairy story, scolding at the boy who complains that he doesn't know how to slip the bread into the oven and bending over to show him. (It is hardly coincidental that when Hänsel and Gretel return after the witch has been killed they find their mother dead.)

As the witch screams in the hot oven, Hänsel and Gretel (the two sides of the child) look at each other and smile. The mouse (the small boy) has escaped roasting; certainly what burns in the oven is nothing dear to him. But his guilt, even in sleep, prompts him to exclaim: "It was the Other," that part of him rebellious to parental approval and to his own better judgment. In the end of the poem, he cannot bear to give up his dream-world and face the mother who tiptoes to the invalid's door and whom he intensely and silently wishes away. Even his nightmare is preferable to waking and meeting her synthetic and paralyzing affection.

Death itself, the mystery at the heart of "King's Hunt" and "A Quilt-Pattern," has lost its reality in these days of abstraction, where the targets of the bombadiers are only names learned in geography classes. In "A Conversation with the Devil" Lucifer himself is appalled by modern man's attitude toward death:

> *I disliked each life, I assure you, for its own sake.*
> *—But to deal indifferently in life and death;*
> *To sell, wholesale, piecemeal, annihilation;*
> *To—I will not go into particulars—*
> *This beats me.**

Indeed, Mephistopheles is a changed devil, an anachronism whose occupation is gone. Contemporary warfare has removed from man his freedom of choice, leaving no room for a devil's operations. And death, which used to have dignity, ritual, cannot be believed in; we only dream that we die.

* *Ibid.*

Thus the flier in "Losses," horrified at the contrast between actuality and the stereotyped war reports, blends dreaming and dying: "It was not dying—no, not ever dying; / But the night I died I dreamed that I was dead."

The life-as-a-dream motif so unusual in Jarrell's poetry finds one of its best articulations in "The Dream of Waking," the first two stanzas of which represent what goes through the mind of a wounded soldier in a hospital as he dreams he is a child waking; he is back home again—the water around the drifting boat from which he was picked up changes into light, then into laughter, then into a blend of himself, his room, and the tree outside the window. In that earlier day, his sun is gold mixed with air, is his own life. Then he really wakes, remembering back to the boat, to the origin of his present plaster cast brown with dried blood, the boat where his friend died in spite of his own frenzied begging. The reality he wakes to now is gruesomely different from the childish reality he woke to in the dream and once used to wake to in life. The interpenetration of self with environment continues throughout the last stanza:

> . . . *the boat is bodies*
> *And the body broken in his broken arms*
> *And the voice, the old voice:* Please don't die—
>
> *His life and their death: oh morning, morning.**

The situation described so movingly here is very much like that in "A Field Hospital," where the patient thinks that he is dreaming after he has awakened—the "old mistake."

In "Absent with Official Leave," the soldier escapes to life through sleep, escapes to civilian lands where death is not organized; where roads hop aimlessly instead of leading to objectives; where hunters sprawl for birds, not men; where fires are lit not to burn down cities but to dry "His charmed limbs, all endearing from the tub." Near the end of the poem Jarrell's devotion to Grimm finds voice in "He

* From *Little Friend, Little Friend* by Randall Jarrell. Copyright 1945 by The Dial Press, Inc.

moans like a bear in his enchanted sleep," with its overtones of the Snow-White and Rose-Red story. The soldier wakes from the spell not to a princess but only to the night, its silence broken by the sighs and breathing of his co-sufferers.

The dreams in these poems speak to their protagonists through images, not through the verbal counters debilitated by waking usage. What they communicate extends as far as the human race extends, and even beyond, since man is the world in miniature; they correspond to prophecy and religious vision; as Joseph Campbell says, they express truths which are eternal and immutable:

> Therefore, in sum: The "monstrous, irrational and unnatural" motifs of folk tale and myth are derived from the reservoirs of dream and vision. On the dream level such images represent the total state of the individual dreaming psyche. But clarified of personal distortions and propounded—by poets, prophets, visionaries—, they become symbolic of the spiritual norm for Man the Microcosm. They are thus phrases from an image-language, expressive of metaphysical, psychological, and sociological truth.*

In the satirical "Blind Sheep," which is a re-telling of Aesop, Jarrell has exploited still another angle of the dream-folktale relationship by his use of the beast-fable. Here the Owl is represented as about to operate on the blind Sheep; however, the latter, after finding out that the world is the same as it was before he became blind, refuses to have his sight restored, since after all he is a sheep, not an ass. About this *genre*, a scholar of Platonic myth, J. A. Stewart, remarks:

> The Beast-Fable is a dream in which men and beasts talk and act together; in which the transformation of a man into a beast, or a beast into a man, is taken as a matter of course; in which beasts, in short, are at once men and beasts. (*The Myths of Plato,* 303.)

* *Grimm's Fairy Tales,* Pantheon Press.

The cynical sheep is of course out of the contemporary world of men, a modern skeptic who can speak out only in the metaphors of dream.

Besides these two major uses of the metamorphosis concept (*Märchen* and dreams), Jarrell utilizes the changes wrought by friendship and connubial love, both traditionally accredited with effecting the union or exchange of souls. This idea is carried out in "Burning the Letters." Here Jarrell puts into the mouth of a war widow an account of the mutation undergone after the death of her aviator-husband:

> *The poor labored answers, still unanswering;*
> *The faded questions—questioning so much,*
> *I thought then—questioning so little;*
> *Grew younger, younger, as my eyes grew old,*
> *As that dreamed-out and wept-for wife,*
> *Your last unchanging country, changed*
> *Out of your own rejecting life—a part*
> *Of accusation and of loss, a child's eternally—*
> *Into my troubled separate being.*

The pilot's life was that of a child—resentful of what reality was doing, forced to give up that wonderful never-never land which his wife was to him as he dreamed about her waking in the hostile airways over the Pacific or sleeping in the doubtful shelter of an island camp; their beings were somehow one in those days, but now she is herself again, *troubled* and *separate*. Out of his death will rise her life, if she wants it:

> *The mourning slaves*
> *In their dark secrecy, come burying*
> *The slave bound in another's flesh, the slave*
> *Freed once, forever, by another's flesh* *

She has lost all faith in religious dogma—the headnote tells us that she was once a Christian, a Protestant—especially in that supreme Metamorphosis, the Holy Eucharist, which

* From *Losses* by Randall Jarrell, copyright, 1948, by Harcourt, Brace and Company, Inc.

now seems to her a nightmare from which she awakens. Her husband is described in lines suggestive of Hart Crane as being beyond change; burning his letters symbolizes the end of their togetherness, the beginning of her own life and the world of her life.

Some Jarrell lyrics use transformation as a primary device; in others it is incidental. "The Emancipators" is addressed to such scientists as Galileo, asking them whether they guessed to what fearful uses their discoveries would be put. What for them was a formula has resulted first in the Industrial Revolution, then in the wars of the present century, since today: "The equations metamorphose into use." The prose-poem, "1914," reminiscent of Auden as is much of Jarrell's earlier work, represents the first World War thus:

> *Now the forts of Antwerp, broken into blocks,*
> *slide into a moat as bergs break off into the sea;*
> *the blocks, metamorphosed into the dead, sprawl*
> *naked as grave-mounds in the stalky fields.**

It reiterates the life-is-a-dream motif discussed above by picturing minutely a photograph of a dead soldier and then pointing up the significance in these words: "Underneath his picture there is written, about his life, his death, or his war: *Es war ein Traum.*" Jarrell goes on to say, fusing the opposites life and death with their meeting place, war: "It is the dream from which no one wakes." This conclusion, however, is not as negativistic as one might think without reading the body of Jarrell's work. Delmore Schwartz, reviewing a book of his verse, says: "If, as one poem declares, this life is a dream from which no one wakes, the dreamer has refused to deceive himself, to let himself go, and to forget what he believes and loves." (*The Nation,* CLXI, 592.)

Another in the military vein, "Leave," traces a soldier's walk through the mountains and refers to the sudden arrival at a cliff thus: "But the plants evolve into a rock, the preci-

* From *Little Friend, Little Friend.*

pice / Habitual, in Chinese ink, to such a scene"; there is, however, no philosopher, usually present in such drawings, to rationalize the instruments of death which intrude even upon this brief escape from combat. Still another war lyric, "Pilots, Man Your Planes," shows air, clouds, planes turning into fire:

> *Flickering through flashes, the stained rolling clouds,*
> *The air jarred like water tilted in a bowl,*
> *The red wriggling tracers—colonies*
> *Whose instant life annexes the whole sky—*
> *Hunt out the one end they have being for,*
> *Are metamorphosed into one pure smear*
> *Of flame . . .**

The rightness of this image for conveying the effect of a direct hit by flak on a plane's gas tanks, literally metamorphosing the target into fire, is typical of Jarrell's accuracy. "Terms," too, uses the transformation motif, presenting through dream technique a living man—a disabled veteran —changing into a grave.

A further example of mutation caused by war is in the lyric called "The Metamorphoses":

> *When I spat in the harbor the oranges were bobbing*
> *All salted and sodden, with eyes in their rinds;*
> *The sky was all black where the coffee was burning,*
> *And the rust of the freighters had reddened the tide.*
>
> *But soon all the chimneys were hidden with contracts,*
> *The tankers rode low in the oil-black bay,*
> *The wharves were a maze of the crated bombers,*
> *And they gave me a job and I worked all day.*
>
> *And the orders are filled; but I float in the harbor,*
> *All tarry and swollen, with gills in my sides,*
> *The sky is all black where the carrier's burning*
> *And the blood of the transports is red on the tide.†*

* From *Losses*.
† From *Little Friend, Little Friend*.

Between the first and the second stanzas peace has been converted into war. The peace was a degenerate, not a healthy one: surplus commodities were being destroyed as an artificial way of keeping up prices (the oranges thrown into the harbor, the burning coffee); idle ships were riding the waters; the protagonist too was idle. Once war breaks out, with its acceleration of the country's economic life, the scene springs to action: oil-tankers dot the bay, crated bombers cover the wharves, the unemployed "I" works all day in the rush caused by war needs. The significance of the title is underlined in the final quatrain. In a ghastly perversion of the prince-flounder idea in Grimm's "The Fisherman and his Wife," the speaker has been changed into a fish—Jarrell's way of describing a swollen corpse, floating upon the "oil-black bay," with wounds in his sides which gape like gills. The "rust of the freighters" has been replaced by the "blood of the transports"; however, whereas the rust blended into the tide, the blood remains separate with a frightful distinctness.

The whole poem emphasizes an idea which permeates several of Jarrell's pieces: war metamorphoses men into things. "The Lines" develops this thought, pursuing it up through the time of discharge from service, when the "things" are changed back into men again: "After the naked things, told they are men, / Have lined once more for papers, pensions. . . ." The horror of regimentation over, the things are free, human beings once again.

The way in which war changes men into things suggests the punitive aspect of metamorphosis, usually present in classical treatments, such as the tales of Ovid and Apuleius (cf. Ovid's account of Actaeon, Io, Narcissus, Lycaon, etc., or Homer's telling of the Circe myth). Jarrell puts but little stress upon metamorphosis as a means of punishment, although there is a suggestion of this in "The Wide Prospect," where he says of native laborers in colonies: "Their lives, enchanted to a thousand forms, / Are piled in holds for

Europe." Changed to new vegetables, tobacco, gold, the lives of the natives are transported in galleons to Europe while their bones go on working the mines and fields. The poem concludes with the "Hohensalzburg" image of the banquet of human flesh: Man, the grisly abstraction, feeds upon the individual men who people the earth.

In "La Belle au Bois Dormant," Jarrell again writes of a human being laboring under the penalty of enchantment; crumpled in a trunk, the murdered wife sleeps away the years:

> *What wish, what keen pain has enchanted her*
> *To this cold period, the end of pain,*
> *Wishes, enchantment: this suspending sleep?* *

The decapitated belle in this difficult lyric, hidden in the checkroom of a big railway station, is pictured in the newspapers, asked for by the State. The man in the poem, half-wishing she were alive again, waits for her to wake, as she in turn waits for the kiss needed to rouse her. But there is no possibility of her doom's being conquered.

World War II brought into the focus of popular attention the truth that a man is at least two persons: the soldier but also the civilian of the past who still exists in the minds of those back home and in dreams. Herman Fränkel classifies one of Ovid's intentions as the split-in-the-ego, so much discussed today: "Furthermore, the theme gave ample scope for displaying the phenomena of insecure and fleeting identity, of a self divided in itself or spilling over into another self. . . . Separation from the self means normally death, but not in a metamorphosis." (*Ovid: A Poet between Two Worlds*, 99.) In the days of old Rome, personal identity was not so fleeting a thing as it is today, after Berkeley's idealism, Locke's sensism, James's flux, Bergson's intuitionism, Sartre's existentialism, and all the other attempts to break down the notion of an abiding self. The most loved of the nineteenth-century children's classics, Carroll's *Alice in*

* From *Seven-League Crutches.*

Wonderland, a book mentioned by Jarrell in his *Kenyon Review* critique of Kafka's *Amerika,* puts the problem thus:
"Who are you?" *said the caterpillar.*
This was not an encouraging opening for a conversation. Alice replied rather shyly, "I—I hardly know, Sir, just at present—
at least
I know who I was when I got up this morning, but I think I might have
been changed several times since then."

The rise of atomic science, with its emphasis on the underlying similarity of all things, may be partially responsible for our modern difficulties in forming a definite idea of personality. Yet this attitude, apparently a progressive one, is anticipated by the savage theory of animism treated above. According to the primitive belief all created things are alive and there are correspondences from level to level in the chain of existence. Relics of such reasoning survive in the animal metaphors used to express the characters of men: "He is a swine."

Mary Holmes, in "Metamorphosis and Myth in Modern Art," stresses this relationship between animism and contemporary physical science. In this stimulating essay published in the quarterly *Perspective* (Winter, 1948), she discusses how we are psychologically involved at present with our universe, then goes on to show our material involvement:

> Physics also has taught us our strict atomic kinship, the ambivalence of energy that binds together the observer and the observed, the playful impermanence of chance configurations to which we give definition and name. But by the grace of probability there go I, and by that same grace, there may I yet be. We may say with St. Francis, our sister the star, our brother the atom, or declare our least cell the universe. (80)

For Saint Francis, such metaphors (that the stars were his sisters and the sun his brother) drew their life from his faith in the Fatherhood of God; for Miss Holmes, they are poetic expressions of scientific theory, used by orphans in an unpredictable world, wherein textbooks of physics contain more marvelous transformations than anything in Ovid: "Our most fanciful metaphors are excelled by the sober scientific descriptions of form alterations in objects moving at the speed of light. We no longer dare assume that the apple is only apple, the lion only beast."

The relation between atomic research and metamorphosis has already been treated in the chapter on *Paterson*. One further expression of the influence of recent discoveries in the creation of elements might, however, serve well here to reinforce the point. The passage is from Erich Kahler's article, "The Persistence of Myth":

> In its recent stupendous advances, physics has arrived at a border region that seems to refuse itself to rational penetration. It has pushed forward into the realms of the submicroscopic, where phenomena can no longer be pictured, but only schematized, that is, symbolized; so deep into the innermost structure of the elements that it has discovered their modes of transformation one into the other and so has come to recognize the elements themselves as being only specific arrangements, linkages of general energies. It has not only shown the total transformation of matter, but matter *as* transformation, and has even reproduced this transformation and made it a tool of man. (*Chimera,* v, 9–10.)

This essay, appearing in the *Chimera* issue devoted to myth, dramatizes the fact that here upon earth change rules everything in a far deeper sense than was dreamed possible before the twentieth century.

With the self-consciousness of the artist, Jarrell approaches this problem of identity, subjects it to poetic examination. One of his favorite symbols in so doing is the mirror. *Die alte Frau, die alte Marschallin* in "The Face" (a character borrowed from *Der Rosenkavalier*) repudiates

what she sees in the looking glass, reflecting that: "It is terrible to be alive," when what you are and what you appear
to be are so different; this creature in the mirror cannot be
she. The protagonist in "A Ghost, A Real Ghost" thought
that he could never survive looking in the mirror and finding
the room empty; yet this happens and he keeps on existing.
Someone in "An Old Song" speaks of "the mirror's lament-
able change." The speaker goes on to wonder, looking into
a grave, if the soul might be deceived into thinking it could
escape punishment or praise in such depths, where it "might
endure / The altering ages in that altered shape." The princess who wakes in the wood, in still another poem, does not
know who she is, though she feels that she is identical with
the universe. "The Venetian Blind," already mentioned in
connection with dreams, reveals a man groping frantically
for his identity, for his niche in the cosmos; for that inexplicable *something* which is his true self, left out in every
account of the world:

> And the Angel he makes from the sunlight
> Says in mocking tenderness:
>
> "Poor stateless one, wert thou the world? . . .
>
> And yet something calls, as it has called:
> "But where am I? But where am I?" *

The italicizing of the personal pronoun shows upon which
facet of the mental agony Jarrell wishes accent to fall.

   That Randall Jarrell is concerned with philosophical ex-
planations of inner and external reality is further evident in
"The Place of Death," which portrays a student walking, his
Spinoza in hand, among the tombstones of a cemetery which
is reminiscent of Robert Lowell's Quaker graveyard in
Nantucket:

* *Ibid.*

He has felt the boundaries of being fade,
These long-outmoded, mounded, dewy modes
Lapse to the seeding and inhuman Substance
Whose infinite, unchanging, and eternal thought
Is here extended in a thousand graves. *

Essence, substance (defined as that which makes a thing
what it is, regardless of accidents) having been rejected by
certain modern philosophers in favor of "A thing is what it
seems to me or what I think it is," the conversion of one
thing into another is no longer exclusively an imaginative
account of origins designed to provide courtly entertain-
ment as in Ovid, or even a poetic representation of the veri-
ties of daily conscious and subconscious experience, as in
the folklore collected by nineteenth-century scholars. It is
an attempt to go back to that principle of change, natural
to the child and common in dreams, in order to live more
adequately our mortal measure of years. It is one of Randall Jarrell's ways of voicing that unfathomable disillusion
which informs his poetry, and at the same time of reaching
a wisdom beyond that proffered by science, a wisdom which
may yet successfully oppose those forces seeking the blood
of Man.

* From *Losses*.

✮

CHAPTER SIX

WILLIAM BUTLER YEATS:

The Road to Tír-na-n-Og

LAST of the seven poets to be considered, William Butler
Yeats might well be called a wandering magician. The life
of every man is a journey. Yeats had his destination constantly in mind: in the earlier verse his goal took the ex-
pressly Irish form of the Land of Tír-na-n-Og, whereas the
later poetry presented a symbolic version of that Paradise at
which all men, by various routes, try tc arrive. The transformations he effected in his lyrics—magic with which he de-
lighted his companion-travelers along the way—were faint
reflections of that transfiguration he expected at journey's-
end.

Metamorphosis in Yeats might be taken as that involved
in the Celtic pagan past (as represented by gods, folk
heroes, *personae*) and that in the Celtic Christian present,
centering about devils and witches, the reverse side of the
dispensation of grace introduced by the early missionaries
to Eire. Further, it might be divided into metamorphosis of
the microcosm, man, both in life and in death; and of the
macrocosm, envisioned first as Ireland and then the world,
the final metamorphosis being that of the land of this earthly
pilgrimage to the Country of the Young.

In 1885, when Yeats was nineteen, he published in the
Dubliner University Review a pastoral play, "The Island of
Statues," interesting as evidence of his early attraction to-
ward metamorphosis as a subject for verse. In Spenserian

manner, it tells the story of the shepherdess Naschina, who by choosing the right flower wakes to life heroes of other days turned to stone by an enchantress; then she and her lover Almintor reign as king and queen of their island Arcadia. Perhaps Yeats dreamed this story in the summers at Sligo where his grandparents lived, as he lay on the slope of Knocknarea near the circle of stones which the peasants believed to be once fairy pipers. At any rate, it was one of his very few experiments in the artificial world of the pastoral; after writing it he turned to what for him was a more real land, that of his Gaelic ancestors. Yet even here he was fascinated by this myth. In *The Celtic Twilight,* after presenting literature as the reflection of moods, he describes the opposite of petrifaction:

> Nay, are there not moods which shall find no expression unless there be men who dare to mix heaven, hell, purgatory, and faeryland together, or even to set the heads of beasts to the bodies of men, or to thrust the souls of men into the heart of rocks? (7)

Ironically, much later on, "Easter 1916," which is concerned with his Celtic present rather than the legendary past, reverses the process: instead of putting living hearts into stone it turns to stone the hearts of men who have sacrificed too long.

Serious writing for Yeats began with a period of preoccupation with Celtic mythology. All the gods of the Sidhe or Tuatha De Danaan were known as Shape-Changers. Mortals had indeed to be on guard against their deceit. The chief weapon against such metamorphoses, Yeats tells us in *Irish Fairy and Folk Tales* (213), is fire. His play, "On Baile's Strand," presents women carrying bowls of fire and chanting:

> *May this fire have driven out*
> *The Shape-Changers that can put*
> *Ruin on a great king's house*
> *Until all be ruinous.*

In their song they go on to represent these transformations as capricious cruelty toward the king on the part of the gods:

> Or, for many shapes they have,
> They would change them into hounds
> Until he had died of his wounds,
> Though the change were but a whim.*

"The Green Helmet," another play, also shows men watching against the Shape-Changers.

The power of transformation, though common to all the gods, seems to be connected with Aengus particularly. The Irish Eros is forever assuming new forms to win his human sweethearts or to facilitate the love affairs of mortals. In "Baile and Aillinn" he first appears as an old man and tells to each lover the tale of the other's death. No change could be more complete than that of the old man, with "ragged long grass-coloured hair," "Knees that stuck out of his hose," "puddle water in his shoes," "half a cloak," and "a squirrel's eye," to the handsome youth who meets Baile and Aillinn after they have been transformed to swans in Tír-na-n-Og. Then "his changed body was / Tall, proud and ruddy," with wings that hovered over the harp-strings woven for him by Edain before Midhir's wife metamorphosed her to a fly (cf. "The Harp of Aengus," and the 1901 version of "The Shadowy Waters," where Forgael calls her a "golden fly.") The passage is reminiscent of the return of Ulysses, prepared for by Minerva's rejuvenation of the hero, a natural resemblance, since the Homeric and Celtic visions of beauty, immortal concepts appearing in various media through the ages, are based on the same absolute.

The romance of Aengus and Edain offers another instance of this disguise of the god as man. "The Two Kings" begins with a terrible battle between Edain's husband, King

---

* The Collected Plays of W. B. Yeats. Copyright, 1952, by The Macmillan Co. Reprinted by permission of The Macmillan Co.

Eochaid, and a marvelous stag who is probably Aengus.
Just as Eochaid is about to plunge his knife into the animal
it vanishes. In discussing Celtic myth J. A. MacCullough
speaks of the frequency of such incidents:

> Shape-shifting was common to deities and Druids. They
> could change their own forms and those of others, and
> no incident is more common than this. To become in-
> visible, to make others invisible, was a frequent magic
> act. (*The Celtic and Scandinavian Religions,* 77.)

On the King's return Edain tells him of how Aengus has
been wooing her in the shape of her brother-in-law, Ardan.
Aengus, having drawn her to an assignation with Ardan,
whom she finds sleeping, appears to her in majesty, with
eyes "Like the eyes of some great kite scouring the woods."
He tries to persuade Edain that as a goddess in the Sidhe
she formerly belonged to him and that she will go back after
death, but she defends the joy she has found in human love.
Just as the stag vanishes, so does the young man. In the end
the royal couple is welcomed by Ardan, dispossessed of the
god's spirit and ignorant that he has been used by Aengus.

Aengus again employs this stratagem in "The Old Age of
Queen Maeve," when he takes the body of the Queen's husband, Ailell, in order to solicit her help in obtaining the
princess Caer. Maeve calls him Aengus of the birds, referring to the time when he changed four of his kisses into
birds, as related by Yeats in *Early Poems and Stories* (282).
A more famous story of his love for Caer is that in which
he becomes a swan since she has been enchanted to that
shape: love seeking conformity with the beloved.

The most familiar metamorphic poem by Yeats on this
god is "The Song of Wandering Aengus," based on a Greek
folk song according to Yeats's notes but actually following
more closely the incidents of "The White Trout" in his
Irish Fairy and Folk Tales. It is an exquisite lyric, all the
delicacy of Celtic fancy caught in its simple three stanzas.
The change from trout to apple-blossom girl is effected as

easily as the change of *something* in line 11 to *some one* in line 12. Here in miniature is the heartbreaking and endless pursuit of the ideal which was to obsess Yeats all his life long. The lady in the poem is really "Eternal beauty wandering on her way." ("To the Rose upon the Rood of Time.") And it is only in hope that this girl is possessed or the silver and golden apples plucked. The fable of the trout-girl is commonplace enough, but

> In Yeats's hands the idea suffers a sea-change and becomes symbolical of the vision of beauty which, mysteriously and unexpectedly, comes to most people at some hour of their lives, and which sets the artist's emotional mind aglow, filling his heart with infinite longing, so that he girds up his loins and goes out to recapture the ravishing phantom. (Willem Van Doorn, *English Studies,* II, 76.)

If the myths of Aengus lead in shape-shifting among stories of the gods, those of Cuchulain take first place among stories of heroes. His birth is a Celtic echo of the Leda myth. The father of Cuchulain was a hawk, as the hero tells his son Conchubar in "On Baile's Strand": "that clean hawk out of the air / That, as men say, begot this body of mine / Upon a mortal woman." In the same poem he himself is pictured as longing for a metamorphosed lover; the Blind Man remarks that Cuchulain is not interested in a conquest of young men. "Now if it were a white fawn that might turn into a queen before morning . . ." Fand, who enticed Cuchulain away from his wife Emer, is known in "Under the Moon" as one who "could change to an otter or a fawn."

Yeats's play, "The Green Helmet," is based upon Cuchulain's adventure with the Red Man, who calls himself the "kindest of all Shape-Changers from here to the world's end." In the beginning, Conall refuses hospitality to the Young Man (Cuchulain) on the grounds that there is a law against the admittance of strangers. Speaking of himself he says, "Who else has to keep the house from the Shape-Changers till day?" Man-headed owls and hare-women have occurred elsewhere in the plays; here Yeats introduces cat-headed men. In the end, the Red Man presents Cuchulain with the magical Green Helmet.

In "At the Hawk's Well" Cuchulain meets a supernatural sweetheart, the Hawk-Woman of the Sidhe, a distant cousin of the bird-girl in *Green Mansions*. At first Cuchulain, called the Young Man again in this play, does not realize the import of the great grey hawk that has attacked him, but the Old Man of the Well tells him that it is the Woman of the Sidhe herself, "The mountain witch, the unappeasable sorrow." Another hero, Oisin, in Yeats's early poem has used the grey wandering osprey as a metaphor for sorrow. Yeats himself in the note to "Meditations in Time of Civil War" tells us that he has a ring depicting a hawk and a but-terfly, the hawk standing for the straight road of logic, mechanism, in contrast to the butterfly's path of wisdom, in-tuition. The temptation by the Hawk Woman accomplishes the testing of the hero.

The hawk mutation is frequent in Gaelic tales. "The Wis-dom of the King" in Yeats's *Early Poems and Stories* begins as crones of the grey hawk with feathers for hair enter the room of a motherless king's son. The first crone lets a drop of her blood fall on the child's lips. As a result he too, as his boyhood progresses, grows feathers for hair, his people con-spiring to keep his monstrous condition from him by putting feathers in their own hair. When the king, as he becomes, discovers their strategy, he vanishes into the world of the Sidhe. Again, Naoise in "Deirdre" talks of Lugaid Red-stripe's wife, who had a seamew's body half the year, and Deirdre herself later compares her tragedy to that of the woman who had "the cold sea's blood in her." Describing fabulous Edens, the speaker in "Under the Moon" mentions "the wood-woman, whose lover was changed to a blue-eyed hawk."

One of the most moving episodes in the Cuchulain legends is that in which the hero unwittingly kills his son, afterward brooding so inconsolably that the men fear he will go mad and destroy them all. Conchubar directs the Druids to "Chaunt in his ear delusion magical, / That he may fight the horses of the sea." To Cuchulain's enchanted eyes the billows turn to horses against which he harmlessly vents his rage. This ironic comparison of the rearing, plunging waves to horses actually needs no magic to explain it. The metamorphosis is private rather than public, as in the Aengus myths: the waves do not really become horses except in Cuchulain's mind. Here, not only the object is metamorphosed but also the very process (the battle). Yeats's sense of the dramatic was attracted to the grief-crazed hero for his own sake—as a noble character reacting in a supreme moment—at the same time that his poet's faculty of symbol-making was seeing in Cuchulain all those who struggle hopelessly against the sorrows of the world.

The hawk-woman comes back to Cuchulain in his death-hour. "The Only Jealousy of Emer" represents her as having dreamed herself into a fisher for men, with dreams as bait. Cuchulain remembers how he once met her beside old thorn-trees and a well, "Half-woman and half bird of prey." "I was that bird of prey, and yet," she assures him, "I am all woman now." In Yeats's final play, "The Death of Cuchulain," the cycle is completed; he who was conceived by a hawk in the womb of a woman wishes to go back after death to his father's form:

> There floats out there
> The shape that I shall take when I am dead,
> My soul's first shape, a soft feathery shape;
> And is not that a strange shape for a soul
> Of a great fighting-man? *

George Henderson in *Survivals in Belief among the Celts* regards this bird as symbolic of the god-soul transmitted to

* *Ibid.*

posterity, a symbolism similar to that of the eagle-tipped sceptre handed down from king to king (93). The last person on the stage in the verse-play "The Death of Cuchulain" is the Morrigu or crow-woman, whose story Lady Gregory tells in *Gods and Fighting Men* (85).

In "Cuchulain Comforted" Yeats follows his hero into eternity. Shades of convicted cowards come to him in the land of the dead and warn him to make a shroud; as he does so they begin to sing, an inhuman sound: "They had changed their throats and had the throats of birds." The passage seems to indicate that his desire to be transformed into a bird was granted.

Yeats had a deeper motive in his Cuchulain series than popularizing these stories out of his Gaelic heritage, though even this is no unworthy aim. The charge of esotericism often leveled against his poems by reviews during the early years of the century is an unfounded one, since the outlines of the saga are quickly fixed in mind by anyone interested enough to spend only a few hours studying Celtic myth. Moreover, why should this remarkable body of folklore be lost to twentieth-century readers, especially those of Irish ancestry? However, Yeats had reasons over and above the preservation of his country's imaginative past. As T. S. Eliot notes, his Cuchulain myths are vehicles for situations of universal significance. (*Southern Review,* VII, 452.) Human love, the transformation stories say, is all very well, but man, who has something of the divine in his genesis, is constantly seeking to transcend the natural. His feet are on the road to Tír-na-n-Og.

And yet, this allegorization in Yeats is never primary. Speaking of his youthful poems about Cuchulain in "The Circus Animals' Desertion," he says:

> *Heart-mysteries there, and yet when all is said*
> *It was the dream itself enchanted me:*
> *Character isolated by a deed*
> *To engross the present and dominate memory,*

Players and painted stage took all my love,
And not those things that they were emblem of. *

His long and rich association with the Abbey Theatre is
evidence of how keenly interested he was in character and
situation. Spenser's manipulation of human beings to illustrate moral points stands as opposite of Yeats's absorption
in the emblems themselves, the men or gods who act out
their dramas within the theater of his imagination.

Oisin, son of the hero Finn and a fawn-woman, also has
his share of metamorphic adventures. Cuchulain's name
(the modern surname Quinn), springing from the animism
of early Celtic belief, means *hound;* Oisin's, *little deer.* He
lives in a marvelous world: "The birds and beasts that cross
his path have been fighting-men or great enchanters or fair
women, and in a moment can take some beautiful or terrible
shape." (*The Cutting of an Agate,* 18.) When he starts out
on his wandering, he is in company with his cousins, Bran,
Sceollan, and Lomair, transformed to hounds. (*Louis Gray,*
The Mythology of All Races, III, 169.) In the course of his
three-hundred-year stay with the goddess Niamh he engages
in the standard transformation combat of heroic legend, to
save a lady held captive by a demon:

> *And when he [the demon] knew the sword of Manannan*
> *Amid the shades of night, he changed and ran*
> *Through many shapes; I lunged at the smooth throat*
> *Of a great eel; it changed, and I but smote*
> *A fir-tree roaring in the leafless top;*
> *And thereupon I drew the livid chop*
> *Of a drowned dripping body to my breast.†*

Finally he kills the monster, who later revives, the struggle
continuing for a hundred years. The battle resembles that in
Yeats's prose sketch, "Dhoya," where the adversary of the
title character turns to a bundle of reeds at the crucial mo-

* *The Collected Poems of W. B. Yeats.* Copyright 1933 by The
Macmillan Co. Reprinted by permission of The Macmillan Co.
† *Ibid.*

ment. (*Early Poems and Stories.*) In the poem Yeats himself is Oisin; the demon, England; and the lady to be saved, Ireland, according to the exegesis given by Richard Ellmann in *Yeats: The Man and the Masks* (52).

But there is a deeper meaning, as Yeats hints in "The Circus Animals' Desertion," where he reviews his career:

> *First that sea-rider Oisin led by the nose*
> *Through three enchanted islands, allegorical dreams,*
> *Vain gaiety, vain battle, vain repose,*
> *Themes of the embittered heart, or so it seems,*
> *That might adorn old songs or courtly shows;*
> *But what cared I that set him on to ride,*
> *I, starved for the bosom of his faery bride?* *

When he wrote "The Wanderings of Oisin," it was love itself that Yeats wanted, an idealized love such as he cherished for Maud Gonne until old age. It takes only a little stretch of the imagination to conceive of the old woman who is Ireland (and Maud Gonne) in *Cathleen ni Houlihan* as belonging also to the same symbolic pattern. As she changes from young to old the lover (Yeats) becomes the warrior, and both step out the door into mystery.

Cuchulain and Oisin are public characters; Red Hanrahan is Yeats's private creation, his other self. Hanrahan's hair, significantly, is red, which is "the colour of magic" in every country and had been so from the very earliest times. The caps of fairies and magicians are well-nigh always red." (*Irish Fairy and Folk Tales*, 61.) "The Tower" is based upon a tale in Yeats's *Early Poems and Stories* that shows Hanrahan and others gathered around an old man shuffling cards:

> . . . And all in a minute a hare made a leap out from between his hands, and whether it was one of the cards that took that shape, or whether it was made out of nothing in the palms of his hands, nobody knew, but there it was running on the floor of the barn, as quick as any hare that ever lived.

* *Ibid.*

Some looked at the hare, but more kept their eyes on the old man, and while they were looking at him a hound made a leap out between his hands, the same way as the hare did, and after that another hound and another, till there was a whole pack of them following the hare round and round the barn.*

These four lines suffice to create the metamorphosis in the poetic version:

> *He so bewitched the cards under his thumb*
> *That all but the one card became*
> *A pack of hounds and not a pack of cards,*
> *And that he changed into a hare.*

Only Hanrahan pursues the hound and hares, fruitlessly of course, as is invariable in the hound-hare or hound-deer myth frequent in Yeats. He comes back from the pursuit of the magic hound and hares to find that his sweetheart has married another. In the prose stories he experiences other transformation adventures: the rope that he is twisting turns to a water-worm who twists him instead; the mist of the valley and the rose leaves become men and women, shadowy and rose-colored.

The best-known variation of the metamorphosed hound theme used in this Hanrahan story is "He Mourns for the Change that Has Come upon Him and His Beloved, and Longs for the End of the World." The "he" in the poem, according to an earlier title, is Mongan, sixth-century king of Ulster, who was the reincarnation of the warrior Find, dead two hundred years before. (H. D'Arbois De Jubainville, *The Irish Mythological Cycle and Celtic Mythology,* 35.) Another former title was "The Desire of Man and Woman," suggestive of the poem's symbolic meaning. In the lyric a man, changed by the hazel wand of Aengus to a hound with one red ear, follows his beloved transformed to a hornless white deer.

* *Early Poems and Stories* by W. B. Yeats. Copyright 1925, by The Macmillan Co. Reprinted by permission of the Macmillan Co.

This same figure of unappeasable desire appears in "The Wanderings of Oisin," as well as in "The Shadowy Waters," where Dectora says, "O look! A red-eared hound follows a hornless deer"; and Forgael answers, "The pale hound and the deer wander forever / Among the wind and waters." C. M. Bowra, in a discussion of this lyric in *The Heritage of Symbolism,* considers the myth a depiction of a spiritual crisis in Yeats himself, whose frustrated desire longs for the destruction of death as represented by the ancient image of the boar (188). Sometimes in Yeatsian lyrics the metamorphic pursuit is successful and temporary (Zeus as Leda's lover); at other times, as in these hound-hare, hound-deer transformations, it is unsuccessful and eternal. One might call the latter motif an example of the Grecian-urn theme: love as frustration, yet never—in contrast to love as it exists outside art—as satiety.

Hanrahan, then, is another figure of Yeats, the Celt in search of the absolute which, evading him at every cross-way, leads him on past the grave. But perhaps the finest expression in Yeats of this theme is his verse-drama, "The Shadowy Waters," wherein the hero, Forgael, is one more *persona* for Yeats. In the program note for the 1906 production, the author summarizes his play thus:

> Once upon a time, when herons built their nests in old men's beards, Forgael, a Sea-King of ancient Ireland, was promised by certain human-headed birds love of a supernatural intensity and happiness. These birds were the souls of the dead, and he follows them over seas toward the sunset where their final rest is. By means of a magic harp, he could call them about him when he would and listen to their speech. (Cited in Thomas Parkinson, *W. B. Yeats, Self-Critic,* 61.)

He goes on to describe the meeting with the ship bearing the lovely Dectora, concluding: "The Sailors fled upon the other ship, and Forgael and the woman drifted on alone following the birds, awaiting death and what comes after, or some mysterious transformation of the flesh, an embodiment of every lover's dream."

The metamorphosed birds, souls of dead lovers, come out of the world of popular belief, where birds represent souls of the dead: "The souls of the righteous appear sometimes as white birds, and those of the wicked as ravens, in Christian documents—a conception which is probably of pagan origin." (Gray, *The Mythology of All Races*, III, 60.) One is reminded of the lover in "The White Birds," who, hungry for death, exclaims, "For I would we were changed to white birds on the wandering foam, I and you!" The birds in "The Shadowy Waters" are flying toward their joy in the Isle of the Blest. Aibric and the other sailors fear them as phantoms, insubstantial decoys to disaster. When the ship of spice appears and the sailors board her, Forgael remains at the tiller listening to the birds:

> *There! there they come!*
> *Gull, gannet, or diver,*
> *But with a man's head, or a fair woman's . . .*
> *And I will hear them talking in a minute.*
> *Yes, voices! but I do not catch the words.*
> *Now I can hear. There's one of them that says,*
> *'How light we are, now we are changed to birds!'*
> *Another answers, 'Maybe we shall find*
> *Our heart's desire now that we are so light.'* *

Then the disembodied lovers go on to speak of how they met their various deaths.

It is illuminating to compare this play as it appears in *The Collected Poems* with the acting version as printed in the second volume of the 1907 *The Poetical Works of William B. Yeats*. In the first mentioned the Second Sailor merely states how he has seen a grey gull on the breast of each corpse adrift on the sea, the gulls rising as he watched, circling with strange cries, then flying westward. His speech in this second version makes the metamorphosis unmistakable:

* *The Collected Poems of W. B. Yeats.*

The dead were floating upon the sea yet, and it seemed as if the life that went out of every one of them had turned to the shape of a man-headed bird—grey they were, and they rose up of a sudden and called out with voices like our own, and flew away singing to the west. Words like this they were singing: "Happiness beyond measure, happiness where the sun died." (490–491)

The Second Sailor goes on to relate how his mother has told him of such birds, "sent by the lasting watchers to lead men away from this world and its women to some place of shining women that cast no shadow, having lived before the making of the earth." It is no wonder that, having the thought of these unnatural birds fresh in his memory, the First Sailor cries out in response to Dectora's promise of nine precious swords for the one first to strike Forgael: "I will strike him first. No! for that music of his might put a beast's head upon my shoulders, or it might be two heads and they devouring one another." (502) This metamorphic idea is also omitted in the closet version.

Still another variation of the play, published in 1901, has Forgael say to Ailbric, "When men die / They are changed and as grey birds fly out to sea." (22) Then, after the battle, when the captain plays his harp, the soldiers, swords out to kill him, see white birds; they say, in turn, "A white bird beats his wings upon my face"; "A white bird has torn me with his silver claws"; "I am blind and deaf because of the white wings." Each of the versions is like a new play, but always there is the prevailing dream, the grey birds drawing mortals toward that land where the white birds of Aengus fly through a scented air.

After Dectora has come under the spell of Forgael's harp, the birds set up a commotion overhead which the Sea-King at first takes for reproach but then realizes it is delight at his success: "And all that tossing of your wings is joy, / And all that murmuring but a marriage-song." Pleading with Dectora, he begs that they follow these grey Pilots so they can at last "put their changeless image on." The play ends as the magic harp cries out of itself to the grey birds, whom the lovers will now pursue together.

By making the union of two natures visible through the man-headed bird image, Yeats gives poetic form to the desire for supernatural powers which lured him down so many blind alleys, if, strictly speaking, any alley can be called blind out of which successful poetry is made. In "The Shadowy Waters" Forgael could have been content with an ordinary human happiness, spending the treasures of the captured ship on a woman in some foreign port, but he prefers the miraculous, even if never attained. About the symbol itself, Howard Baker remarks in the *Southern Review:*

> Bird metaphors always had some compelling interest for Yeats; alongside of his account in the autobiography of his early fascination with Shelley's wise Jew, he professes a still earlier fascination with a passage from Aristophanes "wherein the birds sing scorn upon mankind." Early or late, Yeats makes them the embodiment of forces superior to ordinary human forces; early they are the symbols of extravagant emotions; later, they are symbols of the imperishable creative spirit, and they scorn mere physical life. (VII, 643.)

On another level, these light-winged happy creatures indicate the poet's desire for a bodily resurrection, a longing planted in his heart by God. Tír-na-n-Og, Country of the Young, "for age and death have not found it; neither tears nor loud laughter have gone near it" (*Irish Fairy and Folk Tales,* 200) —what is this but a dream of the heaven that a simple faith promised his orthodox countrymen?

Did Yeats believe in the Celtic myths? Certainly he takes them seriously enough in the detailed notes to his *Irish Fairy and Folk Tales,* where he refuses to explain away a single magical happening. And there is nothing in faeryland more fantastic than some of the tenets of the theosophy and spiritualism to which in his later years he devoted himself. Yet what he really believes in is not the plots of the folk stories but that power of imagination which draws forth the credence of the peasantry. What the artist today does indirectly—casts a spell over those at a distance from him—men of primitive days did directly; amidst a sensitive people this enchantment is still possible. In *Ideas of Good and Evil,* Yeats asks if we shall not some day have to rewrite our histories to admit the reality of the Scholar Gipsy legend, or the escape under the guise of deer of Saint Patrick and his clerics from their enemies, or the metamorphosis of the rod of Moses to a snake. (53–54) Even granted that such enchantment is illusory, to an idealist (and Yeats was such from his youth) the whole world has no more body than its representations which come and go in the human mind.

Modern man is unaware of his power over phenomena. In early ages those who today would be artists gave themselves to contemplation so much so that they thought themselves, and their neighbors along with them, into other realms of being:

> Instead of learning their craft with paper and a pen they may have sat for hours imagining themselves to be stocks and stones and beasts of the wood, till the images were so vivid that the passers-by became but a part of the imagination of the dreamer, and wept or laughed or ran away as he would have them.*

A man practicing enchantment is, after all, Yeats declares in one of his more orthodox moments, only trying to remake the world according to the mind of that Supreme Enchanter, whose voice sounds through all romance, poetry, or intellectual beauty. (*Ibid.,* 68–69.) And if enough people share the same dream, the folk-memory results, that fund from which the individual imagination can draw endlessly. What this type of thinking at bottom really amounts to is an apotheosis of man's imagination.

* *Ideas of Good and Evil* by W. B. Yeats. Copyright 1903, by The Macmillan Co. Reprinted by permission of The Macmillan Co.

Yeats, like Joyce, struggled always to transcend the finite. It is a dangerous struggle, fraught with all the errors that attend man's disregard of his condition as creature. One aspect of this attempt to become godlike is an interest in command over form. Primitive men believed that the gods and goddesses took at their pleasure any shape in the natural world; and that they too by exercise of the creative imagination could change form:

> The hare that ran by among the dew might have sat upon his haunches when the first man was made, and the poor bunch of rushes under their feet might have been a goddess laughing among the stars, and with but a little magic, a little waving of the hands, they too could become a hare or a bunch of rushes, and know immortal love and immortal hatred.*

This blending of natures is a motif repeatedly seen to be a Yeatsian dream as expressed by the individual Celtic myths. In relation to this longing of Joyce and Yeats to become gods, it is significant that in *The Cutting of an Agate* the latter tells about a fabulous book wherein not God but Adam is credited with making the visible world: ". . . he created all things out of himself by nothing more important than an unflagging fancy." (21) Then Yeats goes on to relate this power to that of the Celtic hero, who can make a ship out of a shaving.

The Christianization which brought to the Celtic world the kingdom of light also extended the kingdom of darkness as people became more conscious of evil forces tempting and tormenting the spirit of man. If there are good apparitions in the poetry of Yeats, like Forgael's birds and the angel who took Father Gilligan's place, there are also evil ones. Depictions of witches and devils are but two more manifestations of his efforts to break down the wall between the natural and the supernatural.

* *Ibid.*, p. 280.

Probably the most frequent disguise of the devil is as a cat. The witch in "The Player Queen" had "an imp in the shape of a red cat, that sucked three drops of blood from her poll every night before the cock crew." In *The Celtic Twilight* Yeats tells how demons transform themselves to white cats or black dogs. (33) But diabolical ingenuity is not exhausted by these two forms: "For who can say what walks, or in what shape / Some devilish creature flies in the air." (Aleel in "The Countess Cathleen.") Sometimes the demons take on bird form, like the man-headed owls of "The Land of the Heart's Desire," or even shapes as ridiculous as a newspaper rolling along the road. Summarizing the beliefs of common folk concerning demonology, Yeats says in *Irish Fairy and Folk Tales:* "The Irish devil does not object to these undignified shapes. The Irish devil is not a dignified person. He has no whiff of sulphureous majesty about him." (325) In *Early Poems and Stories,* Yeats reveals that he himself has had a vision of "a quantity of demons of all kinds of shapes—fish-like, serpent-like, ape-like, and dog-like." (264) Occasionally the devil appears in human form, like the Merchants in "The Countess Cathleen," or the young man metamorphosed from the *Irish Times* in "The Devil," a sketch included in *The Celtic Twilight.* (69)

Witches, too, have this property of shape-shifting. In *Irish Fairy and Folk Tales* Yeats calls this power of changing form, usually in Ireland to that of a hare or a cat, the central and universal notion of witchcraft. (148) "The Witch Hare," a story by Mr. and Mrs. Hall in the same collection, tells how Katey MacShane, shot while she is in her hare's form, explains the wound later by saying she has cut herself chopping wood. In discussing fairy doctors, elsewhere in the volume, Yeats remarks: "Perhaps some old hag in the shape of a hare has been milking the cattle." (146) The Fool in "On Baile's Strand" talks about "Hags that have heads like hares, / Hares that have claws like witches." The souls of the dead also can at times take the shapes of hares. (*Irish Fairy and Folk Tales,* 129.)

Do these things really happen? No, says Yeats, they are illusions. He quotes Giraldus Cambrensis, twelfth-century historian of Ireland, as being of the opinion that such a phenomenon as a wolf-woman was an illusion, since only God can change the form, an opinion which coincides with that of tradition. (*Irish Fairy and Folk Tales,* 148.) It is always hard to be sure whether Yeats is speaking for himself in writing of supernatural occurrences or merely reporting results of his folk-lore investigations among the uneducated Irish peasantry. At the end of this essay he comes back to the illusory character of witchcraft changes: "This, then, is to be remembered—the form of an enchanted thing is a fiction and a caprice." (149) In the world of the Sidhe, a noble construct of folk-imagination, changes needed no apology.

Though the realm of Celtic belief, pagan and Christian, absorbed much of Yeats's youthful energies and was never completely forsaken by him, it is only one of the major sources of metamorphosis in his poems. As he gradually developed his own schematized view of human existence, the temporal world for him fell into two cycles: the metamorphosis of man the microcosm, before and after death, and the metamorphosis of the macrocosm in terms of the Platonic year, as well as on both lesser and greater scales. To express the dichotomy another way, life for him involved personal (private) and objective (public) metamorphoses. A dominant influence on the first concept was his Rosicrucianism, made unmistakable in 1890 by his entrance into the Hermits of the Golden Dawn. There was much in this secret society to appeal to his artist's sensibility, though not so much to recommend it to his common sense. But Yeats was one to make mistakes in the grand manner, and so, despite his father's scorn, he dedicated himself to this movement bent on understanding the spiritual forces of the uni-

verse and transforming by will the time-ridden to the timeless. A private transmutation such as the latter is at least
once in the poetry of Yeats affirmed to be possible: in the
lyric "Chosen," where love changes the zodiac into a sphere,
imperfection to perfection.

Toward the end of the century, then, all wisdom, to
Yeats's mind, was locked within the onyx eyes of "Our
Father Rosicross," as the founder of Rosicrucianism is
called in "The Mountain Tomb." "Rosa Alchemica" is a
fictionized account of the sect. It is a first-person narrative,
beginning as Michael Robartes comes to the author's door
and takes him away to a building on the seashore. There the
narrator reads an ancient book that treats of the progress of
six students in alchemical lore. Eventually he takes part in a
ceremony wherein the petals of the mosaic rose on the ceil-
ing of an initiation chamber turn into beautiful Grecian and
Egyptian dancers, who are in reality gods and goddesses.
The villagers attack the rose-worshippers, but the author
escapes, attributing what he has seen to the power of the
devil.

The circumstance that had drawn Robartes to visit the
writer of "Rosa Alchemica" was the latter's publication of a
a book on alchemy. About this he writes:

> I had discovered, early in my researches, that their
> doctrine was no merely chemical phantasy, but a phi-
> losophy they applied to the world, to the elements and
> to man himself; and that they sought to fashion gold out
> of common metals merely as part of a universal transmu-
> tation of all things into some divine and imperishable
> substance; and this enabled me to make my little book a
> fanciful reverie over the transmutation of life into art,
> and a cry of measureless desire for a world made wholly
> of essences.*

A little later he sighs over how far he is from the true dream
of the alchemist, "the transmutation of the weary heart into

* *Early Poems and Stories*, p. 466.

a weariless spirit." (468) It is easier to sympathize with Yeats's ambition than with his cloudy means of effecting it, both as these appeared in his mask as narrator of "Rosa Alchemica," and in his theosophical experiments in actual life.

Yeats was particularly stirred by the central myth of Rosicrucianism, the mystical death and resurrection of the initiate. (Richard Ellmann, *Western Review,* XII, 238.) Transmutation of the elements had been only a symbol of this. His later invention of the phases of the moon as outlined in *A Vision* is related to this in its emphasis on psychical change as man moves from one phase to another; so also is his theory of the mask, by which a man tries ceaselessly to become his antiself.

Death, too, is metamorphosis. Early attracted by the transmigration beliefs of the East, Yeats brings this doctrine into his poems again and again. The earth is haunted by those who once lived upon it ("The Indian to His Love," "To a Shade," "The Cold Heaven"). The lover in "An Image from a Past Life" asks his beloved why she lays her hands over his eyes, and she answers, "A sweetheart from another life floats there." Even before death, according to the age-old belief in a separable soul, shades of lovers wander in gardens they once knew, more real than the present inhabitants ("The New Faces"). As a penance, certain dead must live through their old lives again, or appear to the living in a monstrous image, says "The Dreaming of the Bones." The Three Hermits, in the poem of that name, discuss the forms to which they expect to be changed when they pass the Door of Birth. Sometimes the gods use this shape-shifting as a means of punishing the dead: Attracta in "The Herne's Egg" threatens Congal with being turned to a cat, rat, bat, dog, wolf, or goose; and in the end of the play the divine Herne changes him to a donkey.

The sources of Yeats's interest in transmigration are manifold. Probably the most familiar is his connection with the Theosophical Society founded by Helena Blavatsky in 1875, the members of which believed in a succession of earthly lives through which the spirit advances toward perfection. As one critic, Northrup Frye, says:

> In Yeats the spiritual life in this world is, again like Dante's Purgatory, a gigantic cone, a mountain or tower encircled by a winding stair spiraling upward through one life after another until it reaches an apex. (*University of Toronto Quarterly*, XVII, 13.)

The impact of his meeting with the Brahmin Mohini Chatterji, who visited Dublin in 1866, is recorded in a lyric written forty years later. There Mohini as a dramatic character describes his lives as they range through those of a king, slave, rascal, and lover—a concept which in another context might stand merely for the gamut of experience.

This poem has as a Celtic analogue the early "Fergus and the Druid." Fergus MacRoich, Red Branch warrior and tutor of Cuchulain, follows the Druid all day, watching him change from raven to weasel to man. At last he persuades the Druid to share with him his supernatural wisdom, as symbolized by a little grey bag of dreams. Fergus, the Taliesin of Irish literature, now describes the protean character of his lifetime thus:

> *I see my life go drifting like a river*
> *From change to change; I have been many things—*
> *A green drop in the surge, a gleam of light*
> *Upon a sword, a fir-tree on a hill,*
> *An old slave grinding at a heavy quern,*
> *A king sitting upon a chair of gold—* *

This faith in transmigration, one of the chief tenets in pagan Celtic myth, arose in part from a desire to explain the wonderful knowledge which certain individuals possessed. (De Jubainville, 35.) One lifetime would be all too brief to account for the experience of one wise enough to teach Cuchulain.

* *The Collected Poems of W. B. Yeats.*

Another lyric of transmigration, "He Thinks of His Past Greatness When a Part of the Constellations of Heaven," begins:

> *I have drunk ale from the Country of the Young*
> *And weep because I know all things now:*
> *I have been a hazel-tree, and they hung*
> *The Pilot Star and the Crooked Plough*
> *Among my leaves in times out of mind:*
> *I became a rush that horses tread:*
> *I became a man, a hater of the winds. . . .* *

The Country of the Young is, of course, Tír-na-n-Og; the hazel tree, the Tree of Life; the Pilot Star, the North Star; and the Crooked Plough, the Great Bear. Instead of nuts, the hazel tree in this poem bears star-fruit. From a constellation the speaker is metamorphosed to the lowliest of forms, a rush under the hooves of horses. Eventually he becomes a man, hating the wind; in Gaelic the word for wind is *Sidhe*.

One transmigratory image used by Yeats is that of the soul's emergence as a butterfly, similar to the metamorphosis in Benét's short story, "The Devil and Daniel Webster." The butterfly in "Another Song of a Fool" was once a schoolmaster. In "The Hour-Glass" the Fool says, as an angel enters holding a casket:

> O, look what has come from his mouth—the white butterfly! He is dead, and I have taken his soul in my hands; but I know why you open the lid of that golden box. I must give it to you. There then (puts the butterfly in casket) he has gone through his pains and you will open the lid in the Garden of Paradise.

The change is conventional enough, since the butterfly, part of a metamorphic process, is a standard symbol of resurrection. "If you see one fluttering near a corpse," says Yeats in *Irish Fairy and Folk Tales*, "that is the soul, and is a sign of its having entered upon immortal happiness." (129) An

* *Ibid.*

interesting fact in this connection is that the Greek word for soul is the same as that used for butterfly.

Transmigration, however, is not confined to animal forms. "The stories of trees that grow up from the graves of lovers, such as Tristram and Iseult, and twine themselves together are familiar in Europe." (*Encyclopedia Britannica*, xv, 337.) In 1903 Yeats published a poem about Baile and Aillinn, whose bodies after death were metamorphosed into a yew tree and a wild apple tree that "blossomed to immortal mirth," while their souls wandered with Aengus in Tír-na-n-Og. The poet returned to this legend in one of the Supernatural Songs from *A Full Moon in March*. (1935) Here the old hermit, Ribh, is apparently reading in the pitch-dark night near the tomb of the lovers on the anniversary of their deaths. He explains his folly to a passer-by thus:

> *The miracle that gave them such a death*
> *Transfigured to pure substance what had once*
> *Been bone and sinew; when such bodies join*
> *There is no touching here, nor touching there,*
> *Nor straining joy, but whole is joined to whole;*
> *For the intercourse of angels is a light*
> *Where for its moment both seem lost, consumed.*
>
> *Here in the pitch-dark atmosphere above*
> *The trembling of the apple and the yew,*
> *Here on the anniversay of their death,*
> *The anniversary of their first embrace,*
> *These lovers, purified by tragedy,*
> *Hurry into each other's arms; these eyes,*
> *By water, herb and solitary prayer*
> *Made aquiline, are open to that light.*
> *Though somewhat broken by the leaves, that light*
> *Lies in a circle on the grass; therein*
> *I turn the pages of my holy book.**

In the figure of eternity—the circle—the light of their dis-

* *Ibid.*

embodied common substance is perceptible to one whom mortification and prayer have prepared. Vision is not complete – the light is hindered by the mortal leaves; but even so Ribh's experience shows forth the triumphing power of love.

Could Yeats choose his own form of existence in the life after death, he would select that of a golden nightingale, he says in "Sailing to Byzantium." He who was ever resentful of that "dying animal," the body, would become a deathless (if also lifeless) bird; all the irony implicit in the Grecian-urn theme is operative here. In so far as the nightingale is mechanical it appears to be Yeats's private myth, the only relation to the Ovidian Philomel being that both represent art as contrasted to life. The passion for knowing all things is again present:

> He asks, therefore, not to become a sage like them, but to be turned into a beautiful mechanical bird which will have wisdom placed in its mouth by its fashioner. He will be liberated not only from life but from all responsibilities by being transmuted into an image which in turn will sing not of the world of eternity but of time.*

The companion poem, "Byzantium," extends the theme by metamorphosing the unpurged images of life itself into the purged image of art, just as gold is refined in the goldsmith's fire. The realistic reader will say, "But Yeats isn't serious about this golden nightingale – it's only an image." For the idealist, everything is only an image, if by that is meant an impression on the senses.

For all his dabbling in the doctrine of Karma and related sects, Yeats at times entertained the Christian view of resurrection, as he himself indicates in *The Cutting of an Agate:* "I am orthodox and pray for the resurrection of the body." (115) When he thinks in "Broken Dreams" of the joy which shall attend his contemplation of the glorified Maud Gonne, he becomes incoherent:

* *Yeats: The Man and the Masks* by Richard Ellmann. Copyright 1948 by The Macmillan Co. Reprinted by permission of The Macmillan Co.

But in the grave all, all, shall be renewed.
The certainty that I shall see that lady
Leaning or standing or walking

In the first loveliness of womanhood,
And with the fervour of my youthful eyes,
*Has set me muttering like a fool.**

"From the attempt to achieve personal transmutation 'it was but a brief step," says Richard Ellmann, speaking of Rosicrucianism, "to the attempt to achieve a more general transmutation." (*Yeats: The Man and the Masks,* 239.) The transformation nearest his heart was that of his native land. No one felt more keenly the degradation of her past in submission to a hostile government; none wished more eagerly for her emergence once again as a free woman, accorded all the honors her nobility deserved. The broken old woman who visits the peasant family in "Cathleen ni Houlihan" goes down the road at the play's end with the step of a young queen. All the Irish patriot-heroes ("Easter 1916") are changed utterly, with a terrible new-born beauty; but most of all, Ireland herself rises phoenix-like from the civil war to take her place among the queens of the earth.

Yeats did not stop, however, with Ireland in his vision of a nation transfigured. For him, the world moved through Platonic Years in twelve cycles, each approximately two thousand years. "Nineteen Hundred and Nineteen" summarizes his theory of cyclic rebirth thus: "So the Platonic Year / Whirls out new right and wrong, / Whirls in the old instead." One such Magnus Annus died and another was commenced at the death of Bacchus and the birth of Christ. ("Two Songs from a Play") The first had begun with the conception of Helen of Troy by Leda, the second with the Annunciation to the Blessed Virgin Mary. Now that the Christian cycle was, as Yeats believed, drawing to an end, a new era would be initiated by a new woman and the face

* *The Collected Poems of W. B. Yeats.*

of the earth renewed. Yeats made no distinction between history and fable in this view; the conception of Christ is recorded in documents as reliable as that of the account of Julius Caesar's Gallic Wars, transpiring almost within the same period, whereas the story of Leda's assault by the divine swan is outside of history completely, within the realm of myth.

The story of Leda was Yeats's favorite among Grecian transformations. Making its first appearance in "The Adoration of the Magi," a prose sketch of 1896, it occurs again in "His Phoenix," "Among School Children," "The Player Queen," "On Baile's Strand," "Lullaby," and of course the famous "Leda and the Swan," inspired by Michael Angelo's sculpture now in Florence. The sonnet summarizes that attempt to break down the wall between divinity and humanity which is the key to Yeats, the one continuous thread that runs through his interest in Celtic myth, Rosicrucian ritual, and theosophy. Paradoxically, this poet who, together with Joyce, longed to construct Daedalean wings to soar aloft as a deity, through his creation of forms, spent his heart's blood in the effort to penetrate to the divine mystery that limits man. Indeed, the question that the Leda poem proposes—can mortals share the power and knowledge of God?—is central to his work.

Any tale of divine and human courtship is bound to involve the difference between infinity and finitude, time and eternity; this lyric brings out this cleavage with poignancy and power. Leda is taken in love by Zeus in the guise of a swan, a bird symbolic of Aphrodite, goddess of love, as Lempriere points out in his *A Classical Dictionary*. The metamorphosis, a rather unfair advantage which the king of the gods takes over Leda's husband, Tyndareus, actually had no happy epilogue. As the "white and lithe bridegroom," as Frederick Morgan calls him in "A Swan," goes back to the stars, he leaves behind a desolate bride and an unborn child marked for disaster—ten bloody years of Tro-

jan and Greek warfare. Even though Yeats chooses to disregard these pejorative aspects of his Leda symbol, the un-
dertones remain to condition the reader's response.

In the romance of Leda and Zeus Yeats has found a
legend to connect and dignify individual instances of love.
The swan is an image enchanted by godhead for symbolic
purposes; its history constitutes a legendary theme, the elements of which might be compared to algebraic signs: false
in the sense of not pointing to tangible referents, true in reflecting permanent relations. This theme of passion and
power has a life over and above its appearances (the swan
embracing the beautiful princess); its life is the eternal
story of love conscious of its perfection (Leda) and of Love
incarnate, the activity transformed to the agent (Zeus). One
thinks immediately of the conclusion in that other Ledean
poem, "Among School Children." Yet this metamorphosis
of private experience, successful as it is, is not the chief
reason that Yeats is drawn to the myth.

Leda also symbolizes a turning-point in man's history, an
awful revolution. (Richard Chase, *English Institute Essays,
1947,* 19.) This was Yeats's own intention, as he reveals in
A Vision. Leda begins, through giving birth to Helen, the
cycle of the fall of Troy and thus the rise of Rome. Like
everyone else in the first third of the twentieth century,
Yeats could see a great change approaching, as Commu-
nism grew outward from Russia. If interpreted in this light,
his cyclic theory has more meaning for today's world.
Northrup Frye intimates as much in the essay quoted above
when he says:

> The dove and the virgin are to go and Leda and the swan
> are to come back, in the form of the watchful and ironic
> heron of the Irish marshes and his fanatical priestess
> in "The Hearne's Egg." The new birth is to be however a
> welter of blood and pain, full of the screams of the new
> birds of prey who replace the dove of peace, like the
> leaderless falcon turning in the widening gyre, and full of
> the hound voices of furies in pursuit of blood. (7)

The sonnet itself was not written until 1923, when the shape of things to come was imminent.

In Yeats's myth of the second coming, the new god is not Christ but a sort of anti-Christ. Yet the resurrection of the world is hardly an improvement over the old, as was the expected resurrection of the individual, according to the central dogma of the Rosicrucian Golden Dawn, where the believer lies down in the grave of Christian Rosenkreuz and is reborn. There is something of the terror of prophecy about these lines from "The Second Coming":

> *Things fall apart; the centre cannot hold;*
> *Mere anarchy is loosed upon the world,*
> *The blood-dimmed tide is loosed, and everywhere*
> *The ceremony of innocence is drowned.**

This new god is conceived of as a man-headed lion with a "gaze pitiless and blank as the sun." And from the setting, the riddle he proposes may well be unguessable.

The Platonic changes come about of necessity, with a mathematical regularity. But the imaginative man can—or at least longs to—change his own little square of world, for Yeats the holy land of Ireland and the scenes charged with emotion that it offered. Eliot and the other Laforguians could make poems out of what was ugly in their surroundings, but to Yeats the uncomely and broken and worn out were unendurable. In honor of his love (a perfect rose blossoming in his heart), he wishes in an early lyric to transform the world till it is a proper setting for her beauty:

The wrong of unshapely things is a wrong too great to be told;
I hunger to build them anew and sit on a green knoll apart,
With the earth and the sky and the water, re-made, like a casket
    of gold
For my dreams of your image that blossoms a rose in the deeps
    of my heart.†

("The Lover Tells of the Rose in His Heart")

* *Ibid.*   † *Ibid.*

Over thirty years later, this re-fashioning power is again made the center of a poem, "The Results of Thought." Time has disfigured his friends as it did the old pensioner, wrecked their endowments. He undertakes by meditation to summon back their youthful strength. So well does he succeed that at last he does not even recognize them as they exist apart from his thought—dull-eyed, palsied, bent over. The poet has played Prospero again.

This desire to act as transformer is more than a Petrarchan conceit in Yeats. As Randall Jarrell says, "His life was one long struggle with reality." (*Southern Review*, VII, 653.) Unwilling to bear the positivistic world of his youth, he began early to thumb over roadmaps to Tír-na-n-Og, where he could escape the pressure of science and the menace of change—to a visionary kingdom made concrete in his poetry by images like those of the trees full of painted birds, roses like crimson meteors, windless woods, ever-summered solitudes, and glimmering purple sea of the country where Oisin spent his first hundred years with Niamh. From his journeys over hollow land and hilly land resulted great poetry. And from first to last the subject of that poetry remained constant: the odyssey of the human spirit and its end in glory.

CHAPTER ONE

Ezra Pound and the Metamorphic Tradition

By Ezra Pound

The A B C of Reading. New Haven: Yale University Press, 1934.

"Affirmations." *New Age,* XVI (January 7, 1915), 246–247.

(translator). "The Analects." *The Hudson Review,* III (Autumn, 1950), 9–53.

"Another Chance." *Poetry,* LII (September, 1938), 344–347.

"As Sextant." *Nine* (November 1, 1949), 7.

"The Audience." *Poetry,* V (October, 1914), 29–31.

"A Blast from London." *The Dial,* LVIII (January 16, 1915), 40–41.

Cathay. London: Elkin Mathews, 1915.

"Criterionism." *The Hound and Horn,* IV (October–December, 1930), 113–117.

Culture. Norfolk, Connecticut: New Directions, 1938.

"D'Artagnan Twenty Years After." *Criterion,* XVI (July, 1937), 607–618.

"Emile Verhaeren." *Poetry,* IX (February, 1917), 256–259.

Review of *Ernest Dowson* by Victor Plarr. *Poetry,* VI (April, 1915), 43–45.

"Extract from a Letter." *Poetry,* VII (March, 1916), 321–323.

Exultations. London: Elkin Mathews, 1909.

"For a New Paideuma." *Criterion,* XVII (January, 1938), 205–214.

"From the Editor of 'The Exile.'" *Poetry,* XXX (June, 1927), 174–175.

Gaudier-Brzeska. New York: John Lane Company, 1916.

"The Hard and the Soft in French Poetry." *Poetry,* XI (February, 1918), 264–271.

"Hark to Sturge Moore." *Poetry,* VI (June, 1915), 139–145. Review of *Hark to These Three, and the Vine Dresser, and Other Poems,* and *The Defeat of the Âmazons* by T. Surge Moore.

"Homage to Wilfrid Blunt." *Poetry,* III (March, 1914), 220–224.

"Honor and the United States Senate." *Poetry,* XXXVI (June, 1930), 150–153.

Imaginary Letters. Paris: Black Sun Press, 1930.

Indiscretions. Paris: Three Mountains Press, 1923.

"The Individual in His Milieu." *Criterion,* XV (October, 1935), 30–46.

Instigations of Ezra Pound. New York: Boni and Liveright, 1920.

"Irony, Laforgue, and Some Satire." *Poetry,* XI (November, 1917), 93–97.

"The Island of Paris." *The Dial,* LXIX (October–December, 1920), 406–412.

"The Later Yeats." *Poetry,* IV (May, 1914), 64–69. Review of *Responsibilities* by William Butler Yeats.

Make It New. London: Faber and Faber, Ltd., 1934.

"Mang Tsze." *Criterion,* XVII (July, 1938), 603–625.

"Mr. Dunning's Poetry." *Poetry,* XXVI (September, 1925), 339–346. Review of *The Four Winds* by Ralph Cheever Dunning.

"Modern Georgics." *Poetry,* V (December, 1914), 127–131. Review of *North of Boston* by Robert Frost.

(translator). *The Natural Philosophy of Love* by Remy de Gourmont. London: The Casanova Society, 1926.

'*Noh or Accomplishment: A Study of the Classical Stage of Japan.* New York: Alfred A. Knopf, 1917. (Based on the manuscripts of Ernest Fenollosa.)

"On Criticism in General." *Criterion,* I (January, 1923), 143–156.

"On 'Near Perigord.' " *Poetry,* VII (December, 1915), 143–147.

"Paris." *Poetry,* III (October, 1913), 26–31.

Pavannes and Divisions. New York: Alfred A. Knopf, 1918.

Personae. New York: Horace Liveright, 1926.

Polite Essays. London: Faber and Faber, Ltd., 1937.

"A Possibly Impractical Suggestion." *Poetry,* XXXIV (June, 1929), 178.

"Prologomena." *Poetry Review,* I (February, 1912), 72–76.

Provença. Boston: Small, Maynard and Company, 1910.

"Rabindranath Tagore." *Fortnightly Review,* XCIX (March, 1913), 571–579.

"Remy de Gourmont." *Poetry,* VII (January, 1916), 197–202.

"The Renaissance: I." *Poetry,* V (February, 1915), 246–247.

"The Renaissance: II." *Poetry,* V (February, 1915), 283–287.

"The Renaissance: III." *Poetry,* VI (May, 1915), 84–91.

Review of *Stones of Rimini* by Adrian Stokes. *Criterion,* XIII (April, 1934), 495–497.

Ripostes of Ezra Pound. London: Stephen Swift and Company, Ltd., 1912.

(translator). *The Sonnets and Ballate of Guido Cavalcanti.* Boston: Small, Maynard and Company, 1912.

The Spirit of Romance. London: J. M. Dent and Sons, Ltd., 1910.

"Status Rerum I." *Poetry,* I (January, 1913), 123–128.

"Status Rerum II." *Poetry,* VIII (April, 1916), 38–43.

"Swinburne Versus Biographers." *Poetry,* XI (March, 1918), 322–329. Review of *The Life of Swinburne* by Edmund Gosse.

(translator). *Ta Hio.* London: Stanley Notts, 1936.

"Thames Morasses." *Poetry,* XVII (March, 1921), 325–329.

"Things to Be Done." *Poetry,* IX (March, 1917), 312–315.

"This Constant Preaching to the Mob." *Poetry,* VIII (June, 1916), 144–145.

"This Subsidy Business." *Poetry,* XXXV (January, 1930), 212–214.

"Thomas Macdonagh as Critic." *Poetry,* VIII (September, 1916), 309–312. Review of *Literature in Ireland* by Thomas Macdonagh.

"The Tradition." *Poetry,* III (January, 1914), 137–141.

"T. S. Eliot." *Poetry,* X (August, 1917), 264–371. Review of *Prufrock and Other Observations* by T. S. Eliot.

Umbra. London: Elkin Mathews, 1920.

"Vorticism." *Fortnightly Review,* CII (September, 1914), 461–472.

"William Henry Davies, Poet." *Poetry,* XI (November, 1917), 99–102. Review of *Collected Poems* by W. H. Davies.

"The Wisdom of Poetry." *The Forum,* XLVII (April, 1912), 497–502.

Background References

Amdur, Alice Steiner. *The Poetry of Ezra Pound.* Cambridge: Harvard University Press, 1936.

Barry, Iris. "The Ezra Pound Period." *The Bookman,* LXXIV (October, 1931), 159–172.

Berryman, John. "The Poetry of Ezra Pound." *Partisan Review,* XVI (April, 1949), 368–395.

Blackmur, R. P. "An Adjunct to the Muses' Diadem: A Note on E. P." *Poetry,* LXVIII (September, 1946), 338–347.

————. "Masks of Ezra Pound." *The Double Agent.* New York: Arrow Editions, 1935, 30–68.

Blish, James. "Rituals on Ezra Pound." *The Sewanee Review,* LVIII (Summer, 1950), 185–227.

Cargill, Oscar. *Intellectual America.* New York: Macmillan Company, 1941, 229–238.

Chao, Yuen Ren and Yang, Lien Sheng. *Concise Dictionary of Spoken Chinese.* Cambridge: Harvard University Press, 1947.

Drew, Elizabeth. *Directions in Modern Poetry.* New York: W. W. Norton and Company, Inc., 1940.

Eberhart, Richard. "Pound's New Cantos." *Quarterly Review of Literature,* V (No. 2, 1950), 174–192.

Eliot, T. S. "Ezra Pound." *Poetry,* LXVIII (September, 1946), 326–338.

————. *Ezra Pound: His Metric and Poetry.* New York: Alfred A. Knopf, 1917.

————. "The Method of Mr. Pound." *The Athenaeum,* No. 4669 (October 24, 1919), 1065–1066.

Frankel, Herman. *Ovid: A Poet between Two Worlds.* Berkeley: University of California Press, 1945.

Gordon, Ambrose, Jr. "Low Thought." *Furioso,* VI (Spring, 1951), 84–87. Review of *Parade's End* by Ford Madox Ford.

Gorman, Herbert. "Bolingbroke of Bards." *North American Review,* CCXIX (June, 1924), 855–866.

Gregory, Horace and Zaturenska, Marya. *A History of American Poetry: 1900–1940.* New York: Harcourt, Brace and Company, 1946, 163–182.

Healy, J. V. "Addendum." *Poetry,* LXVIII (September, 1946), 347–349.

————. "The Pound Problem." *Poetry,* LVII (December, 1940), 200–214.

Hughes, Glenn. *Imagism and the Imagists.* Palo Alto: Stanford University Press, 1931.

Kenner, Hugh. *The Poetry of Ezra Pound.* Norfolk, Connecticut: New Directions, 1951.

————. "The Rose in the Steel Dust." *The Hudson Review,* III (Spring, 1950), 66–124.

Macleish, Archibald. *Poetry and Opinion.* Urbana: University of Illinois Press, 1950.

Michelson, Max. "A Glass-blower of Time." *Poetry,* XI (March, 1918) 330–333. Review of *Lustra* by Ezra Pound.

Miller, Frank J. (editor). *Ovid: Metamorphoses.* 2 vols. Cambridge: Harvard University Press, 1939.

Monroe, Harriet. *Poets and Their Art.* New York: Macmillan Company, 1932.

Norman, Charles. *The Case of Ezra Pound.* New York: Bodley Press, 1948.

Paige, D. D. (editor). *The Letters of Ezra Pound.* New York: Harcourt, Brace and Company, 1950.

Read, Sir Herbert Edward. *The True Voice of Feeling: Studies in English Romantic Poetry.* New York: Pantheon Books, 1953, 116–138.

Rice, Wallace. "Ezra Pound and Poetry." *The Dial,* LIV (May 1, 1913), 370–371.

Rouse, W. H. D. (editor). *Shakespeare's Ovid Being Arthur Golding's Translation of the Metamorphoses.* London: De La More Press, 1904.

Russell, Peter (editor). *An Examination of Ezra Pound.* Norfolk, Connecticut: New Directions, 1950.

Sandburg, Carl. "The Work of Ezra Pound." *Poetry,* VII (February, 1916), 249–258.

Schwartz, Delmore. "Ezra Pound's Very Useful Labors." *Po-*

etry, LI (March, 1938), 324–339. Review of *The Fifth Decad of Cantos*.

Shipley, Joseph T. *Trends in Literature*. New York: Philosophical Library, 1949.

Sinclair, May. "The Reputation of Ezra Pound." *North American Review*, CCXI (May, 1920), 658–669.

Stokes, Adrian. "Pisanello." *The Hound and Horn*, IV (October–December, 1930), 5–25.

————. *Stones of Rimini*. New York: G. P. Putnam's Sons, 1934.

————. *Venice: An Aspect of Art*. London: Faber and Faber, Ltd., 1945.

Tate, Allen. *Reactionary Essays on Poetry and Ideas*. New York: Scribner's Sons, 1936, 43–52.

Tietjens, Eunice. "The End of Ezra Pound." *Poetry*, LX (April, 1942), 38–40.

Watts, Harold. "The Devices of Pound's Cantos." *Quarterly Review of Literature*, V (No. 2, 1950), 147–174.

————. "Pound's Cantos: Means to an End." *Yale Poetry Review*, VI (No. 6, 1947), 9–21.

West, Ray B., Jr. "Ezra Pound and Contemporary Criticism." *Quarterly Review of Literature*, V (No. 2, 1950), 192–201.

Yeats, William Butler. *A Vision*. New York: Macmillan Company, 1938.

CHAPTER TWO

Wallace Stevens: His "Fluent Mundo"

By Wallace Stevens

"As at a Theatre." *Wake*, IX (1950), 8.

The Auroras of Autumn. New York: Alfred A. Knopf, 1950.

"Carlos among the Candles." *Poetry*, XI (December, 1917), 115–124.

"Poems, 1899–1901." *The Harvard Advocate*, CXXVII (December, 1940), 5–6.

"Americana." *Wake*, IX (1950), 10.

"The Course of a Particular." *The Hudson Review*, IV (Spring, 1951), 22.

"The Desire to Make Love in a Pagoda." *Wake,* IX (1950), 8.

"Final Soliloquy of the Interior Paramour." *The Hudson Review,* IV (Spring, 1951), 22–23.

Ideas of Order. New York: Alfred A. Knopf, 1936.

Harmonium. New York: Alfred A. Knopf, 1931.

"John Crowe Ransom: Tennessean." *The Sewanee Review,* LVI (Summer, 1948), 367–370.

The Man with the Blue Guitar. New York: Alfred A. Knopf, 1937.

The Necessary Angel. New York: Alfred A. Knopf, 1951.

"Nuns Painting Water-Lilies." *Wake,* IX (1950), 19.

Parts of a World. New York: Alfred A. Knopf, 1945.

"Prologue to What Is Possible." *New Poems by American Poets,* edited by Rolfe Humphries. New York: Ballantine Books, 1953, 154–156.

"The Role of the Idea in Poetry," *Wake,* IX (1950), 10.

"Song of Fixed Accord." *New Poems by American Poets,* edited by Rolfe Humphries. New York: Ballantine Books, 1953, 152.

"The Souls of Women at Night." *Wake,* IX (1950), 10.

"The State of American Writing." *Partisan Review,* XV (August, 1948), 884–886.

"Three Travelers Watch a Sunrise." *Poetry,* VIII (July, 1916), 163–179.

Transport to Summer. New York: Alfred A. Knopf, 1947.

"Two Illustrations That the World Is What You Make of It." *New Poems by American Poets,* edited by Rolfe Humphries, New York: Ballantine Books, 1953, 153–154.

Background References

Baker, Howard. "Wallace Stevens and Other Poets." *Southern Review,* I (Summer, 1935), 373–396.

Benet, William Rose. "Phoenix Nest." *Saturday Review of Literature,* XV (January 16, 1937), 18.

Bewley, Maurice. "The Poetry of Wallace Stevens." *Partisan Review,* XVI (Spring, 1949), 895–915.

Blackmur, R. P. Review of *Notes toward a Supreme Fiction* and *Parts of a World. Partisan Review,* X (May–June, 1943), 297–300.

Breit, Harvey. "Sanity That Is Magic." *Poetry,* LXII (April, 1943), 48–50.

Brinnin, John Malcolm. "Plato, Phoebus and the Man from Hartford." *Voices,* CXXI (Spring, 1945), 30–37.

Colum, Mary. Review of *Parts of a World. New York Times Book Review* (November 29, 1942), 12.

Davie, Donald. "Essential Gaudiness: The Poems of Wallace Stevens." *Twentieth Century,* CLIII (June, 1953), 455–462.

Fitts, Dudley. Review of *Notes toward a Supreme Fiction. Saturday Review of Literature,* XXVI (August 28, 1943), 8–9.

Focillon, Henri. *The Life of Forms in Art.* New Haven: Yale University Press, 1942.

Grant, Elliott M. *French Poetry of the Nineteenth Century.* New York: Macmillan Company, 1932.

Gregory, Horace and Zaturenska, Marya. *A History of American Poetry: 1900–1940.* New York: Harcourt, Brace and Company, 1946, 326–335.

Hays, H. R. "Laforgue and Wallace Stevens." *Romanic Review,* XXV (July–September, 1934), 242–249.

Heringman, Bernard. "Wallace Stevens: The Use of Poetry." *English Literary History,* XVI (December, 1949), 325–337.

Jarrell, Randall. *Poetry and the Age.* New York: Alfred A. Knopf, 1953, 133–148.

Langer, Susanne K. *Philosophy in a New Key.* New York: The New American Library, 1942.

Meyer, G. P. Review of *Esthetique du Mal. Saturday Review of Literature,* XXIX (March 23, 1946), 7–8.

Mizener, Arthur. "Not in Cold Blood." *The Kenyon Review,* XIII (Spring, 1951), 218–225.

Monroe, Harriet. "He Plays the Present." Review of *Ideas of Order. Poetry,* XLVII (December, 1935), 153–157.

――――. *Poets and Their Art.* New York: Macmillan Company, 1932.

Moore, Marianne. "Unanimity and Fortitude." *Poetry,* XLIX (February, 1937), 268–272.

Mornet, Daniel. *Histoire de la Litterature et de la Pensee Francaises Contemporaines (1870–1934).* Paris: Librairie Larousse, 1927.

O'Connor, William Van. *The Shaping Spirit.* Chicago: Henry Regnery Company, 1950.

Pauker, John. "A Discussion of Sea Surface Full of Clouds." *Furioso,* v (Fall, 1950), 34–47.

Schwartz, Delmore. "Instructed of Much Mortality." *The Sewanee Review,* LIV (July–September, 1946), 439–449.

Shepard, Odell. Review of *Harmonium. Bookman,* LXXIV (October, 1931), 207–208.

Simons, Hi. "The Comedian As the Letter C: Its Sense and Its Significance." *Southern Review,* v (Autumn, 1939), 453–468.

———. "Vicissitudes of Reputation." *The Harvard Advocate,* CXXVII (December, 1940), 8–11, 34–44.

———. "Wallace Stevens and Mallarme." *Modern Philology,* XLIII (May, 1946), 235–260.

Southworth, James G. *Some Modern American Poets.* Oxford: Basil Blackwell, 1950.

Untermeyer, Louis. "Departure from Dandyism." *Saturday Review of Literature,* XXV (December 19, 1942), 11.

Vance, Will. "Man Off the Street." *Saturday Review of Literature,* VIII (March 23, 1946), 8.

Viereck, Peter. "Stevens Revisited." *The Kenyon Review,* x (Winter, 1948), 154–157.

Watts, H. H. "Wallace Stevens and the Rock of Summer." *The Kenyon Review,* XIV (Spring, 1952), 122–140.

Winters, Yvor. *In Defense of Reason.* New York: Swallow Press and William Morrow and Company, 1947, 431–460.

Zabel, Morton D. "Wallace Stevens and the Image of Man." In *Essays in Modern Literary Criticism,* edited by Ray B. West, Jr. New York: Rinehart, 1952, 411–417.

CHAPTER THREE

William Carlos Williams: A Testament of Perpetual Change

By William Carlos Williams

"An Approach to the Poem." *English Institute Annual.* New York: Columbia University Press, 1947, 50–76.

The Autobiography of William Carlos Williams. New York: Random House, 1951.

The Clouds, Aigeltinger, Russia, etc. Aurora, New York: Wells College Press, and Cummington, Massachusetts: Cummington Press, 1948.

The Complete Collected Poems of William Carlos Williams, 1906–1938. Norfolk, Connecticut: New Directions, 1938.

"The Fatal Blunder." *Quarterly Review of Literature*, II (No. 2, 1944), 125–127.

"The First President." *The New Caravan.* Edited by Alfred Kreymborg, Lewis Mumford, Paul Rosenfeld. New York: W. W. Norton and Company, Inc., 1936, 563–603.

"Five Prose Sketches." *The Dial*, LXXXIV (June, 1928), 456–462.

"From: A Folded Skyscraper." *The American Caravan.* Edited by Van Wyck Brooks, Alfred Kreymborg, Lewis Mumford, Paul Rosenfeld. New York: Macaulay Company, 1927, 216–222.

"From Queens to Cats." *The Dial*, LXXXVI (January, 1929), 66–67. Review of *Aphrodite and Other Poems* by Wallace Gould.

"Good . . . For What?" *The Dial*, LXXXVI (March, 1929), 250–252. Review of *Good Morning America* by Carl Sandburg.

"How to Write." *New Directions, 1936.* Norfolk, Connecticut: New Directions, n. p.

"Impasse and Imagery." *The Dial*, LXXXV (November, 1928), 431–433. Review of *The Boy in the Sun* by Paul Rosenfeld.

"In Praise of Marriage." *Quarterly Review of Literature,* II (No. 2, 1944), 145–149. Review of *The Phoenix and the Tortoise* by Kenneth Rexroth.

In the American Grain. Norfolk, Connecticut: New Directions, 1925.

Kora in Hell: Improvisations. Boston, Massachusetts: Four Seas, 1920.

"Letter on Pound." *Quarterly Review of Literature,* V (No. 3, 1950), 301.

"Letter to an Australian Editor." *Briarcliff Quarterly,* III (October, 1946), 205–209.

"A Letter Touching the Comintern upon Censorship in the Arts." *Tiger's Eye,* I (June, 1948), 29–32.

Life along the Passaic River. Norfolk, Connecticut: New Directions, 1938.

"Marianne Moore." *Quarterly Review of Literature,* IV (No. 1, 1946), 125–127.

"Marianne Moore." *The Dial,* LXXVIII (May, 1925), 353–401.

Microfilmed Manuscripts, Rolls 21–28. Lockwood Memorial Library. Buffalo, New York: University of Buffalo.

"The New Poetical Economy." *Poetry,* XLIV (July, 1934), 220–226. Review of George Oppen's *Discrete Series,* preface by E. P.

"Notes from a Talk on Poetry." *Poetry,* XIV (July, 1919), 211–216.

"On Burke." *The Dial,* LXXXVI (January, 1929), 6–8.

"Paterson: The Falls." *Selected Poems.* Norfolk, Connecticut: New Directions, 1949, 99–101.

"The Poet and His Public." *Partisan Review,* XIII (September–October, 1946), 488–500.

"Preface." *Quarterly Review of Literature,* II (No. 4, 1944), 346–350. Review of *Transfigured Night* by Byron Vazakas.

"Reply to a Young Scientist." *Directions,* I (Autumn, 1934), 27–28.

"The Round the World Fliers." *Wake,* IX (1950), 22–25.

"Shapiro Is All Right." *The Kenyon Review,* VIII (Winter, 1946), 123–127.

"Some Notes toward an Autobiography." *Poetry,* LXXII (June, 1948), 147–155; (August, 1948), 264–270; LXXIV (May, 1949), 94–111.

"Struggle of Wings." *The Dial,* LXXXI (January, 1926), 22–24.

"The Venus." *The Dial,* LXXXV (July, 1928), 21–29.

The Wedge. Cummington, Massachusetts: Cummington Press, 1944.

"Wide Awake, Full of Love." From *Paterson IV. Quarterly Review of Literature,* IV (No. 4, 1946), 358–359.

"With Forced Fingers Rude." *Four Pages,* (February, 1948), 1–4.

Background References

Bryher, Winifred. "Recent American Poetry." *Life and Letters Today,* XXIX (May, 1941), 145–147.

Burke, Kenneth. "The Methods of William Carlos Williams." *The Dial,* LXXXII (February, 1927), 94–98.

Carruth, Hayden. "Dr. Williams' Paterson." *Nation,* CLXX (April 8, 1950), 331–333. Review of *Paterson III.*

Davidson, Eugene. Review of *Selected Poems. Yale Review,* XXXVIII (Summer, 1949), 724–725.

Davis, Robert Gorham. Review of *Make Light of It. The New York Times Book Review* (December 17, 1950), 1.

Eberhart, Richard. Review of *The Collected Later Poems of William Carlos Williams. The New York Times Book Review* (December 17, 1950), 1.

Ellmann, Richard. Review of *Paterson III. Yale Review,* XXXIX (Spring, 1950), 544–545.

Federal Writers Project. *New Jersey: A Guide to Its Present and Past.* New York: Viking, 1939.

Fitzgerald, Robert. Review of *Selected Poems. The New Republic,* CXX (April 25, 1949), 22.

Flint, R. W. "I Will Teach You My Townspeople." *The Kenyon Review,* XII (Autumn, 1950), 537–543.

Freemantle, Anne. Review of *Paterson I. The Commonweal,* XLIV (October 4, 1946), 601.

Gregory, Horace. "William Carlos Williams." *Life and Letters Today,* XXIV (February, 1940), 164–176.

Hoffman, Frederick J. "Williams and His Muse." *Poetry,* LXXXIV (April, 1954), 23–27.

Honig, Edwin. "The City of Man." *Poetry,* LXIX (February, 1947), 277–284. Review of *Paterson I.*

———. "The Paterson Impasse." *Poetry,* LXXIV (April, 1949), 37–41. Review of *Paterson II.*

Humphries, Rolfe. Review of Selected Poems. *The Nation,* CLXVI (July 9, 1949), 44.

Jarrell, Randall. *Poetry and the Age.* New York: Alfred A. Knopf, 1953, 237–271.

Kenner, Hugh. "With the Bare Hands." *Poetry,* LXXX (August, 1952), 276–290.

Koch, Vivienne. *William Carlos Williams.* Norfolk, Connecticut: New Directions, 1950.

Lowell, Robert. Review of *Paterson I. The Sewanee Review,* LV (Summer, 1947), 500–504.

———. Review of *Paterson II. The Nation,* CLXVI (June 19, 1948), 693.

———. "Thomas, Bishop, and Williams." *The Sewanee Review,* LV (Summer, 1947), 493–504.

Malone, Dumas (editor). *The Dictionary of American Biography,* Vol. XIV. New York: Charles Scribner's Sons, 1934, 291–292.

Martz, Louis. Review of *Paterson I* and *II. Yale Review,* XXXVIII (Autumn, 1948), 148–150.

Mercier, Vivian. Review of *Paterson III. The Commonweal,* LI (March 3, 1950), 564.

Moore, Marianne. "Poet of the Quattrocento." *The Dial,* LXXXII (March, 1927), 213–215.

———. "Things Others Never Notice." *Poetry,* XLIV (May, 1934), 103–106.

Morgan, Frederick. "William Carlos Williams: Imagery, Rhythm, Form." *The Sewanee Review,* LV (Summer, 1947), 675–691.

Nelson, William (editor). *Archives of the State of New Jersey.* First Series, Vol. XXXIX. Trenton, New Jersey: MacCrellish and Quigley Company, 1946.

——— (editor). *Archives of the State of New Jersey.* Second Series, Vol. III. Trenton, New Jersey: John L. Murphy Publishing Company, 1906.

———. *History of the City of Paterson and the County of Passaic.* The Press Printing and Publishing Company. Paterson, New Jersey, 1901.

———. *History of the Old Dutch Church at Totowa: Paterson, New Jersey, 1755–1827.* Paterson, New Jersey: The Press Printing and Publishing Company, 1892.

——— and Shriner, Charles A. *History of Paterson and Its Environs.* 2 vols. New York: Lewis Historical Publishing Company, 1920.

O'Connor, William Van. Review of *Paterson III. Saturday Review of Literature,* XXXIII (May 20, 1950), 41.

———. Review of *Paterson II. Saturday Review of Literature,* XXXI (September 25, 1948), 30.

Parker, Jenny Marsh. *Rochester A Story Historical.* Rochester,

New York: Scranton, Wetmore and Company, 1884, 184–193.

Pearce, Roy. "Poet as Person." *Yale Review,* XLI (Spring, 1952), 421–440.

Pound, Ezra. "Dr. Williams' Position." *The Dial,* LXXXV (November, 1928), 395–404.

Rosenfeld, Isaac. Review of *Paterson I. The Nation,* CLXIII (August 24, 1946), 216.

Shriner, Charles A. *Four Chapters of Paterson History.* Paterson, New Jersey: Lont and Overkamp Publishing Company, 1919.

Spears, Monroe K. "The Failure of Language." *Poetry,* LXXVI (April, 1950), 39–44. Review of *Paterson III.*

Stearns, Marshall W. "Syntax, Sense, Sound, and Dr. Williams." *Poetry,* LXVI (April, 1945), 35–40. Review of *The Wedge.*

Sweeney, John L. Review of *The Broken Span. Yale Review,* XXX (Summer, 1941), 819.

Tyler, Parker. "The Poet of Paterson Book One." *Briarcliff Quarterly,* III (October, 1946), 168–175.

Untermeyer, Louis. Review of *Collected Poems 1906–1938. Yale Review,* XXVIII (Spring, 1939), 612.

Wilson, T. C. "The Example of Dr. Williams." *Poetry,* XLVIII (May, 1936), 105–107. Review of *An Early Martyr and Other Poems.*

CHAPTER FOUR

Eliot and Crane: Protean Techniques

By T. S. Eliot and Hart Crane

Eliot, T. S. *Collected Poems, 1909–1935.* New York: Harcourt, Brace and Company, 1936.

———. "The Comedy of Humours." *The Athenaeum,* No. 4672 (November 14, 1919), 1180–1181.

———. "Dante as a 'Spiritual Leader.'" *The Athenaeum,* No. 4692 (April 2, 1920), 441–442. Review of *Dante* by Dwight Sidgwick.

———. "A Foreign Mind." *The Athenaeum,* No. 4653 (July 4, 1919), 553.

————. *Four Quartets*. New York: Harcourt, Brace and Company, 1943.

————. "Humanist, Artist, and Scientist." *The Athenaeum*, No. 4667 (October 10, 1919), 1014–1015.

————. "The Method of Mr. Pound." *The Athenaeum*, No. 4669 (October 24, 1919), 1065–1066.

————. "The Naked Man." *The Athenaeum*, No. 4685 (February 13, 1920), 208–209. Review of *William Blake, The Man* by Charles Gardner.

————. "Personality and Demonic Possession." *Virginia Quarterly Review*, x (January, 1934), 94–104.

————. "The Preacher as Artist." *The Athenaeum*, No. 4674 (November 28, 1919), 1252–1253. Review of *Donne's Sermons: Selected Passages*, with an essay by Logan Pearsall Smith.

————. *Selected Essays 1917–1932*. New York: Harcourt, Brace and Company, 1932.

————. "War-Paint and Feathers." *The Athenaeum*, No. 4668 (October 17, 1919), 1036. Review of *The Path of the Rainbow* edited by George W. Cronyn.

————. "Whether Rostand Had Something about Him." *The Athenaeum*, No. 4656 (July 25, 1919), 665–666. Review of *Le Vol de la Marseillaise* by Edmond Rostand.

Crane, Hart. "General Aims and Theories." In *Oxford Anthology of American Literature*, edited by William Rose Benét and Norman Holmes Pearson. New York: Oxford University Press, 1938, 1553–1556.

————. "Two Letters on the Bridge." *The Hound and Horn*, vii (July–September, 1934), 676–683.

————. *The Collected Poems*. Edited by Waldo Frank. New York: Liveright, Inc., 1946.

Background References

Baynes, H. G. *Mythology of the Soul*. London: Methuen and Company, Ltd., 1949.

Blackmur, R. P. "New Thresholds, New Anatomies." *The Double Agent*. New York: Arrow Editions, 1935, 121–141.

————. "T. S. Eliot." *The Hound and Horn*, i (Spring, 1928), 187–214; (Summer, 1928), 291–320.

————. *Language as Gesture*. New York: Harcourt, Brace and Company, 1952.

Bodkin, Maud. *Archetypal Patterns in Poetry*. London: Oxford University Press, 1934.

Bowra, C. M. *The Creative Experiment*. London: Macmillan and Company, Ltd., 1949, 159–189.

Bradbury, John M. *"Four Quartets:* The Structural Symbolisms." *The Sewanee Review,* LIX (Spring, 1951), 254–271.

Brooks, Cleanth. *Modern Poetry and the Tradition*. Chapel Hill, North Carolina: University of North Carolina Press, 1939.

Brown, C. S. "T. S. Eliot and 'Die Droste.' " *The Sewanee Review,* XLVI (October, 1938), 492–500.

Bush, Douglas. *Mythology and the Romantic Tradition in English Poetry*. Cambridge: Harvard University Press, 1937.

Butler, Dom Cuthbert. *Western Mysticism*. New York: E. P. Dutton and Company, 1923.

Cargill, Oscar. *Intellectual America*. New York: Macmillan Company, 1941.

Coffman, Stanley K., Jr. "Symbolism in *The Bridge.*" *PMLA,* LXVI (March, 1951), 65–78.

Cowley, Malcolm. "Remembering Hart Crane." *The New Republic,* CIV (April 14, 1941), 504–506.

————. "The Roaring Boy." *The New Republic,* XCI (June 9, 1937), 134.

Deutsch, Babette. *This Modern Poetry*. New York: W. W. Norton and Company, Inc., 1935.

————. "Waste Remains." *Poetry,* LXXXIII (March, 1954), 353–357.

Drew, Elizabeth. *Directions in Modern Poetry*. New York: W. W. Norton and Company, Inc., 1940, 40–55.

————. *T. S. Eliot: The Design of His Poetry*. New York: Charles Scribner's Sons, 1949.

Flint, F. W. *"Four Quartets* Reconsidered." *The Sewanee Review,* LVI (Winter, 1948), 69–82.

Foster, Genevieve. "The Archetypal Imagery of T. S. Eliot." *PMLA,* LX (June, 1945), 567–585.

Fowlie, Wallace. *The Clown's Grail: A Study of Love in Its Literary Expression*. London: Dennis Dobson, Ltd., 1947.

Gardner, Helen. *The Art of T. S. Eliot.* London: Cresset Press, Ltd., 1949.

Ghiselin, Brewster. "A Bridge into the Sea." *Partisan Review,* XVI (July, 1949), 679–686.

Gregory, Horace and Zaturenska, Marya. *A History of American Poetry, 1900–1940.* New York: Harcourt, Brace and Company, 1946.

Hamilton, Edith. *Mythology.* Boston: Little, Brown and Company, 1942.

Hastings, James (ed.). "Metamorphosis." *Encyclopaedia of Religion and Ethics.* Volume VIII. New York: Charles Scribner's Sons, 1916, 593–594.

Herman, Barbara. "The Language of Hart Crane." *The Sewanee Review,* LVIII (Winter, 1950), 52–67.

von Hildebrand, Dietrich. *Transformation in Christ.* New York: Longmans, Green and Company, 1948.

Jarrell, Randall. "A Conversation with the Devil." *The Seven-League Crutches.* New York: Harcourt, Brace and Company, 1951.

Jones, Ernest. *Nightmare, Witches, and Devils.* New York: W. W. Norton and Company, Inc., 1931.

Jung, Carl. *Modern Man in Search of a Soul.* Translated by W. S. Dell and Cary F. Baynes. New York: Harcourt, Brace and Company, 1933.

Krappe, Alexander Haggerty. *The Science of Folk-lore.* London: Methuen and Company, Ltd., 1930.

Lemaitre, George. *From Cubism to Surrealism in French Literature.* Cambridge: Harvard University Press, 1941.

Mesterton, Eric. *The Wasteland Some Commentaries.* Translated by Llewellyn Jones. Chicago: The Argus Book Shop, Inc., 1943.

Moss, Howard. "Disorder as Myth: Hart Crane's *The Bridge.*" *Poetry,* LXII (April, 1943), 32–45.

Raglan, Lord. *The Hero: A Study in Tradition, Myth and Dream.* New York: Oxford University Press, 1937.

Ransom, John Crowe. "Philomela." *Chills and Fever.* New York: Alfred A. Knopf, 1924, 94–95.

Reinsberg, Mark. "A Footnote to *Four Quartets.*" *American Literature,* XXI (November, 1949), 342–344.

Sandys, George (ed.). *Ovids Metamorphosis Englished, My-thologized, and Represented in Figures.* London, 1640.

Schwartz, Delmore. "The Literary Dictatorship of T. S. Eliot." *Partisan Review,* XVI (February, 1949), 119–137.

Shockley, Martin Staples. "Hart Crane's 'Lachrymae Christi.'" *University of Kansas City Review,* XVI (Autumn, 1949), 31–37.

Southworth, James G. "Hart Crane." *Some Modern American Poets.* Oxford: Basil Blackwell, 1950, 159–176.

Swallow, Alan. "Hart Crane." *University of Kansas City Review,* XVI (Winter, 1949), 103–119.

Tate, Allen. "A Poet and His Life." *Poetry,* L (July, 1937), Review of *Hart Crane: The Life of an American Poet* by Philip Horton.

———. "Hart Crane." *Reactionary Essays on Poetry and Ideas.* New York: Charles Scribner's Sons, 1936, 26–42.

Thorold, Algar (tr.). *The Dialogue of the Seraphic Virgin Catherine of Siena.* Westminster, Maryland: The Newman Bookshop, 1943.

Tyler, Parker. *Magic and Myth of the Movies.* New York: Henry Holt and Company, 1947.

Viereck, Peter. "Birth of Song." *Harper's Magazine,* CC (March, 1950), 86–87.

———. "My Kind of Poetry." *Mid-Century American Poets.* Edited by John Ciardi. New York: Twayne Publishers, Inc., 1950, 16–31.

Waggoner, Hyatt. "Hart Crane and the Broken Parabola." *University of Kansas City Review,* XI (Spring, 1945), 173–177.

Weber, Brom. *Hart Crane: A Biographical and Critical Study.* New York: Bodley Press, 1948.

Wells, Henry W. *The American Way of Poetry.* New York: Columbia University, 1943.

Weston, Jessie. "The Grail and the Rites of Adonis." *Folk-Lore,* XVIII (September, 1907), 282–306.

Williamson, George. "The Structure of *The Waste Land.*" *Modern Philology,* XLVII (February, 1950), 191–207.

Williamson, Hugh Ross. "A commentary on T. S. Eliot's *The Waste Land.*" *The Bookman,* LXXXII (July, 1932), 192–195.

CHAPTER FIVE

Jarrell's Metamorphoses

By Randall Jarrell

"Age of Criticism." *Partisan Review,* XIX (March, 1952), 185–201.

"Above the Waters in Their Toil." *American Review,* III (May, 1934), 230.

"All or None." *The Kenyon Review,* XIII (Spring, 1951), 204.

"And Did She Dwell in Innocence and Joy." *Southern Review,* I (Spring, 1935), 84–85.

"An Old Song." *Southern Review,* II (Autumn, 1936), 379.

"Answers to Questions." *Mid-Century American Poets.* Edited by John Ciardi. New York: Twayne Publishers, Inc., 1950, 182–185.

Blood for a Stranger. New York: Harcourt, Brace and Company, 1942.

"Changes of Attitude and Rhetoric in Auden's Poetry." *Southern Review,* VII (Summer, 1941), 326–350.

"The Clock in the Tower of the Church." *The Kenyon Review,* IX (Autumn, 1947), 508.

"Deutsch durch Freud." *Poetry,* LXXVII (December, 1950), 150–154.

"The Development of Yeats's Sense of Reality." *Southern Review,* VII (Autumn, 1942), 653–666.

"Dialogue between Soul and Body." *Southern Review,* III (Summer, 1937), 398–399.

"End of the Line." *The Nation,* CLIV (February 21, 1942), 222.

"Ernie Pyle." *The Nation,* CLX (May 19, 1945), 573–576.

"Falling in Love Is Never As Simple." *Southern Review,* III (Summer, 1937), 396–398.

Review of *Fall of the City* by Archibald MacLeish. *The Sewanee Review,* LI (Spring, 1943), 267–281.

"Fear." *American Review,* III (May, 1934), 228.

"Freud to Paul, the Stages of Auden's Ideology." *Partisan Review,* XII (Fall, 1945), 439–457.

"From that Island." *The Kenyon Review,* I (Autumn, 1939), 468–472. Review of *Modern Poetry: A Personal Essay* by Louis MacNeice.

"From the Kingdom of Necessity." *The Nation,* CLXIV (January 18, 1947), 74–78. Review of *Lord Weary's Castle* by Robert Lowell.

"The Germans Are Lunatics." *The Kenyon Review,* VII (Summer, 1945), 443.

"The Girl Dreams that She Is Giselle." *The Nation,* CLXVIII (June 11, 1949), 664.

"Hohensalzburg." *Poetry,* LXXIV (April, 1949), 1–7.

"The Humble Animal." *The Kenyon Review,* IV (Autumn, 1942), 408–411. Review of *What Are Years* by Marianne Moore.

"January, 1938." *Southern Review,* VII (Spring, 1941), 107–108.

"John Ransom's Poetry." *The Sewanee Review,* LVI (Summer, 1948), 378–390.

"Kafka's Tragi-Comedy." *The Kenyon Review,* III (Winter, 1941), 116–120. Review of *Amerika* by Franz Kafka.

"The Laboratory." *The Sewanee Review,* LI (Spring, 1943), 253.

Little Friend, Little Friend. New York: Dial Press, 1945.

"Looking Back in My Mind." *Southern Review,* I (Spring, 1935), 85–87.

Losses. New York: Harcourt, Brace and Company, 1948.

"Man." *Poetry,* LX (May, 1942), 74–75.

"The Man with the Axe." *American Review,* III (May, 1934), 229.

"News." *The Sewanee Review,* LIII (Summer, 1945), 429.

"To the New World." *The Sewanee Review,* LIII (Summer, 1945), 426.

"The November Ghosts." *The Sewanee Review,* LI (Spring, 1943), 252.

"The Obscurity of the Poet." *Partisan Review,* XVIII (January–February, 1951), 66–82.

"The Other Robert Frost." *The Nation,* CLXV (November 29, 1947), 588. Review of *The Masque of Mercy* by Robert Frost.

"Overture: The Hostages." *The Kenyon Review,* IX (Autumn, 1947), 509.

"O Weary Mariners, Here Shaded, Fed." *American Review*, III (May, 1934), 229.

"A Perfectly Free Association." *The Nation*, CLXVIII (April 30, 1949), 503.

Pictures from an Institution. New York: Harcourt, Brace and Company, 195.

Poetry and the Age. New York: Alfred A. Knopf, 1953.

"The Princess Wakes in the Wood." *Poetry*, LXXVII (December, 1950), 148–149.

"Reflections on Wallace Stevens." *Partisan Review*, XVII (May–June, 1951), 335–345.

"The Refugees." *Partisan Review*, XI (Winter, 1944), 99.

"Scherzo." *Partisan Review*, XI (Winter, 1944), 99.

The Seven-League Crutches. New York: Harcourt, Brace and Company, 1951.

"The Street Has Changed." *The Sewanee Review*, LIII (Summer, 1945), 428.

"Texts from Housman." *The Kenyon Review*, I (Summer, 1939), 260–271.

"Thoughts about Marianne Moore." *Partisan Review*, XIX (November, 1952), 687–700.

"Time and the Thing-in-Itself in a Textbook." *Poetry*, LX (May, 1942), 72–74.

"To the Laodiceans." *The Kenyon Review*, XIV (Winter, 1952), 535–561.

"The Tower." *The Kenyon Review*, XIII (Spring, 1951), 205.

"The Traveller." *Poetry*, LXXVII (December, 1950), 146.

"Up in the Sky the Star Is Waiting." *Southern Review*, IV (Autumn, 1939), 577.

"A View of Three Poets." *Partisan Review*, VI (November-December, 1951), 691–700. Review of *Ceremony and Other Poems* by Richard Wilbur, *The Mills of the Kavanaughs* by Robert Lowell, and *Paterson* by William Carlos Williams.

"Walt Whitman: He Had His Nerve." *The Kenyon Review*, XIV (Spring, 1952), 63–79.

"When Achilles Fought and Fell." *Southern Review*, III (Summer, 1937), 393–394.

"Zeno." *The New Republic*, LXXXI (December 26, 1934), 184.

Background References

Baynes, H. G. *Mythology of the Soul.* London: Methuen and Company, Ltd., 1949.

Beaumont, Cyril W. *Complete Book of Ballets.* New York: Grosset and Dunlap, 1938.

Bradbrook, M. C. and Thomas, M. G. Lloyd. "Marvell and the Concept of Metamorphosis." *Criterion,* xviii (January, 1939), 236–255.

Campbell, Joseph (ed.). *Grimm's Fairy Tales.* New York: Pantheon Books, 1944.

Carroll, Lewis. *Alice in Wonderland.* New York: Modern Library, 1924.

Cowley, Malcolm. "First Blood." *The New Republic,* cvii (November 30, 1942), 718–719. Review of *Blood for a Stranger* by Randall Jarrell.

————. "Poets as Reviewers." *The New Republic,* civ (February 24, 1941), 281–282.

Fiske, John. *Myths and Myth-Makers: Old Tales and Superstitions.* Boston: James L. Osgood and Company, 1875.

Flint, R. W. "Poetry and the Age." *Partisan Review,* xx (November, 1953), 702–708.

Fränkel, Herman. *Ovid: A Poet between Two Worlds.* Berkeley, California: University of California Press, 1945.

Freud, Sigmund. *New Introductory Lectures on Psycho-analysis.* Translated by W. J. H. Spratt. New York: W. W. Norton and Company, Inc., 1933.

Graham, W. S. and Carruth, Hayden. "Jarrell's *Losses:* A Controversy." *Poetry,* lxxii (September, 1948), 302–311.

Holmes, Mary. "Metamorphosis and Myth in Modern Art." *Perspective,* i (Winter, 1948), 79–86.

Jacobi, Jolan. *The Psychology of Jung.* New Haven: Yale University Press, 1943.

James, M. R. (trans.). *Hans Andersen, Forty Stories.* London: Faber and Faber, Ltd., 1930.

Jung, Carl G. and Kerényi, C. *Essays on a Science of Mythology.* Translated by R. F. C. Hull. New York: Pantheon Books, 1949.

Jung, Carl G. *The Integration of the Personality.* Translated by

Stanley M. Dell. New York: Farrar and Rinehart, Inc., 1939.

Kahler, Erich. "The Persistence of Myth." *Chimera,* IV (Spring, 1946), 2–11.

Kenyon, Theda. *Witches Still Live.* New York: Ives Washburn, 1929.

Krappe, Alexander Haggerty. *The Science of Folk-lore.* London: Methuen and Company, Ltd., 1930.

Langer, Susanne. *Philosophy in a New Key.* New York: New American Philosophical Library, 1942.

MacCulloch, J. A. *The Childhood Fiction: A Study of Folk Tales and Primitive Thought.* London: John Murray, 1905.

Malcolmson, Donald. *Ten Heroes.* New York: Duell, Sloan, and Pearce, 1941.

Mills, Charles De B. *The Tree of Mythology, Its Growth and Fruitage.* Syracuse, New York: C. W. Bardeen, 1889.

Read, Herbert. "Myth, Dream, and Poem." *Transition,* XXVII (April–May, 1938), 176–193.

Robert, Grace. *The Borzoi Book of Ballets.* New York: Alfred A. Knopf, 1946.

Schwartz, Delmore. "Dream from Which No One Wakes." *The Nation,* CLXI (December 1, 1945), 590.

Stewart, J. A. *The Myths of Plato.* New York: Macmillan, 1905.

Summers, Montague. *The Vampire His Kith and Kin.* London: Kegan Paul, Trench, Trubner and Company, Ltd., 1928.

Tyler, Parker. "The Dramatic Lyrism of Randall Jarrell." *Poetry,* LXXIX (March, 1952), 335–347. Review of *The Seven-League Crutches.*

Wickwar, J. W. *Witchcraft and the Black Art.* New York: Robert M. McBride and Company, 1926.

Yearsley, Macleod. *The Folklore of Fairy-Tale.* London: Watts and Company, 1924.

CHAPTER SIX

The Road to Tír-na-n-Og

By William Butler Yeats

The Autobiography of William Butler Yeats. New York: Macmillan Company, 1953.

"Away." *The Fortnightly Review,* LVII (April, 1902), 726–741.

"The Broken Gates of Death." *Living Age,* CCXVII (April, 1898), 383–392.

The Celtic Twilight. London: A. H. Bullen, 1902.

The Collected Plays of W. B. Yeats. New York: Macmillan Company, 1952.

The Collected Poems of W. B. Yeats. New York: Macmillan Company, 1953.

The Collected Works in Verse and Prose of William Butler Yeats. Stratford-on-the-Avon: Shakespeare Head Press, 1907.

The Cutting of an Agate. New York: Macmillan Company, 1912.

Early Poems and Stories. New York: Macmillan Company, 1925.

Ideas of Good and Evil. New York: Macmillan Company, 1903.

"Ireland Bewitched." *Contemporary Review,* LXXVI (September, 1899), 388–405.

Letters to the New Island. Cambridge, Massachusetts: Harvard University Press, 1934. Edited by Horace Reynolds.

Per Amica Silentia Lunae. London: Macmillan Company, 1918.

The Poetical Works of William B. Yeats in Two Volumes. New York: Macmillan Company, 1907.

"The Prisoners of the Gods." *The Nineteenth Century,* XLIII (January, 1898), 91–105.

A Vision: An Explanation of Life Founded upon the Writings of Giraldus and upon Certain Doctrines Attributed to Kusta Ben Luka. London: T. Werner Laurie, Ltd., 1925.

Background References

Alspach, Russell K. "Two Songs of Yeats." *Modern Language Notes,* LXI (June, 1946), 395–400.

————. "The Use by Yeats and Other Irish Writers of the Folk-lore of Patrick Kennedy." *Journal of American Folk-lore,* LIX (October–December, 1946), 404–412.

Baker, Howard. "Domes of Byzantium." *Southern Review,* VII (Winter, 1946), 639–653.

Bowra, C. M. *The Heritage of Symbolism.* London: Macmillan Company, 1951, 180–219.

Brown, Forman. "Mr. Yeats and the Supernatural." *The Sewanee Review,* XXXIII (July, 1925), 323–330.

Chase, Richard. "Myth as Literature." *English Institute Essays, 1947.* New York: Columbia University Press, 1948, 3–23.

Drew, Elizabeth and Sweeney, John L. *Directions in Modern Poetry.* New York: W. W. Norton and Company, Inc., 1940, 148–175.

De Jubainville, H. D'Arbois. *The Irish Mythological Cycle and Celtic Mythology.* Dublin: O'Donoghue and Company, 1903.

Eliot, T. S. "The Poetry of W. B. Yeats." *Southern Review,* VII (Winter, 1946), 426–455.

Ellmann, Richard. "The Art of Yeats." *The Kenyon Review,* XV (Summer, 1953), 357–386.

————. *Yeats: The Man and the Masks.* New York: Macmillan Company, 1948.

————. "W. B. Yeats, Magician." *Western Review,* XII (Summer, 1948), 232–241.

Frye, Northrop. "Yeats and the Language of Symbolism." *University of Toronto Quarterly,* XVII (October, 1947), 1–17.

Gray, Louis Herbert. *The Mythology of All Races.* Vol. III. New York: Marshall Jones Company, 1918.

Gregory, Lady Augusta. *Cuchulain of Muirthemne.* London: John Murray, 1934. Preface and note by Yeats.

————. *Gods and Fighting Men.* London: John Murray, 1904.

Gurd, Patty. *The Early Poetry of William Butler Yeats.* Lancaster, Pennsylvania; New Era Printing Company, 1916.

Hall, James and Steinmann, Martin (editors). *The Permanence of Yeats.* New York: Macmillan Company, 1950.

Henn, T. R. *The Lonely Tower: Studies in the Poetry of W. B. Yeats.* London: Methuen and Company, Ltd., 1950.

Hoare, Dorothy M. *The Works of Morris and Yeats in Relation to Early Saga Literature.* Cambridge, England: Cambridge University Press, 1937.

Hone, Joseph. *W. B. Yeats 1865–1939.* New York: Macmillan Company, 1943.

Jarrell, Randall. "The Development of Yeats's Sense of Reality." *Southern Review,* VII (Winter, 1946), 653–667.

Jeffares, A. Norman. *W. B. Yeats: Man and Poet.* New Haven: Yale University Press, 1949.

Johnston, Charles. "Yeats in the Making." *Poet Lore,* XVII (Summer, 1906), 102–112.

Koch, Vivienne. *W. B. Yeats: The Tragic Phase. A Study of the Last Poems.* London: Routledge, Kegan Paul Ltd., 1951.

Leach, Maria (editor). *Funk and Wagnall's Standard Dictionary of Folklore, Mythology and Legend.* New York: Funk and Wagnalls Company, 1950.

Lempriere, J. *A Classical Dictionary.* New York: D. and G. Bruce, 1809, 43.

MacCulloch, J. A. *The Celtic and Scandinavian Religions.* London: Hutchinson's University Library, 1948.

Macleod, Fiona. "A Group of Celtic Writers." *The Fortnightly Review,* LXXI (January, 1899), 34–54.

MacNeice, Louis. *The Poetry of W. B. Yeats.* London: Oxford University Press, 1941.

Menon, V. K. Narayana. *The Development of William Butler Yeats.* London: Oliver and Boyd, 1942.

Morgan, Frederick. "The Swan." *The Sewanee Review,* LVIII (Summer, 1950), 453.

O'Donnell, J. P. *Sailing to Byzantium.* Cambridge, Massachusetts: Harvard University, 1939.

Parkinson, Thomas. *W. B. Yeats, Self-Critic.* Berkeley and Los Angeles: University of California Press, 1951.

Ransom, John Crowe. "The Irish, the Gaelic, the Byzantine." *Southern Review,* VII (Winter, 1946), 517–546.

Rudd, Margaret. *Divided Image: A Study of William Blake and W. B. Yeats.* London: Routledge and Kegan Paul Ltd., 1953.

Shaw, Francis. "The Celtic Twilight." *Studies,* XXIII (March, 1934), 25–41; 260–278.

Stace, W. T. "The Faery Poetry of Mr. W. B. Yeats." *The British Review,* I (January, 1913), 117–131.

Stauffer, Donald. *The Golden Nightingale.* New York: Macmillan Company, 1949.

Stein, Arnold. "Yeats: A Study in Recklessness." *The Sewanee Review,* LVII (Autumn, 1949), 603–627.

Taylor, Josh. "William Butler Yeats and the Revival of Gaelic Literature." *Methodist Review,* LXXXVII (March, 1905), 189–202.

Tschumi, Raymond. *Thought in Twentieth-Century English Poetry*. London: Routledge and Kegan Paul Ltd., 1951.

Unger, Leonard. "The New Collected Yeats." *Poetry,* LXXX (April, 1952), 43–51.

Ure, Peter. *Towards a Mythology: Studies in the Poetry of W. B. Yeats*. London: University Press of Liverpool, 1946.

Van Doorn, Willem. "William Butler Yeats." *English Studies,* II (1920), 65–77.

Witt, Marion. "William Butler Yeats." *English Institute Essays, 1946*. New York: Columbia University Press, 1947, 74–105.

————. "Yeats' 'Mohini Chatterjee.'" *The Explicator,* IV (June, 1946), item 60.

PS
324
Q7
1966

Quinn, Bernetta.
    The metamorphic tradition in modern poetry;
essays on the work of Ezra Pound, Wallace Stevens,
William Carlos Williams, T.S. Eliot, Hart Crane,
Randall Jarrell, and William Butler Yeats.
New York, Gordian Pr., 1966.
    263p.   22cm.

227110
1.American poetry-20th century-Hist. & crit.   2.English
poetry-20th century-Hist. & crit.   I.Title.